Variation in Second Language Acquisition
Volume I: Discourse and Pragmatics

Multilingual Matters

Please contact us for the latest book information:
Multilingual Matters,
Bank House, 8a Hill Rd,
Clevedon, Avon BS21 7HH,
England

MULTILINGUAL MATTERS 49
Series Editor: Derrick Sharp

Variation in Second Language Acquisition Volume I: Discourse and Pragmatics

Edited by

Susan Gass, Carolyn Madden, Dennis Preston and Larry Selinker

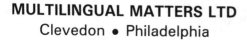**MULTILINGUAL MATTERS LTD**
Clevedon • Philadelphia

Library of Congress Cataloging in Publication Data

Variation in second language acquisition.
(Multilingual matters; 49–50)
Selected papers presented at the XIth Michigan
Conference in Applied Linguistics ... held October 7–9,
1987 at the University of Michigan in Ann Arbor—Pref.
Includes bibliographies and indexes.
Contents: v. 1. Discourse and pragmatics. v. 2.
Psycholinguistic issues.
1. Second language acquisition—Congresses.
2. Language and languages—Variation—Congresses.
I. Gass, Susan M. II. Conference on Applied
Linguistics (11th : 1987 : University of Michigan)
III. Series.

British Library Cataloguing in Publication Data

Variation in second language acquisition.
(Multilingual matters; 49).
Vol. I: Discourse and pragmatics
1. Foreign language skills. Acquisition.
Sociolinguistic aspects
I. Gass, Susan
401'.9

ISBN 1-85359-026-6
ISBN 1-85359-025-8 Pbk

Multilingual Matters Ltd
Bank House, 8a Hill Road   &   242 Cherry Street
Clevedon, Avon BS21 7HH   Philadelphia, Pa 19106–1906
England   USA

Index compiled by Meg Davies, Society of Indexers
Typeset by MCS Ltd, Salisbury, SP1 2AY
Printed and bound in Great Britain by WBC Print, Bristol

Contents

SECTION FIVE: POWER AND SOLIDARITY

Preface

This volume is comprised of selected papers presented at the XIth Michigan Conference in Applied Linguistics 'Variation in Second Language Acquisition', held October 7–9, 1987 at the University of Michigan in Ann Arbor. There were two distinct themes which emerged from this conference: those papers which dealt primarily with Discourse and Pragmatics are published in this volume; those papers which have as their major concern psycholinguistic issues are published in *Variation in Second Language Acquisition Volume II: Psycholinguistic Issues*, also published by Multilingual Matters.

The purpose of the conference was to bring together scholars from two related areas of research. In particular, it was our goal to create a dialogue between sociolinguists and second language acquisition researchers in an attempt to understand precisely where their areas of concerns intersect and how those shared concerns contribute in a broader perspective to the issue of language variation. The conference succeeded in bringing together scholars from North America, Asia, Eastern Europe and Western Europe, representing a wide range of geographical and academic backgrounds.

As usual in such a large undertaking, there are many people to thank. The University of Michigan, continuing its commitment over the years to language teaching and learning, provided through a number of resources the principal funding and the setting for this endeavour. The English Language Institute and its Director, Professor John Swales, gave the essential financial and logistic support. The Interdisciplinary Program in Linguistics, the English Composition Board, The Department of Germanic Languages and Literatures and the Rackham School of Graduate Studies also provided financial support as did the Polish Exchange programme of Eastern Michigan University and the English Language Center of Michigan State University. Many colleagues, students and staff helped with the running of the conference, and we are grateful to them as well.

Section One:
Introduction

1 Introduction

Variation is central to the discipline of sociolinguistics. Recently, there has been a growing interest in establishing connections between sociolinguistics, on the one hand, and second language acquisition, on the other, the goal being to determine the relevance of each discipline to the concerns of the other. One can find in the literature a clear intersection of interests, yet until now there has been little mutual contact. Important advances in the study of variation have been made in both sociolinguistics and second language acquisition studies, with each separate area having implications for the other (see Preston, in press). These books specifically address those areas which are of concern to both disciplines.

A primary goal of sociolinguistics is to account for the facts of variation within a theory of language. Second language acquisition researchers extend variation studies into acquisition settings. This book and the accompanying volume provide an initial impetus for understanding the range of phenomena to be considered and, consequently, for reformulating models of variation.

Two basic connections between these two fields of inquiry form the framework for these two books: variation external to the learner and variation internal to the learner. The first provides the basis for this volume; the second the basis for Volume II. The inclusion of a chapter in Volume I or Volume II is our attempt to highlight that chapter's major contribution rather than imply a limitation of its scope.

The focus in this volume is on second language variation as determined by the social and situational context in which language is used. Earlier views of acquisition held that one first learned the grammar of a language and then used the social context as a vehicle for practice. That is, the external setting was not seen as instrumental in the shaping of a learner's second language grammar. However, in recent years it has been proposed (e.g.

Wagner-Gough & Hatch, 1975) that it is indeed the interactions in which learners engage which shape their language and determine their language development.

This latter perspective spawned a number of studies representing a shift in orientation of second language research. Much research in this decade has focused on the input to the learner (see Gass & Madden, 1985) as a means of understanding the relationship between input and intake (Corder, 1967) as well as on the types of interactions in which a learner is engaged. Long (1980) distinguished between (1) modified input, the language used by native speakers of a language when addressing a non-proficient second language speaker, and (2) modified interaction which refers to the difference in the structure of conversations in which non-native speakers participate. Detailed analyses of the way conversation takes place have revealed structural differences between native speaker/native speaker interactions, on the one hand, and native speaker/non-native speaker interactions on the other (see Day, 1986). From this point of view, it is assumed that the social interactional patterns in which learners engage are basic to acquisition. Thus, one cannot understand how learning takes place apart from the interactions in which a learner is engaged. In fact, one cannot consider input separate from the learner since the input itself is, in the final analysis, mutually created.

If we assume that processes of social interaction are crucial to language acquisition, variation in interactional patterns then becomes central to acquisition research. This volume furthers this perspective by examining such external variables as status, purpose of interaction, native language background of one's interlocutor, proficiency level of one's interlocutor, and topic of conversation. Such variation in interactional patterns is important both descriptively and theoretically, for we cannot begin to understand the causal variables of acquisition until we can determine the range and limits of these patterns.

The chapters in this volume approach the issue of variation from different perspectives. It will become clear upon reading them that the divisions do not imply a narrow focus to chapters. On the contrary, the chapters are highly interrelated. Sections two through five, which comprise the body of the volume, deal with a variety of treatments of variation as a result of external factors.

Section two includes one chapter dealing with the complex issue of standards for pedagogical norms. In this chapter Valdman is concerned with the sociolinguistic interface between the classroom and the world. The pedagogical norms of instruction, though they must be derived from studies of native speaker performance, must also refer to what he characterises as '... a dynamic process of gradual approximation to selected target norms in which transitional replicas—some of which may be sociolinguistically stigmatized—are not only tolerated but sometimes proposed as intermediate targets.' Valdman goes on to note the special problems which obtain in the classroom learning of nonstandardised or vernacular languages where the so-called monitored variety of the native speaker is not available as a model and where the diglossic or continuum nature of the target language imposes considerable responsibility on the learner. Valdman cautions that learners and native speakers alike do not refer to one variety, even in diglossic speech communities, as *the* norm. He uses a multi-norm model for second language studies, exactly as Gumperz and others have urged consideration of social identity and metaphoric shifting as important concepts in mono-lingual sociolinguistic studies. In natural language learning situations, competing norms will influence learners precisely to the degree that they catch their attention and allegiance; in classrooms, however, there is an opportunity for selection. Based particularly on his knowledge of language and culture in Haiti, Valdman outlines how one might select from the competing norms of a creole language and offer pedagogical norms for the developing interlanguages of learners at various stages of development.

Section three includes chapters which investigate a variety of concerns in second language acquisition—speech acts, politeness, conventionalised expressions and attention to perlocutionary matters. Kasper begins her chapter with a review of interlanguage pragmatics, clarifying basic notions and discussing several central theoretical issues, including that of contextual variation. She lists the learner's 'pragmatic tasks' as primarily learning (a) new speech act categories, (b) new distributions of speech acts and (c) new means for speech act realisations. Her data come from a discourse completion task of the speech act of requesting as realised by second language learners. She finds a preference by non-native speakers for longer 'propositional explicitness' where native speakers prefer shorter and more implicit request statements, a higher variation in non-native directness level, learner-specific behaviour in directness levels, and higher non-native frequency in use of 'external modification' in request realisation.

The chapter by Olshtain and Blum-Kulka investigates the function of bilingual code-switching and code-mixing. As in the chapter by Kaufman and Aronoff (Volume II), the data come from Hebrew—English bilinguals with the specific focus on language use (as opposed to language attrition in the work by Kaufman and Aronoff). The setting for investigation was family dinner table conversations. They consider the context in which code-switching occurs, including the status of the two languages and the proficiency of speakers and hearers. In addition to contextual variables, they investigate the function which code-switching serves. Their research distinguishes between code-switching and code-mixing. The distinction is determined by the level of the unit of alternation, with code-*switching* involving alternation between grammatical clauses or sentences and code-*mixing* alternation between lower level units, such as idioms or lexical items.

In examining code-mixing data, Olshtain and Blum-Kulka considered where alternation occurs and the resultant syntactic and morphological behaviour of the 'guest' unit. Their results confirm those of previous research: when alternation occurs at morpheme boundaries, the rules of the guest or host language are followed.

Olshtain and Blum-Kulka's analysis of code-switching data, on the other hand, differs from previously reported studies in that equal status is attributed to both languages. To account for their findings, they developed a framework within which to place their results. In particular, they propose three functional levels of code-switching: pragmatic, textual and interpersonal. The first refers to the effect code-switching has on the listener. The second is based on talk across speakers and the function this speech has on the coherence of the discourse. Code-switching thus contributes to intertext coherence. Through investigations of the interpersonal function of code-switching, the authors find that code-switching contributes to a sense of unity among the participants, in their particular case, a family. Therefore, a bond is formed through the use of code-switching.

In the next chapter, Kleifgen, adapting a framework set up by Gumperz, presents a study of ways in which teachers and limited English proficiency students negotiate meaning such as speaker values, beliefs and attitudes, as well as background knowledge, especially classroom knowledge and linguistic and non-verbal codes. Through ethnographic data she considers inferencing processes and further shows that 'shared educational goals' and knowledge can crucially influence interpretation in this setting. Interaction with 'contrasting frames' is exemplified with teacher awareness of such frames stressed as a crucial variable for successful communication in the absence of common linguistic structure.

The chapter by Beebe and Takahashi discusses the face-threatening acts of disagreeing and giving embarrassing information. Their focus is on the language of Americans and Japanese ESL speakers in face-threatening situations. Of particular interest is the difference in status between interlocutors and the resulting effect on the language used. Their results, compiled from questionnaire data (as in Kasper's study), suggest a rethinking of stereotypes of Japanese ESL speakers and stereotypic comparisons between American and Japanese speakers. It is not the case that Americans are consistently more direct and explicit than Japanese (see also the chapter by Kasper for different results). As an explanation, Beebe and Takahashi consider the role of the native language as well as the limited English language proficiency of the Japanese speakers although more definitive results await further research. Their study, like those of Woken and Swales, Zuengler, and Takahashi, reaffirm the important effect of sociolinguistic variables on the nature of non-native speech.

Section four contains studies which base their analyses on the structure of text: in the case of Basham and Kwachka and Stalker and Stalker, the basis is the written text, whereas Williams and Fiksdal deal with oral discourse.

The Basham and Kwachka chapter provides a look at ESL composition data produced by Native American children in Alaska. Cultural transfer is explored. For example, they present evidence of 'unique uses' of modals by these students. They see these uses as an intersection of native cultural concepts of social values and pragmatic properties (even when the native students have lost the ability to communicate in their native American language) with some inherent properties of modality. An interesting result concerns rhetorical effects on modal/tense sequence. The student begins a paragraph, for example, with present tense usage followed by several sentences with a modal word. At the point of topic shift, there appears in the text a concomitant shift back to the present tense followed again by several sentences with the same modal word.

Stalker and Stalker draw on the parallel between native and non-native speakers' development as writers of academic prose. At both sentence and organisational levels, they find a number of errors in common, errors, in fact, often attributed to non-natives as evidence of interference or other aspects of a developing interlanguage. They illustrate with prepositional errors that sentence-level facts (including article deletion, lexical choice and punctuation) which might distinguish native from non-native practice do not, in fact, noting that both type and frequency of errors are similar. At the discourse level they show that the structure of an introductory paragraph, which was intended to specifically include a thesis sentence, was more often missing that element among native speakers than among non-natives. Evidence of crosscultural rhetorical strategies was found for only one writer, and he appeared to be quite conscious of his choice in following a non-native style.

Stalker and Stalker conclude that their non-native subjects may be more skilled at language learning and therefore more adept at following the rhetorical advice on paragraph construction than their native speaker classmates, although they admit that their particular native subjects were not used to reading academic prose. In general, they conclude that problems at every level for native and non-native acquirers of academic prose may not be so different and question the need for separate instruction in advanced writing for these two groups.

Williams' chapter presents a study of linguistic devices used to introduce and/or maintain reference in discourse. Native speakers and two non-native speaker groups (second language learners in the USA, a classic learner variety, and speakers of Singapore English, a non-native 'institutionalised variety') are contrasted from a discourse functional perspective. She is primarily concerned with pronoun copies, pronoun anaphora and zero anaphora. The latter is interestingly contrasted with pronoun omission, which covers the same data but implies different interpretations. The function of these devices in three groups appears relatively constant, though in the non-native groups they have spread to new contexts. Variation occurs in the second language learners, where there is extensive use of pronoun copies. Language transfer enters the Singapore English case with regard to zero anaphora. Variables such as planned/unplanned discourse and shared/surprising information are explored. These variables may intersect in that some communications breakdowns seem to be attributable in unplanned discourse to an overuse of zero anaphora. This may occur in the case where the speaker encodes what is most important, and, perhaps inappropriately, assumes too much shared background information. This situation leaves some referents to be decoded through contextual information in a way that the hearer cannot fulfil.

The final chapter in this section also deals with participants of different status. Fiksdal provides a microanalysis of what goes on in gate-keeping interviews. In particular she gives a microanalysis of uncomfortable moments in discourse based on native language background and the topic under discussion. Unlike the previous chapters in this section, the data are not only from native speaker/non-native speaker interactions, but also from native speaker/native speaker interactions. Importantly, it is the native speaker (a foreign student adviser) who is of higher status. Fiksdal finds that in talk between two native speakers, uncomfortable moments are framed by rhythmic changes in the conversation and by verbal metastatements. Non-native speakers appear to use a different repair system which more seriously affects the timing of the discourse.

In Section five there are three chapters which are concerned with the relationships among individuals within a conversation and the kind of talk which results. Woken and Swales challenge the traditional assumption of native speaker dominance in conversations with non-native speakers. The non-native speakers in their study were advanced graduate students in computer science; the native speakers had little experience with computers. The data come from the non-native speakers instructing the native speaker on the use of a word processing system. The results show that the non-native speaker did indeed dominate in numerous aspects of conversation; the participation of native speakers in the conversation was generally confined to seeking information. An important contribution of this study is the questioning of assumptions of dominance prevalent in the second language literature; topic control and expertise variably affect conversation. How roles of status, expertise and other power relationships relate to actual learning is a question of central relevance to second language acquisition research.

Zuengler's chapter treats similar issues to those discussed by Woken and Swales. She also questions the concept of dominance and control particularly as they relate to negotiation of meaning and second language learning. Her study deals with topic knowledge and the degree of participation in native speaker/non-native speaker interactions. Her data base consists of native speaker and non-native speaker pairs involved in two conversations, one in which one of the members had greater topic knowledge and the other in which topic knowledge was equal. In determining varying degrees of interlocutor behaviour, she considers interruptions, in terms of the actual interruption as well as the resulting behaviours, and amount of talk. In the case in which topic knowledge was equal, there were no differences; in the case in which topic knowledge was unequal, the quality of talk was determined to a large extent by the degree of expertise of a speaker. As with the Woken and Swales paper, domination was found to be less controlled by language proficiency and to a greater extent determined by topic knowledge.

Takahashi's chapter is concerned with non-native/non-native interactions, focusing specifically on the effect that ethnic background and proficiency level of one interlocutor has on the speech of another. The subjects were Japanese women who participated in separate interviews with native speakers of Japanese (high and low proficiency), native speakers of Spanish (high and low proficiency), and a native speaker of English. Takahashi found that the effect of an interlocutor's talk on the speech of a non-native speaker was manifested both linguistically and psychologically.

Speaking to someone of lower proficiency level and/or of the same ethnic background resulted in less speech, speech that was less fluent, speech that reflected greater domination and greater discomfort. On the other hand, speaking with someone of a different proficiency level and/or a different ethnic background resulted in a greater quantity of meaning negotiations. This chapter contributes to the growing body of research on face-to-face interactions by showing the importance of a non-native speaker's perception of the speech of an interlocutor.

We hope this volume helps clarify the notion 'context' in second language acquisition and mainstream sociolinguistics. We further hope that it has contributed to an expanded data-base for further investigation of language variation in the multifold contexts that exist. Future research will have to come to grips with an understanding of the ways in which native language variation and interlanguage variation are similar and ways in which they are dissimilar. An empirical question with important theoretical and applied implications is whether or not a theory of language variation can account for second language data (both developing and fossilised) and, more importantly, whether the two phenomena are sufficiently similar to necessitate a unified theoretical approach to account for both.

Of course, not every theme in language variation that is of importance to second language acquisition is taken up in this and the accompanying volume, but we do hope that the chapters summarise much important work which has been done, reveal current interests and point out likely directions. More abstractly, but no less sanguinely, we hope they serve to place second language studies solidly inside the concerns of general linguistics. Second language acquisition scholars, while recognising the importance of variation to their own interests, need to establish even more firmly the centrality of the study of developing second language systems to general linguistics, particularly in showing how such work entails modification and re-evaluation of sociolinguistic claims formulated in a more limited setting. We will also be pleased if these volumes contribute to the realisation of that position.

References

CORDER, S. P., 1967, The significance of learners' errors, *International Review of Applied Linguistics*, 5 (4), 161–70.

DAY, D. (ed.), 1986, *Talking to Learn: Conversation in Second Language Acquisition*. Rowley, Mass.: Newbury House.

GASS, S. and MADDEN, C. (eds), 1985, *Input in Second Language Acquisition*. Rowley, Mass.: Newbury House.

LONG, M., 1980, Input, interaction and second language acquisition. Ph.D. Dissertation, U.C.L.A.

PRESTON, D., (in press), *Sociolinguistics and Second Language Acquisition*. Oxford: Basil Blackwell.

WAGNER-GOUGH, J. and HATCH, E., 1975, The importance of input data in second language acquisition studies, *Language Learning*, 25, 297–307.

Section Two:
Models and Standards

2 The elaboration of pedagogical norms for second language learners in a conflictual diglossia situation

ALBERT VALDMAN
Indiana University

Introduction

Learning a foreign language (FL) formally, whether it be in the classroom or in the target language community with the provision of some guidance, differs substantially from untutored acquisition in situations of language contact. In characterising the classroom environment W. J. Edmonson (1985:162) invokes an analogue of the Labovian paradox, stated as: '... we seek in the classroom to teach people how to talk when they are not being taught.' But this characterisation of formal language learning fails to stress one of the main differences between it and naturalistic acquisition, the fact that it entails metalinguistic, metadiscursive, and metacommunicative activities. Formal language learning also requires the definition of special norms for the target language. As Soulé-Susbielles (1984) remarks: '... the language that is produced [in the FL classroom] must be evaluated in terms of its own natural context and not according to external norms.'

The notion of the interlinguistic continuum has led to research that has underscored the ubiquity and centrality of variation in the acquisition of the target language (TL) on the part of FL learners. Traditionally, in the teaching of highly standardised languages, particularly the so-called languages of culture such as English, French, German and Spanish, the monitored speech of educated native speakers has been set as the target appropriate for FL learners. I have argued elsewhere (Valdman, 1987) that this definition of the target is too restrictive, and that, instead, attainment of near-native proficiency in a FL entails the capacity to perceive the total *repertoire* of target speakers rather than a particular norm. I have also developed the notion of *pedagogical norms*. Although they are grounded on the observation of the actual speech of target speakers, these special learner norms take into account sociolinguistic and psycholinguistic factors, notably the attitude of both native speakers and learners toward TL variants and learner replicas of TL variable features. Unlike traditional classroom norms, pedagogical norms are not static. On the contrary, they define a dynamic process of gradual approximation to selected target norms in which transitional replicas—some of which may be sociolinguistically stigmatised—are not only tolerated but sometimes proposed as intermediate targets.

If we extend the notion of formal language learning broadly to include not only classroom instruction in standardised languages of culture (which I prefer to label *referential languages*) but also the guided learning of vernacular and vehicular languages (Gobard, 1976), the definition of pedagogical norms poses greater problems. Because norms for these languages are more fluid, the target set for learners is more variable. In addition, it would seem that, in view of the types of situations in which they are expected to use the TL and the types of TL speakers with whom they are expected to interact, learners of vernacular languages would be expected to master less monitored speech forms. But in most multilingual communities whose language behaviour has been closely scrutinised, vernacular languages seldom exist in isolation. In fact they are more likely to constitute the low member of a diglossic pair.[1] In order to communicate effectively with all segments of multilingual communities, foreign learners need to control a linguistic repertoire that includes features of both the low and the high speech varieties.

The linguistic cleavages of multilingual societies reflect deeper under-lying social differences and conflicts which necessarily affect access to the coexisting varieties, the degree of functional complementarity which exists between them, and their hierarchical relationship. All diglossic relationships are at least potentially conflictual since the constituent social groups of multilingual communities have differential access to the coexisting speech varieties and, as a result, they are differentially placed in the dominance–subordination relationship inherent in hierarchically ranked language vari-eties. For these reasons, I prefer to operate with the notion of *linguistic conflict* put forward by Catalan and Occitan sociolinguists (Aracil, 1965;

Kremnitz, 1983; Ninyoles, 1960; Valverdú, 1979), which I have relabelled *conflictual diglossia*. For these sociolinguists, situations of linguistic conflict may be resolved by *assimilation*, a shift toward the dominant (high) variety, or by *normalisation*, the functional expansion and upgrading of the subordinate (low) variety that trigger its standardisation and instrumentalisation.

Charles Ferguson (1959) includes the coexistence of French and Haitian Creole (HC) in Haiti as one of the four prototypical cases of diglossia. But unlike the German-speaking Swiss and Greek situations, these two languages are neither genetically related nor mutually intelligible and only a small minority of the population has effective control of the two languages (Dejean, 1980; Valdman, 1978). Yet, although only about 10% of the Haitians habitually use the two languages in a complementary fashion, the fact that HC depends on its lexifier language (French) for lexical enrichment and the existence of a deep ambivalence toward both languages on the part of all segments of the population make the label of conflictual diglossia eminently appropriate to describe the linguistic situation of the country as a whole. As we will see, the Haitian linguistic situation is paradoxical in that the dependence of HC on the French lexicon increases in proportion to its spread to functional domains heretofore reserved for its lexifier language. As a consequence, a *decreolisation continuum* is forming which threatens its autonomy.

Because they represent the more complex cases of conflictual diglossia, situations where creole languages coexist with their lexifier language provide an interesting test case for the extension of the notion of pedagogical norm beyond the relatively simple case of the teaching of standardised referential languages in the classroom. Theoretical and methodological considerations that emerge from this test case should be applicable to the formal learning of vernacular languages existing in situations of conflictual diglossia. In this chapter, I will discuss the elaboration of pedagogical norms for variable features of HC. I will attempt to show that in the teaching of the language to foreigners the decreolisation continuum that is forming between that language and French, as well as the attitudes of monolingual speakers of HC toward French, preclude the adoption of the most obvious solution, namely, targeting learners' speech on the speech of the 90% of the population who master only the vernacular. In this chapter I will adhere to the following order. First, I will review the concept of pedagogical norm and the theoretical view of interlinguistic variation on which it is based. Second, I will describe the structural relationship between HC and French, and I will show that a variety of factors conspire to reduce the line of demarcation between the two languages. Third, I will apply the notion of pedagogical norm to several HC linguistic variables situated on the decreolisation continuum.

The notion of pedagogical norm

Early IL variationist studies

Early attempts to account for interlinguistic (IL) variability have focused inwardly, as it were. L. Dickerson (1975) and W. Dickerson (1976) showed that approximation to the TL model proceeds in wave-like fashion. Learners produce a variety of replicas for individual TL features, each replica predominating in a particular environment. Tarone (1979, 1983) hypothesised that second language learners' productions constitute a continuum analogous to the vernacular-standard continuum of the early Labovian sociolinguistic model (Labov, 1966). She showed that variation in interlinguistic replicas correlates with degree of attention to speech form. The most deviant yet systematic IL features, analogous to Labov's vernacular, are produced under conditions of reduced monitoring of speech form. At the opposite pole, heightened monitoring leads to forms that more closely approximate target models but which show least internal consistency. However, a shortcoming of these early studies is that they assumed invariable TL models.

A multi-norm model of language variation

In his study of urban black English, Labov (1972:249) accounts for the persistence of stigmatised forms in the vernacular speech of black youths by invoking a set of covert norms that attribute positive value to the vernacular. An analogous observation was made by Léon (1973) who reported shifting among alternative norms in a small village in Touraine. He noticed that a group of male speakers from farmer and worker backgrounds shifted away from the local apical r in two directions: they replaced it either with the velar resonant typical of Standard French or by a pharyngal resonant found among working class Parisians. The latter variant coincided with macho behaviour and took place typically in a café run by a retired railway worker from Paris. Such shifts in norm orientations cannot be accounted for exclusively in terms of relative attention to speech form. They reflect acts of social identity triggered by social relationships among interlocutors, as well as various social and psychological factors present in the communicative situation.

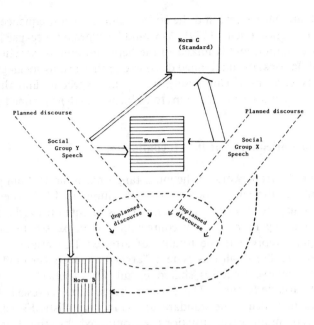

FIGURE 1. *Multi-target model of language variation*

As an alternative to the unidirectional vernacular-standard model I offer the multi-norm model represented in Figure 1. All social groups in a speech community have available a range of speech styles determined by coexisting norms. In Figure 2 the square boxes labelled Norm A, Norm B and Norm C, respectively, represent alternative norms available to the various social groups of a speech community. For the sake of simplicity only two social groups are posited, X and Y. The widths of the arrows reflect the relative power of attraction exercised on a particular social group by a given norm. Shifts in norm orientation are determined by the social identity speakers wish to signify in the course of a particular speech event. In daily communicative interactions with their peers, speakers make use of their vernacular. In complex communities one of the norms becomes associated with political power and/or prestige. It undergoes a gradual process of uniformisation and gains the status of *standard*.

In addition to reflecting multiple norm orientation a speaker's verbal production varies between planned and unplanned discourse. Unplanned discourse, which characterises conversational interaction, reflects reliance on the situational context and the lexicon and, as a consequence, it shows syntactic reduction (Ochs, 1979). As would be expected, because it relies on shared information and is linked to the here and now of specific communicative situations, the unplanned discourse of the various social groups in a community converges. Conversely, we would expect to find the greatest differentiation among social groups to be located in their planned discourse.

The multiple orientation of the IL continuum

Within the framework of the multi-target norm model I am proposing to account for the variation present in the input to FL learners, the IL continuum may be viewed as a vector which is oriented toward a particular norm by filtering input and by controlling feedback, see Figure 2. The largest square represents the totality of attested TL variants. Following Chaudenson (1986) I call this system Target Language Zero (TL0).[2] This system encompasses features shared by all TL varieties, as well as the totality of variable features. The three smaller squares represent competing norms, one of which is the standard norm. In naturalistic FL learning the types of communicative situations encountered by the learners will determine in large part the orientation of their IL continuum. In formal FL learning, however, the IL continuum may be controlled to a certain extent by selection and sequencing of linguistic features, by instructional procedures, and—last but not least—by the elaboration of pedagogical norms.

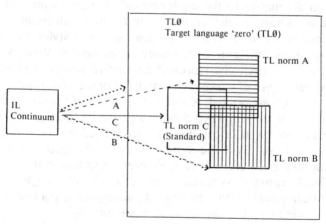

FIGURE 2. *Possible orientations of IL continuum toward various TL norms*

Learner perception of appropriate TL norms

The varieties of the TL which are appropriate for foreign learners are determined by the attitudes of the TL community as well as those of the learners themselves. From casual observations and anecdotal reports it would seem that TL speakers expect foreigners who have learned their language formally to speak 'better' than they do, that is, to evidence control of the TL community linguistic repertoire characteristic of formal usage and written discourse. They generally ascribe lower social status to foreigners who use devalorised variants. Whereas there exists a considerable body of research on native speakers' reactions toward learners' deviant IL features (see d'Anglejan 1983 for a review of the literature), little attention has been paid to their reactions toward learners' choice among variants of TL variable features.

In the absence of a substantial body of empirical research that bears on defining sociolinguistically acceptable learner norms, we must resort to extrapolation from other areas of interlinguistic research. Ryan (1983) has proposed a model involving the parameters of status and solidarity to account for TL speakers' reactions to foreign accents. Accents and other interlinguistic features are highly salient markers of out-groups. This fact would lead us to exclude from pedagogical norms features symbolising in-group membership, such as socially or regionally marked variants. Appeal to the notion of linguistic capital (Bourdieu, 1977) also supports the selection for foreign learners of norms associated with dominant social and political status and formal usage. The learning of a FL may be viewed as an economic investment whose value increases in direct proportion to the status conferred by variant forms: the higher the social status associated with a variant, the more remunerative the investment.

Defining principles of pedagogical norm

Four principles guide the elaboration of pedagogical norms. First, they should reflect the actual speech of TL speakers in authentic communicative situations. Second, they should conform to native speakers' idealised view of their speech use. Third, they should conform to expectations of both native speakers and foreign learners concerning the type of linguistic behaviour appropriate for foreign learners. Fourth, they should take into account processing and learning factors.

Illustration of a pedagogical norm

I will illustrate the application of these four principles to the selection and sequencing of French WH-interrogative constructions, a notoriously variable area of French syntax (Valdman, 1975; 1976; 1983). Traditionally, two WH-constructions are selected for the teaching of French as a foreign language: *est-ce que* and *inversion*. However, as the data in Table 1 show (Behnsted, 1973), these constructions are relatively rare in vernacular speech. Instead, French speakers most frequently use variants often characterised as 'ungrammatical' but which are syntactically less complex, *pronominalisation* and *fronting*. It is noteworthy that Behnsted's middle-class informants overestimated their use of the most valorised construction and, on the other hand, underestimated their use of the two stigmatised variants.

There are no studies of native speakers' attitudes regarding the relative appropriateness of WH-question variants for foreign learners. Invoking the criteria of status and solidarity (Ryan, 1983), one may assume that French educated middle-class speakers would expect foreign counterparts to adhere

TABLE 1. *Relative frequency of the distribution of interrogative constructions in a representative corpus of spoken French (Behnsted, 1973)*

	Production			
	Fr. Pop.	Fr. St. I.	Fr. St. F.	Perception
Pronominalisation				
Tu vas ou?	12%	33%	25%	20% −
Fronting				
Ou tu vas?	36%	46%	10%	30% −
Est-ce que				
Ou est-ce que tu vas?	8%	12%	3%	20%(+)
Est-ce que variants				
Ou c'est que tu vas?	45%	4%	—	
Inversion				
Ou vas-tu?	9%	5%	62%	30%(+)
	N-587	N-446	N-436	

closely to their own subjective norm and to favour *inversion* which they associate with formal style and written discourse. The two most frequent types—*pronominalisation* and *fronting*—appear to be the most easily learnable. A study of the acquisition of French WH-questions by American English learners (Valdman, 1975; 1976) revealed a high proportion of *fronting* despite the fact that this variant had not been part of the input. Its presence in learners' output represents a case of creative construction (Dulay *et al.*, 1982).

The first three principles of pedagogical norm elaboration converge to identify *inversion* as the most highly valued variant from a sociolinguistic perspective. No doubt native speakers would deem it most suitable for foreigners who have acquired the language by a formal process. Bourdieu's view of language as capital would also lead learners to assign inversion the highest surrender value. On the other hand, it is highly marked, both from the syntactic and the sociolinguistic perspectives. In addition, the numerous syntactic constraints that apply to that variant (Valdman, 1975) made it difficult to learn and to use with accuracy. The sociolinguistically neutral status and relative syntactic regularity of *est-ce que* designate it as the choice for first-level target approximation. However, since fronting appears as a case of creative construction, it is a likely candidate for transitional use in early stages of learning, see Figure 3.

As was pointed out above, the notion of pedagogical norm makes it possible to progressively orient the IL continuum toward the ultimate target norm selected. The TL variant chosen for initial presentation is the one learners can most easily process. Should it be a stigmatised feature, it is progressively replaced by a sociolinguistically neutral or valorised variant. In the case at hand, *fronting* would be the variant presented first. It would be progressively faded out in favour of the more neutral and valorised *est-ce*

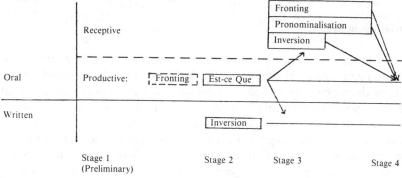

FIGURE 3.

que construction. *Inversion* would be introduced in written and formal discourse and in final stages of instruction. All four variants would be presented for recognition and active control in appropriate situational contexts.

Variation in conflictual diglossia

The linguistic situation of Haiti

All of the approximately six million Haitians speak the country's vernacular, HC, but only about 10% of them have proficiency in the referential and politically dominant language, French. HC has steadily encroached on the functions that previously were the exclusive domain of French; for example, it is now the classroom medium for the first five years of instruction in a third to half the country's primary schools and, in the 1986 constitution, it is recognised as an official language together with French. Yet the vernacular language does not yet enjoy full promotion by the government and members of the social groups with social, economic and political power. As is the case for all creole languages that coexist with their lexifier language, it still tends to be perceived as a debased variant of French. More importantly, and partly as a consequence of this deep-rooted attitude, HC is subject to strong structural pressures from its lexifier language which most strongly affect its lexicon but which appear at the phonological and morphosyntactic levels as well. I will attempt to show that these two aspects of the relationship between HC and French in Haiti determine a general pattern of variation in HC in which variable features will align themselves on a continuum whose mesolectal pole is oriented towards French. This pattern of variation constitutes a central factor in the elaboration of a pedagogical norm for the teaching of HC to foreigners.

Variation in HC

Although there are local differences, in particular sharply differentiated variants in the north and the south, HC is remarkably homogeneous, in spite of the absence of a good road network that condemns a large part of the rural population (nearly 75% of the population) to relative isolation. Such variants as have been identified fall into two categories: a central form characteristic of the capital Port-au-Prince region but spreading out gradually; a peripheral variant attested in increasingly remote areas. Some of these contrasting central vs. peripheral variants are not located on the basilectal HC-French decreolisation continuum.[3]

Gloss	French	Central	South	North
		(*Port-au-Prince*)		
peanut	arachide		pistach	amizman
pot	marmite		mamit	kanistè
to joke, to fool around	plaisanter	jwe	badinen	jwe
progressive verb marker	(après)	ap	ape/pe	ap

But a large number of HC variable features orient themselves on the decreolisation continuum: the central variant approximates the French corresponding form and the peripheral variant diverges from it. The fact that it alternates with the peripheral form in remote regions shows the strong attraction exerted by the central, French-oriented variant.

Gloss	French	Central	Peripheral
		(*Port-au-Prince*)	
thirst	soif	swaf	swaf/swèf
box	boîte	bwat	bwat/bwèt/brèt
already	déjà	deja	dija
wise	sage	saj	saj/say/chaz/chay
garlic	aïl	lay	laj
orange	orange	zoranj	zoranj

Although the variants listed in the two sets above correlate mainly with geographical factors, they also involve a social dimension. In a given area the central variant is more likely to be found among urban dwellers, and in towns, among members of the bilingual middle classes. For example, in the south-western town of Les Cayes, for the progressive verb marker, speakers alternate between the local form *pe* and the central variant *ap*. (Interestingly, some informants when commenting on these forms declared that *pe* was the HC form and *ap* the French one!) But some variants correlate with social class membership. For the variables listed below the variant approximating the French cognate tends to be found among middle class bilinguals, although—a fact which is crucial to our argument—any monolingual speaker may alternate between the two variants.

Gloss	French	Urban	Rural
		(*bilingual*)	(*monolingual*)
rice	(du)riz	duri	diri
sister	sœur	sèu	sè
two	deux	deu	de
family	famille	famiy	fanmiy
leg	jambe	janb	janm
ashes	cendre	sand	sann

HC lacks front-rounded vowels, it assimilates all voiced stops to the preceding nasal consonant, and although vowel nasalisation has phonemic value, vowels tend to become nasalised in the context of a nasal consonant. The first two features are strongly associated with class status, and, as we would expect, they are subject to hypercorrection. This tendency to hypercorrection affects particularly the front-rounded vowels and their front-unrounded equivalent; these in fact function as shibboleths, effectively filtering out monolingual speakers with rudimentary knowledge of French. For example, once, in a small town of the Port-au-Prince region I asked a schoolgirl for the name for the bow she was wearing in her hair (the term varies greatly in Haiti: *papiyon, kokad, ne/neu*). She responded with the mesolectal variant *neu*. But when I pointed to my nose and asked her to give the HC name, she provided the hypercorrect form *neu* instead of the basilectal form *nen* or the mesolectal form *ne*.

That no mutual intelligibility exists between HC and French stems from their profound differences at the morphosyntactic level. For example, HC lacks inflectional categories: there is no gender agreement in the nominal system and tense and aspectual categories are expressed by the adjunction of free verb markers to invariable verb bases. HC has remained relatively impervious to syntactic encroachments from French, except for a shift from parataxis to hypotaxis. Unlike French, HC does not require a complementiser for sentential complements. Thus, in (1) HC does not have any function word matching French *que*:

(1) *M kwè* [ ] *yo pati*. Je crois **qu'**ils sont partis. 'I think they've left.'

Frenchified varieties of HC increasingly contain the complementiser *ke* (often pronounced with the corresponding front-rounded vowel). This is not a new development, as is attested by the following excerpts from early nineteenth century texts. (2a) is abstracted from a play written in 1818 by Emperor Christophe's court poet, a certain Juste Chanlatte, who held the title of count. The second text is an excerpt from one of the proclamations posted by the commander of the French expeditionary force dispatched by Napoleon Bonaparte to subdue the slave revolution in Saint-Domingue. The distinctly basilectal flavour of the first excerpt, depicting the words of a servant, stems in part from the absence of the complementiser. It contrasts with the administrative tone of (2b), which in fact constitutes the first attested use of HC in the official sphere.[4]

(2a) Play by Juste Chanlatte, Comte de Rosiers, 'L'entrée du Roi en sa capitale en janvier 1818.'

A force nou brûlé d'envie et d'impatience, mo craire [ ] *têt à toute monde va tourné folle* quand à coeur à moé li après palpité, li dans délire tant comme prémié fois gié à moé té contré quienne à toé ... n'a pas pitit composé li va composé dans tête à li, tant mo vlé [ ] *toute zoiseaux pé dans bois* pour io tendé mo chanté. (So much we burn of desire and impatience, I think that head of everybody *future* turn crazy; so far as is concerned heart of me it *progressive* flutter, it in delirium the same as first time eye-my *past* meet those of you ... *negative* + have not little composition he *future* compose in head-his, so much I want [ ] all bird quiet in wood for they listen to me sing.)

(2b) Proclamation of General Leclerc, 1802.
Lire Proclamation primié Consul Bonaparte voyez pour zote. Zote à voir **que** *li vélé nègues resté libre*... Li va mainteni commerce et culture, parce que zote doit conné **que** *sans ça, colonie pas cable prospéré.* Ça li promé zote li va rempli li fidellement. (Read proclamation [of] first Consul Bonaparte send for you. You *future* see that he want negroes remain free... He *future* maintain commerce and agriculture, because you should know that without that colony not able [to] prosper. What he promise [to] you he *future* fulfil it faithfully.)

Conflict of norms in the standardisation of HC

Together with functional expansion HC has undergone a moderate amount of standardisation and instrumentalisation. It is now provided with an autonomous systematic phonologically-based spelling, and it is undergoing a process of informal codification. However, standardisation is proceeding in two opposite directions: toward and away from the mesolectal pole of the decreolisation continuum, respectively. The first direction, based on the principle of maximal differentiation between HC and its lexifier language (Baissac, 1880; Bernabé, 1983), is defining a norm oriented towards the basilectal pole of the decreolisation continuum. In the absence of any governmental agencies engaged in language planning, the responsibility for standardisation has fallen on the shoulders of religious groups. These groups, representing both Protestants and Catholics, have taken the lead in introducing HC in the educational sphere, and they also produce the bulk of written material in HC, including translations of the Bible and two monthly magazines which jointly reach from 50,000 to 200,000 persons. The norm developed by this private sector is relatively homogeneous. It systematically eliminates Frenchified features and attempts to steer a middle course between urban and rural varieties of the vernacular. On the other hand, the media and private sectors not affiliated with the church groups engaged in large-scale standardisation and instrumentalisation promote a norm oriented toward the mesolectal pole. The texts (oral and written) they produce are replete with nonce borrowings from French and Frenchified features.

The two texts below, abstracted from news notices released by the United States Information Service office in Port-of-Prince in the spring of 1985, illustrate the two norm orientations. These texts have been produced by two translators who not only differ with regard to norm orientation but also with regard to choice of autonomous spelling. (3a) uses a variant of the older Faublas–Pressoir spelling; (3b) opts for the now officialised IPN system. It is noteworthy that the translator who favours Frenchification fails to adhere rigorously to spelling conventions and slips into occasional graphic Frenchification:

(3a)   Basilectal, Faublas–Pressoir spelling[5]
       Yon lòt bagay ankò Ambasad la ta vle fè nou **chonjé**: depi konsil la dakò pou bay viza-a, l ap **ri**n**mèt** moun lan yon ti kat. Se kat-sa-a **pou** *li prezante nan konsila-a* pou yo ka **ri**nmèt li paspò ak tout viza-a ...
       (An other thing also Embassy-the would want make us/you reflect on: since consul-the in agreement for give visa-the, he *progressive* hand over person-the a small card, it's card-this for he present at consulate-the for they able hand over [to] he passport with all visa-the)

(3b)   Mesolectal, IPN spelling
       ... senk lot moun ki t'ap eseye rantre anbachal Ozetazni. Gad kot ameriken yo fè yon rapò sou yon ti bato **ke** *yon bato patrouy yo jwenn sou lanmè Ozetazini a minwi pase.* Kidonk, yo te considere yo kankou etranje **ke** *yo gen dwa ekspulse.* (... five other person who *past progressive* try enter clandestinely [to the] United States. Coast guard American-*plural* make a report about a little boat which a boat patrol [patrol boat] find on sea [in the] United States at midnight past. Thus, they past consider them like foreigner which they have right [to] deport.)

These two samples show opposite choices among some of the variables discussed above: the use of the complementiser *ke* in the mesolectal text (3b) whereas (3a) shows the basilectal complementiser *pou* 'for' zero. The nasalisation of vowels in the context of nasal consonants (the mesolectal equivalent of *rinmèt* would be *remèt*); in (3a) 'consul' appears with the basilectal variant of the diaphoneme *u* realised as front-unrounded [i] or front-rounded [y].

However, the same persons who espouse a basilectal norm in language planning activities will show orientation toward the competing Frenchified mesolectal norm. Most of the private sector language planners and language developers I have interviewed in Haiti use front-rounded vowels and lace their speech with the complementiser *ke*. Yet these are features they systematically eliminate from texts they produce or edit that are destined for consumers of HC materials, many of whom are monolinguals. In (4) I provide a sample of speech produced by one of these persons when he was interviewed on the radio (the discussion concerned sexual symbolism in Carnival costumes):

(4) ... tout bagay ki pwent**u** ... senbolikman li r**eu**prezante ... donk on sòt d**eu** rapò antr**eu** fiy **e** gason menm si moun nan pa panse **a** sa d**u** tou ... menm enkonsyaman nan sans pwofon se sa l senbolize bagay sa yo menm si nou pa konsyan d**eu** sa. (every thing which [is] pointed ... symbolically it represent ... therefore a sort of relationship between woman and man even if person-the not think about that at all ... even subconsciously in deep sense it's that it symbolise thing-this-*plural* if we not conscious of that.)

So far as monolingual speakers are concerned, they distinguish two varieties of HC which, interestingly, they describe metaphorically with dichotomous terms describing hair types: *swa* and *rèk*. The latter refers to Negroid kinky hair, the former to smooth Caucasian hair. When asked to describe or characterise these two varieties, speakers will produce doublets situated on the decreolisation continuum, for example *chonje* vs. *sonje* (songer) 'to think', *mouche* vs. *misye/msye/msyeu* (monsieur) 'man'. Examples of **kreyòl rèk** they offer will usually consist of stereotypical rural basilectal forms, such as *mouche*.

Toward the elaboration of a pedagogical norm for HC

The application of the principles that determine pedagogical norms to the variable features of HC discussed in the preceding section is rendered difficult by the lack of information. Few empirical studies are available that describe variation in HC. The diglossic relationship between HC and French requires, in addition to studies on the use of variables by monolingual speakers, the observation of dyadic interactions between bilingual speakers, between bilingual and monolingual speakers, and between both categories of Haitians and foreign users of HC. Among the factors that might influence norm orientation are attitudes of speakers toward the norms themselves. For example, are language planners and developers involved in the standardisation of HC toward the basilectal norm more likely to accommodate toward that norm when they interact with monolinguals than fellow members of the middle classes who are unconcerned about linguistic matters or who still hold strongly the view of HC as a debased and corrupted version of French?

The intense political activity that has followed the overturning of the Duvalier regime has led to an explosive increase in the public use of the vernacular, for example in posters and tracts. Paradoxically, since this increasing use has not been matched by greater attention to standardisation and lexical enrichment of HC, it has resulted in a higher degree of Frenchification and the potential destabilisation of HC as an autonomous language variety.

Foreigners who learn HC intend to use it to communicate more effectively with monolingual speakers in the countryside or in the urban slums of Port-au-Prince. A basilectal norm would seem to meet their needs better. However the diglossic relationship between HC and French and the increasing decreolisation that the vernacular is undergoing suggest that monolingual Haitians would view foreign learners more favourably if they spoke 'better' than they, that is, if they were oriented toward the more prestigious mesolectal norm. For rural and lower class urban monolinguals, foreigners are associated with the bilingual middle classes of the country, and they would be expected to share the same norm orientation.

Thus, foreign learners would have to be trained to borrow freely from French, particularly in discourse dealing with technological and administrative matters. In view of the highly symbolic value of the complementiser *ke*, foreigners might be well advised to utilise it in constructing complex sentences. On the phonological level, they should favour vowel denasalisation in contexts where oral and nasal vowels alternate freely and front-rounded over their unrounded counterparts. For learners, however, who have not acquired the ability to distinguish between these two series of vowels, the fourth principle of pedagogical norm elaboration—the consideration of acquisitional factors—would indicate designating instead basilectal features as learning targets. For example, American learners would find it difficult to distinguish front-rounded [y] from [u]. In attempting to produce words like *ju/ji* they would be likely to confuse them with matching words containing back-rounded [u]. In order to differentiate minimal pairs like *ji/ju* 'juice' vs. *jou* 'cheek', they could, as a transitional step, produce the former with its unrounded, basilectal variant.

Conclusion

Commenting on the relationship between research and teaching, Fishman (1965:121) declared: 'There is nothing as practical as a good theory

... [and] ... there is nothing as theoretically provocative as sensitive practice.' I have tried to show that to help foreign language learners acquire an appropriate variable repertoire requires some degree of intervention in the form of defining special pedagogical norms. From the disconcerting array of variants found in the speech of target language speakers a choice must be made that leads eventually to variable behaviour deemed appropriate for foreigners who have learned the language in a non-naturalistic context. The judiciousness of the choice will be in direct proportion to the soundness and insightfulness of the models proposed to account for variation in the target language itself, as well as to the richness of the data collected.

Heretofore there has been a distinct monolingual/monocultural bias to interlinguistic variation. As a consequence it may have only limited relevance to the multilingual situations which—we must remind ourselves—are the norm rather than the exception in the world. To extend interlinguistic research so that it may be pedagogically relevant to such complex situations as the case of conflictual diglossia I have discussed is a challenge that second language acquisition variationists cannot fail to accept.

Notes to Chapter 2

1. I am using the notion of diglossia in the more narrow sense attributed to it by French hellenists who first coined the term (Psichari, 1928) and by C. A. Ferguson in his seminal article (1959). Unlike later definitions broadened to include the complementary use of any two speech varieties (Fishman, 1972; Fasold, 1984), in its original sense diglossia described a situation in which the two complementary varieties are closely related and, in addition, hierarchically ranked: the low variety assumes primarily vernacular and local vehicular functions; the high variety exclusively serves referential functions. As a corollary only the high variety is likely to undergo standardisation and to be endowed with a systematic written representation. Classic diglossia, as defined by Ferguson, is in a sense asocial. It presupposes a static social situation in which all members have equal access to the coexisting varieties.

2. Chaudenson deals exclusively with French varieties. He introduces the notion of French Zero to encompass all attested variants of variable features, including those of the standard variety.

3. HC forms are represented with the orthography officialised in 1979 by a decree issued by the then lifelong president Jean-Claude Duvalier which permitted the use of the vernacular as main pedagogical vehicle in the nation's primary schools. The orthography was devised by a team of specialists comprising linguists from The University of Paris-V (René Descartes) working at the National Pedagogical Institute of Haiti (I.P.N.), hence the label IPN which I use to refer to it.

4. These early HC texts are reproduced in the original etymological spelling. Note, however, the scribe's attempts to show some of the salient distinctions between HC forms and their French cognate. Instead of contextual equivalents I provide a transliteration in which grammatical morphemes are represented in italics. Note that in HC determiners and possessive adjectives are post-posed and the verbs and nominals (nouns, adjectives, determiners) are uninflected.

5. The Faublas–Pressoir spelling was devised in the late 1940s by the Haitian journalist Charles-Fernand Pressoir and adopted in 1951 by the Ministry of Education's programme of adult literacy directed by Lélio Faublas. It stemmed from a reaction to the first systematic phonologically-based spelling proposed for HC by two 'Anglo-Saxons', a North Irish Methodist minister, Ormonde McConnell, and the American adult literacy specialist Frank Laubach. Pressoir objected to a small number of orthographic conventions that departed from those of French, especially the use of the circumflex accent, instead of diagraphs composed of vowel + *n* to represent nasal vowels. Compare: [vãn] 'to sell' *vân* vs. *vann*; [vã] 'wind' *vâ* vs. *van*. Pressoir also strongly objected to the use of the so-called Anglo-Saxon letters *y* and *w* to render the semivowels [j] and [w], respectively. For *y* he substituted *y* in words not traceable to French etyma and *i* elsewhere; for *w* he used *ou*: [pje] 'foot' *pjé* vs. *pié* but [jo] '3rd person plural pronoun' *yo*: [lwa] 'vaudoun spirit' *lwa* vs. *loua*, [wanga] 'vaudoun charm' *wanga* vs. *ouanga*.

An important factor in the polemics surrounding the elaboration of an autonomous spelling for HC is the diglossic relationship between that language and French. To understand the nationalist anti-American overtones of Pressoir's reaction to some of the choices of the McConnell–Laubach spelling it should be remembered that in the 1940s Haiti was emerging from a nineteen year occupation and pacification by the US Marines (1915–1934).

On the other hand, it is difficult to understand the decision to replace the Faublas–Pressoir spelling, viewed by Haitians committed to the upgrading of HC as a national creation, by one perceived as French-inspired. As may be seen from the texts cited in (3a) and (3b), only a half-dozen conventions distinguish the two systems, notably the use of *e* instead of *é* [e], *en* instead of *in* [e], and a return to the Anglo-Saxon letters *y* and *w* to represent the semivowels.

References

ARACIL, L., 1965, *Conflit linguistique et normalisation linguistique dans l'Europe nouvelle*. Nancy: Centre Universitaire Européen.

BAISSAC, C., 1880, *Etude sur la patois créole maricien*. Nancy: Imprimerie Berger-Levrault et Cie.

BEHNSTED, P., 1973, *Viens-tu, est-ce que tu viens? Formen und Strukturen des direkten Fragesatzes im Französischen*. Tübingen: Gunter Narr.

BERNABÉ, J., 1983, *Fondal-natal: Grammaire basilectale approchée des créoles guadeloupéen et martiniquais*, Vols 1–3. Paris: L'Harmattan.

BOURDIEU, P., 1977, L'économie des changements linguistiques, *Langue Française*, 34, 17–34.

CHAUDENSON, R., 1986, Norme, variation, créolisation. *AILA Review*, 2, 68–88.

D'ANGLEJAN, A., 1983, Introduction to special issue, native speaker reactions to learner speech, *Studies in Second Language Acquisition*, 5, vii–ix.

DEJEAN, Y., 1980, *Comment écrire le créole d'Haiti?* Outremont, Québec: Collectif Paroles.

DICKERSON, L., 1975, The learner's interlanguage as a system of variable rules, *TESOL Quarterly*, 9, 401–7.

DICKERSON, W., 1976, The psycholinguistic unity of language learning and language change, *Language Learning*, 26, 215–31.

DULAY, H., BURT, M. and KRASHEN, S., 1982, *Language Two*. New York: Oxford University Press.

EDMONSON, W. J., 1985, Discourse worlds in the classroom and foreign language learning, *Studies in Second Language Acquisition*, 7, 159–68.

FASOLD, R., 1984, *The Sociolinguistics of Society*. Oxford, New York: Blackwell, Ch. 2.

FERGUSON, C. A., 1959, Diglossia, *Word*, 15, 325–40.

FISHMAN, J., 1965, The implications of bilingualism for language teaching and language learning. In A. VALDMAN (ed.), *Trends in Language Teaching*. New York: McGraw-Hill, pp. 121–32.

——, 1972, *The Sociology of Language*. Rowley, MA: Newbury House.

GOBARD, H., 1976, *L'aliénation Linguistique. Analyse Tétraglossique*. Paris: Flammarion.

KREMNITZ, G., 1983, *Français et Créole ce qu'en Pensent les Enseignants, le Conflit Linguistique à la Martinique*. Hamburg: Buske.

LABOV, W., 1966, *The Social Stratification of English in New York City*. Arlington, VA: Center for Applied Linguistics.

——, 1972, *Sociolinguistic Patterns*. Philadelphia: University of Pennsylvania Press.

LAFONT, R., 1984, Pour retrousser la diglossie, *Lengas*, 15, 5–36.

LÉON, P. R., 1973, Réflexions idiomatologiques sur l'accent en tant que métaphore sociolinguistique, *French Review*, 46, 783–9.

NINYOLES, R. L., 1960, *Conflict Linguistic Valencià*. Barcelona: Ed. 62.

OCHS, E., 1979, Planned and unplanned discourse. In T. GIVÓN (ed.), *Discourse and Semantics*, Vol. 12 (Syntax and Semantics). New York: Academic Press, pp. 51–80.

PSICHARI, J., 1928, Un pays qui ne veut pas sa langue. *Mercure de France*, 1–9, 63–120.

RYAN, E. B., 1983, Social psychological mechanisms underlying native speaker evaluations of non-native speech, *Studies in Second Language Acquisition*, 5:2, 148–59.

SOULÉ-SUSBIELLES, N., 1984, La question, un outil pédagogique dépassé? *Le français dans le monde*, 183, 26–34.

TARONE, E., 1979, Interlanguage as chameleon, *Language Learning*, 29, 181–91.

——, 1983, On the variability of interlanguage systems, *Applied Linguistics*, 4, 149–63.

VALDMAN, A., 1975, Error analysis and pedagogical ordering. In S. P. CORDER & E. ROULET (eds), *Some Implications of Linguistic Theory for Applied Linguistics*. Paris: Didier, pp. 105–26.

——, 1976, Variation linguistique et norme pédagogique dans l'enseignement du français langue étrangère, *Bulletin de la Féderation Internationale des Professeurs de Français*, 12–13, 52–64.

——, 1978, *Le Créole: Structure, Statut et Origine*. Paris: Klincksieck.

——, 1983, Language variation and foreign language teaching: Issues and orientations. In L. MACMATHUNA & D. SINGLETON (eds), *Language across Cultures*. Dublin: Irish Association for Applied Linguistics, pp. 171–84.

——, 1987, The problem of the target model in proficiency-oriented foreign language instruction. In A. VALDMAN (ed.), *The Proceedings of the Symposium on the Evaluation of Foreign Language Proficiency*. Bloomington, IN: CREDLI, Indiana University, pp. 131–50.

VALVERDÚ, F., 1979, *La Normalitzacio Linguistica a Catalunya*. Barcelona: Ed. Laia.

Section Three: Pragmatics

3 Variation in interlanguage speech act realisation

GABRIELE KASPER
University of Aarhus, Denmark

Compared to other areas of second language research, interlanguage (IL) pragmatics is still a young discipline. The first studies into non-native speakers' (NNS) perception and performance of speech acts appeared ten years ago, both in North America (e.g. Borkin & Reinhart, 1978) and Europe (Hackmann, 1977). Since then, a number of investigations into IL speech act realisation have been conducted, examining how different types of speech acts are performed by NNSs with a variety of language backgrounds and target languages (cf. the overview in Blum-Kulka *et al.*, in press). While the information collected by these empirical studies contributes significantly to our understanding of speech act realisation across cultures and languages, it seems timely to take a more theoretical view of IL pragmatics, in order to re-examine some central notions and to suggest some directions for future research. This chapter, then, has the following goals:

(1) To provide some conceptual clarification of the notions 'pragmatics' and 'speech act', and to determine the type of variability that is most interesting in the context of IL pragmatics.

(2) To identify NNSs' *learning* tasks in their acquisition of pragmatic knowledge, as a prerequisite for outlining some of the central *research* tasks for IL pragmaticists.

(3) Based on some results from a descriptive study into IL speech act realisation, to discuss what further research questions such results suggest with regard to *explaining* variability in IL pragmatics.

Defining 'pragmatics', 'speech act', and 'variability'

As linguistic pragmatics has its roots in a number of quite different philosophical, sociological, linguistic and psychological traditions, it is not surprising that the area has been defined in many different ways (see Wunderlich, 1972; Schlieben-Lange, 1975; Levinson, 1983; for historical and systematic overviews). According to the currently most influential citation authorities, Geoffrey Leech and Stephen S. Levinson, pragmatics concerns 'the study of meaning in relation to speech situations', dealing with 'utterance meaning' (rather than sentence meaning, which is the domain of semantics) (Leech, 1983:6, 14); it comprises 'the study of language usage' (Levinson, 1983:5). In their respective books on pragmatics, both authors explicate these very general definitions, partly discussing the relative merits of alternative explications (Levinson, 1983:5 ff), partly delimiting pragmatics from neighbouring disciplines (Leech, 1983: 5 ff). A still broader concept of pragmatics is suggested by Verschueren (1987), who argues that rather than regarding pragmatics as defined by a specific research object, it should more appropriately be viewed as a perspective on language. In recent Chomskyan theory, 'pragmatic competence' has been opposed to 'grammatical competence', the latter referring to 'the knowledge of form and meaning' and the former to 'knowledge of conditions and manner of appropriate use, in conformity with various purposes' (Chomsky, 1980:224). Since a large number of grammatical structures, notably pronouns, determiners, tense, aspect, modality, expressions of location, and topicalisation devices, cannot be adequately described without reference to their deictic properties (the speaker's ego-hic-nunc origo, in Karl Bühler's (1934) terms), it has been argued that 'pragmalinguistics' (also: performance linguistics) ought to function as some sort of a linguistic superscience, comprising formal linguistics as one of its specialised areas (e.g. Maas, 1972).

Even though it is true that descriptive adequacy often requires the inclusion of contextual and deictic constraints into the analysis of syntactic structures and the lexicon, this does not invalidate the distinction between otherwise dissimilarly structured types of linguistic knowledge. Rather than perpetuating the fashionable concept of pragmatics as anything related to context and use (or, as one alternative, invoking a semiotic approach along the lines of Peirce and Morris), my suggestion is to revert to the philosophical notion of pragmatics, as developed in the late Wittgenstein's concept of 'Sprachspiel' (language play), in speech act theory as proposed by Austin and Searle, and in Habermas' universal pragmatics. The common ground for these otherwise different traditions is the view of language as *action*

(Greek *pragma* = acting, action, activity). Pragmatics is thus the study of acting by means of language, of doing things with words. In this view, linguistic pragmatics constitutes a subset of a more comprehensive theory of human action (e.g. v. Wright, 1965). Its research object is language users' pragmatic knowledge, its use and development, as studied, for example, in the philosophy of language, linguistics, developmental psychology, and second language research.

I propose to conceive of pragmatic knowledge as a component of language users' communicative competence in the sense of Hymes (1972) and Canale & Swain (1980). Pragmatic knowledge is distinct from other types of declarative communicative knowledge, such as discourse knowledge, semantic, grammatical and phonological knowledge, and also from types of declarative knowledge that are not in themselves 'communicative', but clearly communicatively relevant, such as sociocultural and world knowledge (Færch & Kasper, 1986). Pragmatic knowledge interacts with these other knowledge types, and the language user's task in performing verbal action is to select and combine elements from these areas in accordance with her illocutionary, propositional and modal (or 'social', 'politeness') goals (Leech, 1983; Færch & Kasper, 1984).

Given this rough definition, or demarcation, of pragmatics, it follows that the notion of *speech act* (SA) is central to pragmatic theory. Recently, the adequacy of SA as a theoretical and analytical category in linguistic pragmatics has been disputed, e.g. by Levinson (1981), Thomas (1989) and Candlin (1987); cf. also the excellent summary of the speech act controversy in Verschueren (1985). The main objection is that speaker meaning often cannot be unambiguously identified. Discussing multiple illocutionary force, Thomas (1985) distinguishes four such types:

(1) Ambiguity, where speaker A intends force X, while the addressee B computes force Y, e.g.

A: You're drinking a beer there.
B: Yes.
A: Erm er well er I might er if you were kind enough to offer me one I probably wouldn't say no.
(from Kasper, 1981: 187)

— as obvious from A's second (metacommunicative) utterance, the illocutionary goal of his first utterance was a request, whereas B construed it as a statement.

(2) Ambivalence, where the illocutionary force is deliberately indeterminate—i.e. it is up to the addressee to pick and choose the illocution she

likes. Thus, the utterance

A: I'm sorry but I'm afraid you're in my seat.
(from Kasper, 1981:162)

is ambivalent between a reproach and a request.

(3) Bivalence or plurivalence, where two or more non-related forces are co-present, all of which have to be decoded.
Thomas' example is the back-hand compliment, as in

A: Your hair looks so nice when you wash it.

— where the overt compliment carries a covert insult.

(4) Multivalence, where the utterance has two (or more) different receivers, for instance a direct addressee and another receiver (hearer, audience, overhearer, bystander; Thomas, 1989), a different illocutionary force being addressed to each of them through the same utterance. Thus a showmaster's utterance

A: And now, ladies and gentlemen: Mr Bruce Springsteen.

has the force of an announcement for the (directly addressed) audience, while at the same time functioning as a cue (a specific form of instruction) to the artist to appear on stage.

Since these instances of multiple illocutionary force are both interesting descriptive and explanatory problems for pragmatic theory, and likely sources of misunderstanding in crosscultural communication, they clearly deserve closer study in IL pragmatics. However, I cannot see why they should oblige us to abandon the notion of SA. The co-presence of different illocutionary forces suggests that individual illocutions, as in the examples of pragmatic multifunctionality, will have to be computed. This, however, is no evidence against the identifiability of distinct illocutions: just as illocutionary *multi*functionality is a fact of linguistic communication, so is the unambiguously *mono*functional occurrence of SAs. Indeed, the risk of communication breakdowns would be dramatically enhanced, were it not for the fact that a great number of standardised speech events allow for unambiguous assignment of illocutionary value. Unlike the types of speech event favouring multifunctionality, which are characterised by a predominantly *interpersonal* orientation, speech events with a strong *task* orientation and a fixed distribution of social roles and actional goals, such as service encounters, highly rule-governed work contexts, or bureaucratic institutions, favour illocutions which speaker, addressee and possible third parties immediately agree upon. Thus in a legal trial, an exchange such as *'Objection, your honour'*—*'Objection sustained'*, uttered by participants endowed with the relevant institutionalised rights, is just as little open to illocutionary negotiation as exchanges by mechanics during a car repair task (cf. the exchanges reported in Holmqvist & Andersen (1987) for illustration). An analogy to the identification of lexical meaning suggests itself: the occurrence of semantic ambiguity is not a valid argument against the notion of word, or lexical item. In fact, as Verschueren (1985) convincingly argues, the psychological reality demonstrated for prototypical instances of a variety of lexical items also applies to illocutionary verbs ('linguistic action verbials'), in that they express, in the codes of individual languages, the conceptual space of verbal action. It is by no means compulsory to allege incompatibility of the prototypical *cognitive* representation of illocutionary acts, as reflected in linguistic action verbials, with the fuzzy, multifunctional *communicative* illocutionary values emphasised by Thomas (1989) and others. Metapragmatic statements, performed by participants on the occurrence of co-present illocutionary forces, testify to the contrary, as in exchanges such as *'Mark is bringing his bongos to the party'—'Is that a promise or a threat?'* However, I agree that the *term* 'speech act' has certain infelicitous connotations, suggesting static, clear-cut entities without interrelations and context-embedding. The German term *Sprechhandlung* more appropriately emphasises the dynamic, process character of the notion, as Verschueren successfully captures in his expression 'linguistic action'. Yet, in order not to contribute to an unnecessary terminological inflation, I prefer to retain the received term 'speech act', but use it with the proposed dynamic reading.

The third theoretical issue that deserves comment is the one of *variability* in IL pragmatics. The variation in learners' performance observed in early IL studies was taken by some researchers as counterevidence of the systematicity claimed for ILs, and thus as an embarrassment for IL theory and its fundamental tenet that IL is natural language (e.g. Bertkau, 1974; Ickenroth, 1975; but see for different views Adjemian, 1976; Tarone *et al.*, 1976; and the discussion of the latter in Brown, 1976). That variation at the time was considered more of an oddity than a regular fact of human language appears to be a direct consequence of the prevalent theoretical orientation of second language research towards Chomskyan linguistics and studies into first language acquisition. Since the object of linguistics was defined as a homogeneous system stripped of any social and psychological relations, variation deriving from precisely those relations could not be accommodated within the theory. In his influential elaboration of the IL hypothesis, Corder (1978) makes the observation that linguistic variability along sociological and situational parameters (systematic variability) constitutes no deviation from natural languages but rather one of their most prominent features—a point that is, and was then, obvious enough from a sociolinguistic perspective, but was news to mainstream IL research. A linguistic theory based on the assumption of heterogeneity, as developed, for instance, in sociolinguistics and stylistics, and epitomised in models of *communicative* rather than *linguistic competence*, therefore provides a more adequate framework to account for variability in IL data. Understandably, what was regarded as a problem for IL grammar and phonology was never considered embarrassing for IL pragmatics. Rather than struggling with an alleged opposition between systematicity and variability, IL pragmatics, from its very outset, was firmly based on the sociolinguistic assumption that in order to carry out verbal action, NNSs make *systematic* choices from their repertoire of realisation procedures and linguistic means, and that these choices vary according to relevant factors in the speech event. Uncovering the principles of *contextual variability*, in Ellis' (1986) terms, of SA selection and realisation, is thus the core issue of IL pragmatics. Extending the notion of IL to refer to language learners' developing communicative rather than formal-linguistic competence provided a fundamental prerequisite for investigating NNSs' development and use of pragmatic knowledge within the same theoretical framework as other types of IL knowledge.

Research tasks in IL pragmatics

Next, I wish to outline what I consider the most pertinent research tasks in IL pragmatics. In the tradition of IL research generally, we have said that IL pragmatics seeks to describe and explain learners' development and use of pragmatic knowledge. The learner's task is not very different from that of the pragmaticist: She has to discover the contextual (situational) and co-textual (linguistic) constraints governing SA selection and modes of realisation in the target language and culture. In Hymes' (1971) terms, she has to discover what is possible, feasible, appropriate and done in carrying out SAs in L2.

In principle, acquiring pragmatic knowledge in L2 comprises the following subtasks:

(1) Learning new SA categories, e.g in communication domains with highly culture-specific content and organisation, as in games, religious and profane ceremonies, legal trials, and other institutionalised events. These subtasks interact with the acquisition of sociocultural knowledge about the target society.

(2) Learning new contextual and co-textual distributions of SAs, such as

when to thank whom for what. In Danish culture, for instance, guests are required to offer their hosts ritualised thanks for the meal and 'for the last time' (on the first encounter after having received hospitality). As an immigrant to Denmark, I still have a hard time remembering these rituals. However, immigrants and refugees to the Scandinavian countries with culturally more distant backgrounds are obviously faced with considerably more demanding learning tasks. To give but one example from an important type of gatekeeping encounter, they have to learn that in Scandinavian classrooms, making suggestions, contradicting the teacher, asking for clarification, etc., is not considered as lack of respect, and therefore to be avoided, but rather evaluated as active participation and as such appreciated by the teacher. In Scollon & Scollon's (1983) terms, the precondition for 'leakage' in Scandinavian educational contexts is for the non-member to adopt a solidarity politeness strategy rather than a deference strategy, as may be in accordance with the NNS's native cultural norms. As was the case with the first subtask, learning distributional constraints of SA performance thus requires an understanding of target social structure and values.

(3) Learning new procedures and means for SA realisation. This task is largely dependent on the learner's linguistic L2 knowledge, as it requires availability of and access to at least two types of linguistic knowledge:

(a) 'Productive' grammatical, lexical and prosodic structures, which for the purpose of realising illocutionary intent can attain 'acquired meanings'. For instance, the past perfect of the modal *shall* can be used to express a reproach, given the pragmatic conditions for this illocution are satisfied (i.e. H did event p/p is at a cost to S): *You should have switched off the printer before going to bed.*

(b) 'Frozen' routines functioning as conventionalised realisations of specific speech acts, such as (in English) routines for greeting, thanking, apologising, interrupting.

(4) Learning how these realisation procedures and means are contextually and co-textually distributed. This involves knowledge of how principles of politeness operate in the target culture, and what politeness values pertain to the alternative realisation procedures—in other words, how face-work is carried out in accordance with target sociopragmatic and pragmalinguistic norms.

Which of these tasks require new learning for the NNS depends to a large extent on the distance between the culture(s) familiar to the learner, and the target culture. However, it would be naïve to assume automatic similarity–facilitation and difference–difficulty effects, as in the heyday of the contrastive analysis hypothesis. Rather, transferability constraints have been shown to operate on pragmatic knowledge in a similar fashion as on linguistic knowledge (e.g. Kasper, 1981; Olshtain, 1983). Still, the first tasks—SA categories and their distribution—may be of no or little importance in the case of related languages and cultures. By contrast, realisation procedures and means will have to be newly learned by any NNS. It may be due to the prevalence of SA realisation as a learning task in L2 acquisition that IL pragmatics has concentrated on this area, which is also what the empirical part of this chapter will be concerned with.

Based on the outline of NNSs' learning task in pragmatics, we can now delineate research tasks for IL pragmaticists. Currently, empirical IL pragmatics is focusing on two activities:

(1) collecting and systematising observational facts about variation in NNSs' use of procedures and means for SA realisation;

(2) determining the factors and principles underlying the observed systematic variation. Such factors and principles are:
(a) the configuration of factors in the communicative events, as detailed in the ethnography of communication;
(b) the properties of the SA in question;
(c) the Cooperative Principle à la Grice;
(d) principles, maxims and strategies of politeness, as suggested in the different models of Brown & Levinson (1977), Leech (1983), and others.

Theories formulated within this second area are claimed to have explanatory function for the sociopragmatic and pragmalinguistic variation described in the first area. Unlike studies into the pragmatics of individual languages or contrastive pragmatics, however, matters in IL pragmatics are complicated by the fact that the factors and principles comprised by the second area have to be analysed in relevant cultural manifestations which are unlikely to coincide completely with either the NNSs' L1 or L2.

A study into IL request realisation: some results and research questions

I shall now present some results from a descriptive study into IL SA realisation, with the purpose of discussing two questions: What information about NNSs' systematic variation of their requestive behaviour do such results from cross-cultural and IL pragmatic data provide? What further research questions do they suggest with regard to *explaining* variability in IL SA realisation?

The data comprise request realisations under five different contextual conditions, collected in the Cross-Cultural Speech Act Realisation Project by means of a written Discourse Completion task (cf. Blum-Kulka *et al.*, in press). They are from speakers of six closely related languages and language varieties:

Three groups of NSs:
    Danish (*N* = 163) (D)
    German (*N* = 200) (G)
    British English (*N* = 100) (E)

Three groups of NNSs:
    L1 Danish, L2 German (*N* = 200) (DG)
    L1 Danish, L2 English (*N* = 200) (DE)
    L1 German, L2 English (*N* = 200) (GE)

The request contexts were the following:

1. A policeman asking a driver to remove her car (Policeman)
2. A student asking his flatmate to tidy up the kitchen (Kitchen)
3. A student asking a fellow student for her lecture notes (Notes)
4. A young man asking his neighbour for a lift (Lift)
5. A professor asking a student to present his paper a week earlier (Paper).

As a prerequisite for the analysis, it is assumed that requestive force can be modified on three major dimensions:

(1) by choosing a particular *directness level*;

(2) by modifying the request *internally* through the addition of mitigating or aggravating *modality markers* (syntactic or lexical 'downgraders' or 'upgraders');

(3) by modifying the request *externally* by means of *supportive moves* introductory or subsequent to the Head Act (the request proper).

For the present purpose, results relating to the first and third modificatory dimensions will be considered.

Directness levels

Following Blum-Kulka & House (in press), we can distinguish three degrees of directness, depending on the extent to which the illocution is transparent from the locution: direct, conventionally indirect, and indirect requests. With direct requests, the illocutionary force is indicated in the utterance by grammatical, lexical or semantic means; conventionally indirect requests express the illocution via fixed linguistic conventions established in the speech community; and indirect requests require the addressee to compute the illocution from the interaction of the locution with its context. Within these types of directness, we distinguish the following nine directness levels (or request strategies):

1. Mood Derivable: the grammatical mood of the utterance signals illocutionary force (Move your car!).

2. Explicit Performative: the illocutionary force is referred to by a performative verb (I'm asking you to move your car).

3. Hedged Performative: as (2), with the performative verb modified by a hedging expression (I have to ask you to move your car).

4. Obligation Statement: the hearer's obligation to perform the act referred to in the proposition is stated (You have to move your car).

5. Want Statement: the speaker's wish that the hearer carries out the act referred to in the proposition is stated (I want you to move your car).

6. Suggestory Formula: illocutionary force is indicated by a semantic formula expressing a suggestion (How about moving your car).

7. Preparatory: a preparatory condition for performing the request is referred to, such as the hearer's ability or willingness to carry out the act (Can/would you move your car).

8. Strong Hint: the requestive force has to be inferred from the context; however, at least one element pertaining to the proposition is explicitly mentioned (Your car is in the way).

9. Mild Hint: the requestive force has to be inferred from the context; no mention is made of elements relevant for the proposition (We don't want any crowding).

According to the definitions offered above, direct requests comprise directness levels 1–5, conventionally indirect requests, levels 6 and 7, and indirect requests, 8 and 9 (cf. Blum-Kulka, in press, and Weizman, in press, for further discussion).

Due to the frequencies with which these directness levels are used in the data, they have been grouped for the present study as follows:

1. Mood Derivable   2. Performatives/Obligation Statement/Want Statement/Suggestories   3. Preparatory   4. Hints.

Figures 1(a)–(e) indicate the distribution of the four directness level categories in the six language groups, each figure representing one of the five request contexts.

In the *Policeman* situation, it is noticeable that, with two exceptions, all language groups use *Preparatories* most frequently, though with considerable intergroup variability. The British NSs use Preparatories in as much as 90% of their responses, whereas the three learner groups and the Danish NSs choose this directness level only in 15–56% of their responses. For all groups but the English NSs, direct realisations (Mood Derivables) are possible alternatives in this situation (between 16 and 29%); the German NSs even show a clear preference for Mood Derivables over Preparatories. The Danish learners of German have a still lower choice of Preparatories—only 15%—; they prefer Hints instead (which they use with the amazing frequency of 40%). The choice of directness level thus varies considerably in the Policeman situation.

Moving on to the *Kitchen* situation (Figure 1(b)), the picture becomes more homogeneous. There is still clear intergroup variation in the choice of directness level, but more impressive perhaps is the intergroup agreement: Mood Derivables and the Performative/Obligation/Want/Suggestory levels are chosen between 6 and 24%, Hints between 0 and 6%, and Preparatories are the clear favourites (between 53 and 85%).

As we go on to the remaining requests contexts, this trend towards similar choices becomes most pronounced in the *Notes* situation (Figure 1(c)), whereas both the *Lift* (Figure 1(d)) and the *Paper* situation (Figure 1(e)) show a bit more diversity: some groups make modest choices of the Performative/Obligation/Want/Suggestory levels, and to a lesser extent, Hints are again chosen somewhat more often—but without at all challenging the absolute dominance of Preparatory realisations.

To summarise the most significant descriptive facts:

In all situations and for all language groups (with the exception of the German NSs and the Danish learners of German, cf. Færch & Kasper (in press) for discussion), the most frequently chosen directness level is Preparatory. In the literature, reasonable explanations have been offered to account for this fact, which is corroborated by many other studies (e.g. Rintell, 1979; Fraser & Nolen, 1981; Kasper, 1981): Preparatories as the most pervasive realisation of conventional indirectness strike a convenient balance between the conventional maxim of clarity and marking for politeness, i.e. the requestive force is brought out unambiguously while at the same time social requirements for face-saving are observed (cf. Blum-Kulka in press for further discussion).

(a)

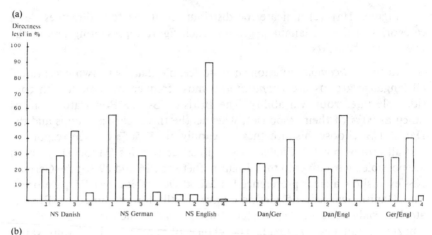

(b)

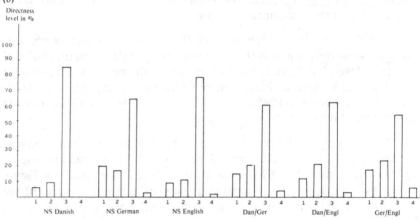

(c)

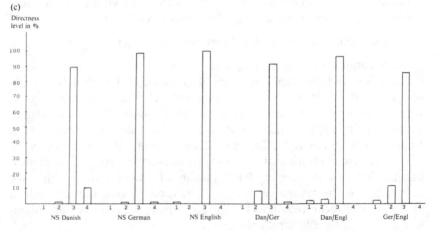

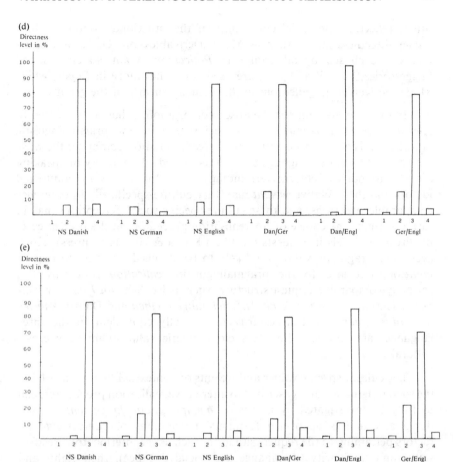

FIGURE 1. *Directness levels in (a) 'Policeman', '(b) 'Kitchen', (c) 'Notes', (d) 'Lift', (e) 'Paper'*
1 = Mood Derivable   2 = Performative/Obligation/Want/Suggestory
3 = Preparatory   4 = Hints

Throughout the language groups and situations, the choice of directness levels follows a consistent pattern: few choices of Mood Derivables, somewhat more of the Performative/Obligation/Want/Suggestory levels; the single most frequent directness level is Preparatory, and the frequency of Hints is roughly between Mood Derivables and Performative/Obligation/Want/Suggestories. Within this overall pattern, contextual and interlingual variation is observable. The NSs of British English indicate least contextual variation in their choice of directness level: in over 85% of cases, they choose Preparatories. All other groups opt for alternative choices more often, reflecting the social constraints of the situational contexts. Thus, higher directness levels, such as Mood Derivables and Obligation Statements, are chosen by all groups in *Policeman*, Want Statements and Suggestories, as well as Hints, are used somewhat more in *Paper*, whilst Mood Derivables are ruled out in this context for any of the groups.

In order to account for the observed variation, it has to be related to relevant aspects in language users' sociopragmatic and pragmalinguistic knowledge. The sociopragmatic knowledge in question comprises the ways the parameters in the language users' internalised ethnography of speaking are set, to borrow current terminology. Both the *values* of contextual factors and their relative *weight* may vary culture-specifically in otherwise comparable situations, and these culture-specific social perceptions may in turn determine the choice of SA realisation procedure, in the present case, of directness levels in requests (cf. Blum-Kulka & House, in press). However, sociopragmatic values are likely to be attached not only to request *contexts*, but also to the pragmalinguistic *realisation procedures*. A formally comparable request structure, such as English *can I borrow your notes,* German *kann ich deine Aufzeichnungen leihen* and Danish *kan jeg låne dine noter* is not necessarily functionally equivalent in the three languages and cultures, i.e. its sociopragmatic value might vary cross-culturally.

The culture-specific values and weights of contextual factors, as well as the sociopragmatic values ascribed to alternative realisation procedures, can usefully be investigated by means of *metapragmatic judgements*. Situational assessments uncover informants' perceptions of context-*external* factors pertaining to the request situation, such as the interlocutors' relative status and familiarity (dominance and social distance), their rights and obligations, and context-*internal* factors relating to the degree of imposition associated with the request goal, the likelihood for the addressee to comply with, and the difficulty for the speaker to perform, the request. In the situational assessment studies of the five request contexts conducted by House (1986) and Blum-Kulka & House (in press), it was found that NSs of German, Hebrew and Argentine Spanish distinguish between types of interaction which are prearranged by social contract, and interactions where 'setting the social parameters' is more open to negotiation. Thus the Policeman and Kitchen context stand out against the remaining three situations in that they were found to exert on the addressee high obligation and therefore likelihood for compliance, while at the same time endowing the speaker with a strong right to carry out the request, and consequently associated with low difficulty of request performance. House (1986) distinguishes such *standard situations* from the Notes, Lift and Paper contexts as *non-standard situations,* characterised by relatively low obligation for the addressee to comply and equally low rights on the part of the requester, thus resulting in greater difficulty in performing the request.

The differential social perceptions of the request contexts have been shown to importantly determine language users' choice of directness level. The studies by House (1986) and Blum-Kulka (in press) suggest that standard situations allow for greater directness, whereas non-standard situations call for more indirect realisation strategies with their inherent potential for negotiation. For native Hebrew, German and Argentine Spanish, the most effective directness predictor was demonstrated to be the degree of the requestee's obligation. Context-internal factors were found to determine the preference for conversational indirectness in the non-standard situations (Notes, Lift, Paper), where the addressee's ability and willingness to comply, as brought out in the semantics of Preparatories, constitute prerequisites for compliance, and are appropriate aspects to focus on in 'asking a favour'.

To apply these findings to the present study, one may ask whether the lower degree of variability in the British NS data suggests that British language users would *not* assign different degrees of imposition, and different distributions of rights and obligations, to the Policeman and Kitchen situations as opposed to the other three contexts? Or does the higher variability in directness level selection shown by the learner groups indicate that the NNSs perceive even greater differences between the five request contexts than the Danish and German NSs, and if so, what factors do they ascribe such differences to? To date, situational assessment studies with NNS informants have not yet been conducted. Their availability will provide one important source of information to account for learners' contextual variation in the choice of request strategies.

The other explanation of variable choices of directness levels relates to the requestive behaviour itself: the sociopragmatic value of modification procedures may be perceived differentially by different language groups. Metapragmatic judgement studies on request realisation have been carried out, e.g. by Fraser & Nolen (1981), in order to assess different modification alternatives in English, and by House (1986) and Blum-Kulka (1987), investigating crossculturally the relationship between indirectness and politeness. While House's and Blum-Kulka's studies grosso modo confirmed the psycholinguistic validity of the directness scale used in CCSARP for NSs of German, British English, Hebrew and American English, the politeness values attached to the individual directness levels were found to vary crossculturally, though with the important shared feature that all four groups perceived conventional indirectness, rather than hints, as the most polite request strategy.

Again, replicating these sociopragmatic assessment studies with NNSs would yield another valuable source of information to explain variable choices of directness level, as learners' perception of the relative directness and associated politeness value may well differ from native assessments, i.e. be IL specific. Furthermore, preferences for alternative directness levels should be related to relevant contextual variables. For instance, it is conceivable that a Mood Derivable level, while presupposing pre-existing obligations for all language groups in the present study, is associated with status *difference* by the German NSs, with status *equality* (emphasising solidarity) by the English NSs, and with either by the learner groups.

Methodologically, then, to test hypotheses about the principles underlying observed contextual variation (here, in the use of directness levels), two types of metapragmatic judgement data are required, namely *contextual* assessment data, probing for the value and weight of context-external and context-internal factors, and *textual* assessment data, providing judgements on modification procedures.

External modification: Supportive Moves

By Supportive Moves we refer to additions to the context of the request that upgrade or downgrade its force. Aggravating Moves can, for instance, be threats, insults or moralising utterances. Mitigating Moves, which are the ones I will consider here, comprise preparing the request (I'd like to ask you something), prerequesting (Are you free this evening?), Imposition Minimisers (Can you give me a lift? *But only if you're going my way*), and Grounders, giving justifications for the request (*I missed the bus*. Could you give me a lift?). In our data, the Grounder is by far the most frequently used Supportive Move.

The distribution of Supportive Moves across the five request contexts and six language groups is represented in Figure 2. With the exception of the Policeman situation, a clear increase in the use of Supportive Moves is noticeable for all groups from the Kitchen context over Notes and Paper to Lift. In these four contexts, the learners modify their requests externally in 18–85% of their responses, whilst the two target language groups, English and German, only use 2–44% supportive moves. The Danish NSs, however, modify their requests externally with up to 80%. A first explanation for the Danish learners' tendency towards external modification could

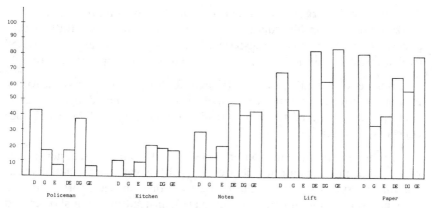

FIGURE 2. *Supportive Moves in %*
D = NS Danish   DE = NNS Danish–English
G = NS German   DG = NNS Danish–German
E = NS English   GE = NNS German–English

therefore be transfer from their L1. Transfer cannot account for the German learners' indulgence in Supportive Moves though, as such a tendency is absent from the native German data. Furthermore, in a study involving American learners of Hebrew, Blum-Kulka & Olshtain (1986) found a similar over-use of Supportive Moves in the IL data as compared to the target language, and again there was no transfer effect. The observed preference for learners to use external modification thus appears to be IL specific communicative behaviour, which they display independently of their L1. This finding raises a number of questions, of which I wish to address two.

(1) Do learners perceive the impositive force of requests as more face-threatening than NSs, and if so, why?

It has been argued that they do, and that the difference in using external modification is an expression of the learners' self-perception as non-members of the target culture. As a consequence of their foreigner role (as discussed, for instance, in Janicki 1986), learners may feel a stronger need than NSs to establish, rather than presuppose, common ground. Instead of relying on the interlocutor's co-operation in reconstructing the implicit justification for requesting, and consequently performing the request without external modification, NNSs may therefore prefer to explicitise the reasons for exerting an imposition on their interlocutor.

According to this argument, learners do not only invest more energy in face work— which, after all, could be done in many other ways. Rather, they appear to prefer a more transparent communicative style than do NSs (which might be considered as a specific kind of face-supportive activity).

As we observed elsewhere (Færch & Kasper, in press), learners' inclination towards 'verbosity', which was already noted by Levenston (1971), is not confined to request realisation, or even to SAs where face concerns are essentially involved.

In her study of cohesion in NS–NNS discourse, Stemmer (1981) reports that intermediate learners of English display a tendency towards 'complete responses', i.e. repeating (part of) their interlocutors' initiating act when this is not functionally motivated, instead of using shorter and more efficient procedures such as ellipsis and pro-forms. In the same data, Kasper (1981) notes the learners' preference for propositional explicitness where NSs would prefer shorter and more implicit modes of expression (e.g. 'Would you like to drink a glass of wine with me' instead of something like 'How about a glass of wine'). Moreover, in their studies of compensatory strategies used by NNSs for solving referential problems, Bongaerts *et al.* (1987) and Tarone & Yule (forthcoming) observe that the learners produce overcomplex and longwinded utterances as compared to NSs of English. These results from different areas of IL discourse tentatively suggest a universal trend for language learners to give preference to the conversational maxim of manner (or clarity), over the maxim of quantity (or parsimony) when these two maxims are in conflict. From the learners' point of view, explicitising may function as a playing-it-safe strategy of communication. Implementing such a strategy presupposes, of course, a rather well-developed linguistic competence, a condition met by the intermediate to high intermediate learner groups reported on in the literature and in the present study.

(2) How is this learner-specific behaviour to be evaluated?

Blum-Kulka & Olshtain (1986) suggest that by adhering to the conversational maxim of clarity rather than quantity, the learners violate the quantity maxim, thus producing instances of pragmatic failure. From the point of view of NS communication, which largely rests on a principle of parsimony, or least effort, this is a convincing analysis. However, as Janicki (1986) has pointed out, it may not be adequate to invoke the same criteria for assessing native and non-native communicative behaviour. For NNSs' contributions to be successful and efficient, they may have to follow different conversational principles. What would count as over-elaboration in native discourse may fulfil a useful metalingual and metacommunicative function in crosscultural communication, serving to clarify the learner's intended semantic and pragmatic meaning. From other areas of IL discourse, it has become apparent that rather than following target norms in crosscultural communication, it may be more appropriate to use conversational procedures that take account of the increased risk of miscommunication. To take but one example, I found in an earlier study (Kasper, 1981) that in conversations with NSs, intermediate learners used considerably more hearer back-channel signals than NS controls in equivalent discourse roles. Through this increased phatic activity, the learners contributed to maintaining the discourse in a situation where mutual comprehensibility could not be taken for granted.

Returning to learners' high frequencies in the use of external modification in request realisation, two types of studies seem necessary to look into the questions raised.

(1) It should be tested in performance studies whether the absence or presence of Supportive Moves in learners' requests is decisive for the success of the interaction, and what other factors they interact with in contributing to communicative efficiency, or lack of the same.

(2) Assessment studies should be carried out with NSs and NNSs as informants, examining how differential use of Supportive Moves as a function of membership vs. non-membership is perceived by native and non-native language users. Because, if learners assess their tendency toward external modification as appropriate, while NSs perceive the same learner behaviour as inappropriate, then this would indeed strongly indicate a source for pragmatic failure, and hence potential breakdown, in crosscultural communication.

References

ADJEMIAN, C., 1976, On the nature of interlanguage systems, *Language Learning*, 26, 297–320.
BERTKAU, J. S., 1974, An analysis of English learner speech, *Language Learning*, 24, 279–86.
BLUM-KULKA, S., 1987, Indirectness and politeness in requests: same or different? *Journal of Pragmatics*, 11, 145–60.
——, (in press), Playing it safe: The role of conventionality in indirect requests. In S. BLUM-KULKA, J. HOUSE & G. KASPER (eds), *Cross-Cultural Pragmatics*, Norwood, N.J.: Ablex.

BLUM-KULKA, S. and HOUSE, J., (in press), Cross-cultural and situational variation in requestive behaviour in five languages. In S. BLUM-KULKA, J. HOUSE & G. KASPER (eds), *Cross-Cultural Pragmatics*. Norwood, N.J.: Ablex.

BLUM-KULKA, S., HOUSE, J. and KASPER, G., (in press), Investigating cross-cultural pragmatics: An introductory overview. In S. BLUM-KULKA, J. HOUSE & G. KASPER (eds), *Cross-Cultural Pragmatics*, Norwood, N.J.: Ablex.

BLUM-KULKA, S. and OLSHTAIN, E., 1986, Too many words: length of utterance and pragmatic failure, *Journal of Pragmatics*, 8, 47–61.

BONGAERTS, T., KELLERMAN, E. and BENTLAGE, A., 1987, Perspective and proficiency in L2 referential communication, *Studies in Second Language Acquisition*, 9, 171–99.

BORKIN, A. and REINHART, S. M., 1978, Excuse me and I'm sorry, *TESOL Quarterly*, 12, 57–79.

BROWN, H. D., 1976, Discussion of 'Systematicity/variability and stability/ instability in interlanguage systems', In H. D. BROWN (ed.), *Papers in Second Language Acquisition* (Special Issue of *Language Learning*), 4, 135–40.

BROWN, P. and LEVINSON S., 1978, Universals in language usage: politeness phenomena. In E. M. GOODY (ed.), *Questions and Politeness*. Cambridge: Cambridge University Press, pp. 56–289. Reissued version: *Politeness*. Cambridge: Cambridge University Press 1987.

BÜHLER, K., 1934, *Sprachtheorie*. Jena: Fischer (2nd edition Stuttgart: Fischer 1965.)

CANALE, M. and SWAIN, M., 1980, Theoretical bases of communicative approaches to second language teaching and testing, *Applied Linguistics*, 1, 1–47.

CANDLIN, C., 1987, What happens when applied linguistics goes critical. Paper presented at 8th AILA World Congress Sydney.

CHOMSKY, N., 1980, *Rules and Representations*. New York: Columbia University Press.

CORDER, S. P., 1978, Language-learner language. In J. C. RICHARDS (ed.), *Understanding Second and Foreign Language Learning*. Rowley, Mass.: Newbury House, pp. 71–93.

ELLIS, R., 1986, *Understanding Second Language Acquisition*. Oxford: Oxford University Press.

FÆRCH, C. and KASPER, G., 1984, Pragmatic knowledge: rules and procedures, *Applied Linguistics*, 5, 214–25.

——, 1986, Procedural knowledge as a component of foreign language learners' communicative competence, *AILA Review*, 3, 7–23.

——, (in press), Internal and external modification in interlanguage request realisation. In S. BLUM-KULKA, J. HOUSE & G. KASPER (eds), *Cross-Cultural Pragmatics*. Norwood, N.J.: Ablex.

FRASER, B. and NOLEN, W., 1981, The association of deference with linguistic form, *International Journal of the Sociology of Language*, 27, 93–109.

HACKMANN, D., 1977, Patterns in purported speech acts, *Journal of Pragmatics*, 1, 143–54.

HOLMQVIST, B. and ANDERSEN, P. B., 1987, Work language and information technology, *Journal of Pragmatics*, 11, 327–58.

HOUSE, J., 1986, Cross-cultural pragmatics and foreign language teaching. In K.-R. BAUSCH, F. G. KÖNIGS & R. KOGELHEIDE (eds), *Probleme und Perspektiven der Sprachlehrforschung*. Königstein: Scriptor, pp. 281–95.

HOUSE J. and KASPER, G., 1987, Interlanguage pragmatics: requesting in a foreign language. In W. LÖRSCHER & R. SCHULZE (eds), *Perspectives on Language in Performance*, Festschrift for Werner Hüllen, Tübingen: Narr, pp. 1250–88.

HYMES, D., 1971, Toward ethnographies of communication: the analysis of communicative events. In P. P. GIGLIOLI (ed.), *Language and Social Context*. Harmondsworth: Penguin, pp. 21–43.

——, 1972, On communicative competence. In J. B. PRIDE & J. HOLMES (eds), *Sociolinguistics*. Harmondsworth: Penguin, pp. 269–93.

ICKENROTH, J., 1975, *On the Elusiveness of Interlanguage*. Progress Report. Utrecht.

JANICKI, K., 1986, Accommodation in native speaker–foreigner interaction. In J. HOUSE & S. BLUM-KULKA (eds), *Interlingual and Intercultural Communication*. Tübingen: Narr, pp. 169–78.

KASPER, G., 1981, *Pragmatische Aspekte in der Interimsprache*. Tübingen: Narr.

LEECH, G., 1983, *Principles of Pragmatics*. London: Longman.

LEVENSTON, E., 1971, Over-indulgence and under-representation—aspects of mother-tongue interference. In G. NICKEL (ed.), *Papers in Contrastive Linguistics*. Cambridge: Cambridge University Press, pp. 115–21.

LEVINSON, S., 1981, The essential inadequacies of speech act models of dialogue. In H. PARRET, M. SBISA & J. VERSCHUEREN (eds), *Possibilities and Limitations of Pragmatics*. Amsterdam: Benjamins, pp. 473–89.

——, 1983, *Pragmatics*. Cambridge: Cambridge University Press.

MAAS, U., 1972, Grammatik und Handlungstheorie. In U. MAAS & D. WUNDERLICH, *Pragmatik und sprachliches Handeln*. Frankfurt: Athenäum, pp. 189–276.

OLSHTAIN, E., 1983, Sociocultural competence and language transfer: the case of apology. In S. GASS & L. SELINKER (eds), *Language Transfer in Language Learning*. Rowley, Mass.: Newbury House, pp. 232–49.

RINTELL. E., 1979, Getting your speech act together: the pragmatic ability of second language learners, *Working Papers on Bilingualism*, 17, 97–106.

SCHLIEBEN-LANGE, B., 1975, *Linguistische Pragmatik*. Stuttgart: Kohlhammer.

SCOLLON, R. and SCOLLON, S. 1983, Face in interethnic communication. In J. C. RICHARDS & R. SCHMIDT (eds), *Language and Communication*. London: Longman, pp. 156–88.

STEMMER, B., 1981, *Kohäsion im gesprochenen Diskurs deutscher Lerner des Englischen* (= Manuskripte zur Sprachlehrforschung 18). Bochum: Seminar für Sprachlehrforschung der Ruhr-Universität.

TARONE, E., FRAUENFELDER, U. and SELINKER, L., 1976, Systematicity/variability and stability/instability in interlanguage systems. *Language Learning Special Issue* No. 4, 93–134.

TARONE, E. and YULE, G., (forthcoming) *Focus on the Language Learner: Approaches to Identifying and Meeting the Needs of Second Language Learners*. Oxford: Oxford University Press.

THOMAS, J., 1989, Complex illocutionary acts and the analysis of discourse. In J. THOMAS (ed.), *The Dynamics of Discourse*. London: Longman.

VERSCHUEREN, J., 1985, *What People Say They Do with Words*. Norwood, N.J.: Ablex.

——, 1987, The pragmatic perspective. In J. VERSCHUEREN & M. BERTUCELLI-PAPI (eds), *The Pragmatic Perspective*. Amsterdam: Benjamins, pp. 3–8.

WEIZMAN, E. (in press) Hints as a request strategy. In S. BLUM-KULKA, J. HOUSE & G. KASPER (eds), *Cross-Cultural Pragmatics*. Norwood, N.J.: Ablex.

v. WRIGHT, G. H., 1965, The logic of action. In N. RESCHER (ed.), *Introduction to Value Theory*. Englewood Cliffs: Prentice Hall.

WUNDERLICH, D., 1972, Sprechakte. In. U. MAAS & D. WUNDERLICH, *Pragmatik und sprachliches Handeln*. Frankfurt: Athenäum, pp. 69–188.

4 Happy Hebrish: Mixing and switching in American-Israeli family interactions

ELITE OLSHTAIN
Tel Aviv University

SHOSHANA BLUM-KULKA
Hebrew University in Jerusalem

Introduction

The following conversation was overheard when an American-Israeli family, Americans who have come to live permanently in a Hebrew speaking environment in Israel, were arguing among themselves:

(1) **Child A (to Child B):** You're talking gibbish!
   Father: Hebrish.
   Child A: Oh, yeah.

The members of this American-Israeli family are aware of the fact that they often speak a mixture of Hebrew and English and they refer to it as 'Hebrish'.

Two interactants who share more than one language might under certain circumstances switch from one language to the other or they might mix words or phrases of one language into the wider syntactic structures of the other. Such communication strategies employed by bilinguals enable them to take advantage of the language resources of both codes which they share. Haugen (1956, 1969) distinguishes among three cases: 'switching' which is the alternate use of two languages, 'interference', the overlapping of two languages, and 'integration', the use of words and phrases of one language that have historically become a part of the other language. This chapter concerns itself primarily with Haugen's area of language 'switching' which takes place according to Gumperz (1982) when there is '... juxta-position within the same speech exchange of passages of speech from two distinct grammatical systems or subsystems'.

The phenomena of code-mixing and code-switching have been reported for a variety of multilingual or multidialectal speech communities: in Paraguay (Rubin, 1968), New Guinea (Sankoff, 1972), Mexican American communities (Fishman, 1972; Gumperz, 1970, 1976; Pfaff, 1979), North India (Gumperz, 1958), Austria (Gal, 1979), Israel (Berk-Seligson, 1986), France (Dabene & Billiez, 1986).

According to Sankoff (1972) two basic approaches to the study of code-switching can be discerned: the predictive approach and the interpretive approach. The predictive approach seeks to answer questions relating to social factors present in the communicative situation which might influence the amount and type of code-switching, or in Fishman's (1972) words, 'Who speaks what language to whom and when'. The interpretive approach, on the other hand, as represented by Gumperz, seeks to discover the functions which the language used plays in the ongoing interaction. According to Gumperz, code-switching signals significant information concerning momentary attitudes, speaker's intent and emotions. This is particularly prominent in minority language communities where there seems to be an ingroup 'we' code as opposed to the 'they' code of the majority group which is perceived as more formal, stiff and distant. Switching codes can therefore carry important social meaning. In terms of accommodation theory (Giles *et al.*, 1987) code-switching might be viewed as convergence towards the minority group when switching is done by speakers of the majority group to the minority language, and vice versa, maintaining the distinction between the two codes might result in divergence.

In our own work on code-mixing and code-switching we have adopted both approaches since we believe that predictor variables present in the social context play an important role in the selection of such communication strategies, but once such strategies have been employed they have an impact on the nature of discourse which develops. Furthermore, we would like to suggest a sharper distinction between code-mixing (CM) and code-switching (CS), two terms which are often used interchangeably in the literature. In our work, we have assigned the term 'code-switching' to instances when the speaker alternates units from different codes that are higher level constituents, at least grammatical clauses or sentences. Thus, a speaker who shares both Hebrew and English with the hearer might start out in Hebrew and suddenly switch over to a whole stretch of speech in English and then return to Hebrew. In this case there was a CS from Hebrew to English and back again. Gumperz (1982) comments on such conversational CS which makes full use of two separate linguistic systems: 'Speakers communicate fluently, maintaining an even flow of talk. No hesitation pauses, changes in sentence rhythm, pitch level or intonation contour mark the shift in code. There is nothing in the exchange as a whole to indicate that speakers don't understand each other. Apart from the alternation itself, the passages have all the earmarks of ordinary conversations in a single language' (1982:57−8). A single interactional unit is being created, with the two languages (potentially) subservient to the same discourse-functions. But the availability of the two languages for signalling conversational functions also means that the juxtaposition of the two codes might be used as a signalling device, just as any other linguistic means.

Code-mixing (CM) as opposed to CS refers to smaller units, usually words or idiomatic expressions, which are borrowed from one language and inserted into the sentence of another language. Thus, we may speak of the host language (Sridhar & Sridhar, 1980) represented by the larger syntactic unit and of the guest element, the part which was taken from another language and inserted into the first. When the speaker produces the following sentence in English including one word in Hebrew:

(2) 'Did you speak to the *GANENET* (nursery teacher) today?'

English acts as host language and Hebrew as guest language. CM therefore refers to the transition from using linguistic units of one language to using those of another language within the original sentence. CM, as defined here, is similar to Pfaff's (1979) 'borrowing' which can also occur in the language of monolinguals who are familiar with certain words and expressions in another language which they don't really know.

The linguistic context

The present study focuses on CM and CS as occurring in family interactions among American-Israelis. These are immigrants to Israel who have lived in the new environment from nine to nineteen years and thus all members of the family have acquired Hebrew to various degrees of competence. The parents remain dominant in their mother tongue, English, even though some of them have become very near native in Hebrew. The children, on the other hand, spend most of their time in a Hebrew speaking environment at school and in any other context outside the family and so it can be assumed that they are Hebrew dominant. It was surprising, therefore, to find that even young children born in Israel had a very high level of fluency in English. The typical range of use of the two languages was well expressed by an eight-year-old: 'I speak English at home all day and I speak Hebrew at school and at summer camp'.

In the particular context of bilingualism and 'languages in contact' as described above for the American-Israeli families, and within the restriction of our data-collecting framework, four predictor variables seem to be at work in terms of CM and CS:

(a) the *status* of the two languages in question, Hebrew and English.

(b) the level of *proficiency* in each of the two languages as shared by the speaker (S) and the addressee (A) within the family.

(c) the presence of other hearers, *outsiders*, who do not have equal competence in both languages.

(d) the interactional/linguistic *domain* within which the data are collected.

Status

In terms of the status of the two languages, although Hebrew is an official language of the State of Israel and English is not, English enjoys special status as a language of wider communication (Fishman *et al.*, 1977). It is perceived by the educational system as a compulsory subject throughout elementary and high school and as a major component of the entrance exams to universities. Furthermore, most white collar positions require a good knowledge of English. Interactions with outsiders, tourists, diplomats are always conducted in English. It is obvious therefore that knowing English is a social asset to anyone living in Israel and English speaking immigrants are strongly motivated to maintain their language, even when full acculturation in the new community is aspired to. It is therefore to be expected that there would be a considerable amount of CS and CM between English and Hebrew and even monolingual Hebrew speakers may have a certain amount of English CM. For the subjects participating in the study, English has, in some sense, both the ethnic 'we' from the homeland and the extended family in the country of origin and part of the new 'we' since it is the prestigious second language in the new community.

The American-Israeli families that participated in this study are strongly motivated to maintain English as the dominant language of the family and to ensure that their children are bilingual, which will be an asset in the new community. A clear indication of success in this effort is evident in the fact that most children participating in our study reported that they read for pleasure in both languages.

The interactions collected for this study were predominantly English. This was surprising considering the fact that many of the children were born in Israel and know Hebrew better than their parents do. Fluent interactions in English were very much the typical situation for all members of the family with some CM and CS to Hebrew. Yet, some parents were aware of the difficulty the children might encounter in using English only. The following is an example of such awareness on the mother's part:

(3) **Mother (to 10 year old daughter)**: Rina, if you're more comfortable speaking Hebrew, so speak Hebrew, because I know you generally speak Hebrew, OK?

Proficiency

All members of the family, but particularly parents, are concerned with the fact that the children should be quite proficient in both languages. They often provide suitable equivalents for various words and expressions in the two languages, providing a type of scaffolding for the younger children. The following example illustrates such a scaffolding technique employed by a parent in order to ensure the child's equal command of Hebrew and English, with obvious focus on enriching the child's English vocabulary:

(4) **Father**: How do you say GEVES in English?
   Child: I don't know.
   Father: Cast.
   Child: Cast?
   Father: Uh-uh.
   Child: cast, cast, cast, ...[1]

It is interesting to note that example (4) also indicates very willing co-operation on the child's part.

A similar kind of scaffolding also works for the parents' Hebrew proficiency. In this case the children are the experts and they help the parents acquire better Hebrew, as in the following example where even a five-year-old can play the expert:

(5) **Daniel (15) (to younger sister)**: A hamster, no?
   Father: OGER, no, no, it's a ŠOREK.

Ilana (13): A ŠOREK is a guinea-pig.
Father: Oh.
Daniel: Or, a XAZIRIN, whatever.
Naomi (5): XAZIR YAM.

It seems that all members of the family are aware of this unique situation in which two languages serve equally as valid sources for communication. In the following language teaching game which a five-year-old plays with his eighteen-month-old baby brother, we see how natural it is for these subjects to use any one of the two languages:

(6) **Yair (5)**: Say Grandma!
    Zivi (1½): Gramma
    Yair: Say TODA (thank you)
    Zivi: TODA
    Yair: TODA. Say bottle.
    Zivi: Bah

Outsiders

In the particular speech event recorded for this study all members of the family participated in their usual dinner conversation yet there were one or two technicians present recording the event. Some of these technicians were native speakers of Hebrew while others were native speakers of English. In the case of technicians who were Hebrew speakers, some accommodation was obvious where all the members of the family tended to switch to Hebrew when addressing the technician although the latter had a very good command of English. The following is such an example where the switching from English to Hebrew is done for accommodation and convergence:

(7) **Wife (to husband)**: Dick, do you think you want some wine?
    (to technician): ITZIK, ATA ROCE LIŠTOT YAIN IM
                    HAOXEL? (Itzik, do you want to drink
                    wine with the food?)

Domain

All the data were collected during regular dinner conversations at home.[2] This particular context seems to be the most suitable domain within which the American-Israeli families are likely to consciously preserve the use of English. Table 1 presents quantitative data on the dominance of

TABLE 1. *Language dominance and amount of CM and CS during dinner conversations of American-Israeli families*

Family	Total number of utterances	Hebrew %	English %	Utterances in which CM and CS occurred	
				N	%
1	1835	37	63	156	8.6
2	1380	20	80	158	11.0
3	1500	19	81	37	2.4
4	1600	10	90	38	2.4
5	1200	43	57	193	16.0
6	960	38	62	73	7.6
7	1030	36	64	117	11.3
8	2600	45	55	210	8.0
9	1220	45	55	67	0.5
10	530	47	53	30	0.6
11	600	42	58	123	20.0

English for the eleven families which served as the research population in this study.

From the Table we can see that for all families more than 50% of the utterances are in English, for family 4 it is as high as 90%. The amount of mixing and switching in this context varies from as little as 0.5% in family 9 to as high as 20% in family 11. It is interesting to note that the amount of CM and CS is independent of the level of language dominance. Thus, family 2, for example, has a very high level of dominance (80%) as well as a rather high level of CM and CS (11%), while family 3, with a similar level of dominance (81%), has only a very low amount of CM and CS (2.4%).

The study

Four research questions relevant to the type of data collected (family dinner conversations) in the American-Israeli context described above, were examined in this study:

1. How does the speaker's role in the family affect the amount of CM and CS which s/he engages in?

2. How is the direction of switching affected by relative roles of S (speaker) and A (addressee)?

3. What is the context and structure of CM?

4. What are the discourse functions of CS?

The first two questions relate to the overall pattern of switching and mixing as evidenced in our data. The findings are presented in Tables 2 and 3.

As can be seen from Table 2, parents tend to switch more when addressing children than when addressing each other (83% as opposed to 17%) and children tend to switch more when addressing parents than when addressing their siblings (63% as opposed to 37%). These differences are statistically significant ($X^2 = 145.82$; df = 1; $p < 0.001$; $\phi = 0.44$). The explanation for this unique situation is quite obvious: parents maintain English at home among themselves but when addressing children, especially the younger ones, they often feel the need to make sure that they are fully understood and so they switch to Hebrew for their children's sake. Sometimes such switching is an exact repetition of what was said in English first. Children, on the other hand, tend to speak Hebrew among themselves but will switch to English when speaking to their parents in order to accommodate them and play by the rules of language maintenance.

A very similar picture becomes evident from Table 3 concerning code-mixing. Since the interactions were predominantly in English, the mixing was of Hebrew words and expressions into English. Parents mixed significantly more when speaking to children than to each other (72% as

TABLE 2. *Amount of code-switching by role in the family*

Parents addressing		Children addressing	
parents	children	parents	other children
17%	83%	63%	37%

$X^2 = 145.82$ df = 1 $p < 0.001$ $\phi = 0.44$

TABLE 3. *Amount of code-mixing by role in the family*

Parents addressing		Children addressing	
parents	children	parents	other children
28%	72%	76%	24%

$X^2 = 94.48$ df = 1 $p < 0.001$ $\phi = 0.48$

opposed to 28%) and children mixed significantly more when speaking to their parents rather than to their siblings (76% as opposed to 24%). These are statistically significant ($X^2 = 94.48$; df = 1; $p < 0.001$; $\phi = 0.48$). It is plausible to assume that parents were motivated to mix so as to preserve the authenticity and full meaning of culturally bound expressions. Children, on the other hand, may have utilised mixing as a communication strategy since most of the Hebrew expressions were more easily available to them than the English equivalent. In some instances, these children do not even know the English word.

In order to answer questions (3) and (4) we shall first discuss code-mixing and second code-switching.

Code-mixing

When discussing the context and structure of CM in our data, we must break the question down into two parts:

(a) Where is CM most likely to occur within the sentence?

(b) What happens to the 'guest' unit in terms of syntactic and morphological behaviour as compared to the 'host' sentence?

In our data, CM occurred only with English as the host language and Hebrew as the guest element. The question thus focuses on where Hebrew mixes are most likely to occur in the English sentences. Previous studies ask similar questions; however, they often lack a clear distinction between CS and CM and therefore it is difficult to compare results.

When one examines examples of CM published by researchers, one detects a general trend towards preference for certain linguistic categories which are more susceptible to mixing. Pfaff (1979) found that 84% of all code-mixes in the utterances of her Spanish-English bilinguals involved single lexical items—74% nouns, 6% verbs, 4% adjectives; 10% were phrases (6% noun phrases) and 6% whole clauses.

Poplack (1978), who also investigated Spanish-English bilinguals in New York, found the following breakdown: tag switches 22.5%, sentence switches 20.3%, phrase switches 18.7%, noun switches 9.5%, clause switches 8.4%, interjections 6.3% and others 14.4%. It is difficult to compare these studies since their categories are differently defined and Poplack states that she, for instance, did not include habitual lexicalised borrowing, nor food names, place names, explanations or comments about the language. This raises a serious issue of defining members of the various categories when investigating CM, an issue which will be subsequently addressed in this chapter.

Berk-Seligson (1986), who studied speakers of Spanish and Hebrew living in Israel, followed Poplack's example of excluding items already integrated into the other language. She distinguishes between switching intersententially and intrasententially. The latter can be viewed as similar to our definition of CM yet she also included clauses which in our case are considered CS. Berk-Seligson's results show the following: the single most often switched (mixed) constituent was the noun—comprising 40% of all code-switches. Her next most frequently switched constituents were what Berk-Seligson calls intersentential and we would prefer calling discourse fillers (tags, interjections, exclamations, etc.).

In our study we found that within the constituents that are relevant to our definition of CM, namely constituents smaller than clauses, the breakdown is as given in Table 4.

To the extent that these results can be compared to Berk-Seligson's findings, we see that the first most frequent categories are the same, namely noun phrases and discourse fillers. It seems that our subjects use the strategy of CM primarily for naming objects, events and activities with which they have a daily experiential encounter in Hebrew. For such elements the Hebrew name seems to surface more easily and its semantic content seems well defined. In example (8) below, a bilingual youngster uses the Hebrew words for 'test' and for a score of 'one hundred'. These two Hebrew terms have a well-defined meaning in her daily school activities and

TABLE 4. *Percentage of total code-mixing according to grammatical categories*

Category	%
Noun phrases	60
Discourse fillers	14
Expressions of cultural context	12.5
Verb phrases	4
Idiomatic expressions	3
Others	6.5
	100

the English equivalents, which she probably knows, lack for her such definite reference.

(8) **Naomi (13):** They are going to do me a MIVXAN (test) in English and in the MIVXAN they'll see I'll get MEA (a hundred).

Many of the Hebrew mixes in our data represent culturally bound elements that are part of Israeli life. In the following three exchanges carried out by bilingual youngsters, we see that they are all fluent and speak English with ease, yet there are some Hebrew words which have come to represent certain institutions or objects in the Israeli context which they would not think of naming in English:

(9) **Boy (15) to five year old sister:**
At Malka's or on the way back from your GAN?
(nursery)
Girl (5): Right in back of my GAN.

(10) **Girl (13) to younger brother:**
What does ADOM   mean in a RAMZOR?
(red)   (traff.c light)

(11) **Boy (15):** Mom, you know what I'm going to have everyday for breakfast at SABA and SABTA's
(grandpa) (grandma's)

The term GAN (nursery school) has become so well established in Hebrish and stands for the Israeli version of such a school that when it resembles an American nursery school the mother says:

(12) **Mother:** It's an American-style GAN.

The second category which was rather productive were the discourse fillers (14%). In this case subjects tended to use Hebrew fillers within regular English utterance, as can be seen from examples (13) and (14):

(13) **Mother (to technician):** Oh, wait... who do we seek if we're both North DAVKA (particularly, specifically)—it has to be North Americans.

(14) **Child (to parent):** AVAL, (but, however) I did it fast.

Some of these discourse fillers do not have exact equivalents in English and therefore have gained special status in Hebrish.

The question of syntactic and morphological changes resulting from mixing refers to the incorporation of the 'guest' element into the 'host' sentence. Poplack (1978) proposes a general constraint—the free-morpheme constraint which states that a switch cannot take place between the stem of a word and its affix (bound morpheme) unless the stem has been phonologically integrated. In most of our data these two constraints were maintained. However, there are exceptions. Since most of our examples are noun phrases, one way to test to what extent this constraint is active in our type of CM would be to examine plural formation: do the plural forms follow the rules of the guest language or the host language? We will see in our data that within the same conversation both possibilities appear as is demonstrated in examples (15) and (16):

(15) **Mother:**   What do I have to do when I go to your GAN (nursery school)?

   Son (15):   Wait, they're on strike, the GANIM?

   Mother: No, the OZROT (assistants) are on strike. In order not to close down the GAN the mothers are taking TOROT (turns) to help the GANENETs. (nursery teachers; Hebrew stem with English plural suffix) The assistants to the GANENETS. They're young women who have taken a year's course to be an OZERET for GANIM.

   Son: So why are they going on strike and not the GANANOT? (nursery teachers; Hebrew stem and Hebrew plural (suffix).

(16) **Youngster:** I bought two KARTIVs (popcicle)
                  I had two KARTIVIM.

We see that most of the time there is simple incorporation of the guest element into the syntactic structure of the host language with the morphological form of the guest constituent left intact, maintaining Poplack's boundary constraint. Yet, there are cases where the stem in its guest language form is preserved but a host affix is added to it making up a new form such as GANENETs or KARTIVs.

It seems that CM in our data can be of three different types:

(a) CM can act as a communication strategy and enable bilinguals to quickly retrieve a word in whichever language is momentarily more available;

(b) CM is used for naming elements which relate specifically to cultural and experiential contexts and which have taken on specific local meanings—these are always preferred in the host language;

(c) some CM is used for accommodation purposes to ensure comprehension on the hearer's part when the speaker thinks that the hearer is not fully proficient in the language in which the interaction is taking place.[3]

One of the major difficulties encountered by studies in the area of CM is the distinction between 'true mixes' used for one of the above three processes and borrowing from the guest language into the host language beyond the bilingual context. In our case it has been useful to distinguish between English as spoken in a regular English speaking setting, where no borrowing from Hebrew is to be expected, and English as it is spoken by the American-Israelis. If we accept the fact that a unique type of dialect is developing here, then many of the CM cases might be considered borrowing since they represent tendencies among all American-Israelis and they are not specific to the families recorded for the purpose of this chapter. In analysing our data we have excluded only names of places, and of local parties which would have to be used in their original version even by English monolinguals.

Conversational code-switching: discourse functions

Conversational code-switching in the American-Israeli families resembles the cases described by Gumperz (1982) on two accounts: in structure, it is interwoven into conversation with no visible effort or overt signalling of alternation, and in function it serves a rich variety of discoursal-goals, theoretically achievable just as well by other means. It is when we come to analyse the macro-function of code-switching in these families that we notice a difference; in contrast to the cases described by Gumperz as noted above, the tacit presuppositions in our case assume an equal status for both languages, and separation along the dimension of 'we' language as opposed to 'they' language does not hold. Against this background, we began to wonder whether code-switching in the American-Israeli families carries any specific meaning for the family-group as such, and if it does, how we can distinguish between this specific level of meaning and other functions of code-switching.

To answer these questions we need a general framework for the analysis of the functions of code-switching. We propose to base this framework on making a distinction in the analysis between three functional levels: pragmatic, textual and interpersonal. By 'pragmatic' we mean the effects achieved by the utterance via the alternation between languages, as felt by the listener, whether *intended or not by the speaker*. In trying to detect the pragmatic functions of CS, we are considering a stretch of discourse uttered by a single speaker, to one or more addressees. By 'textual' functions we mean the effects code-switching can have on the coherence of whole conversational segments, as felt by both participants and bilingual overhearers to the interaction (including the discourse-analyst). For this level, the relevant unit of analysis is the exchange, or a whole conversation, regardless of its number of participants. By 'interpersonal' we mean the functions carried by the free, fully licensed alternation of two languages for a particular socio-cultural group, as felt by its members (in our case the American-Israeli families) over time. It follows from this definition, that the context to be considered at this level can be flexible and indeterminate.

Theoretically, code-switching can operate simultaneously on all three levels; in practice, functions achieved on a specific level might gain salience over functions achieved on another. We assume, as others before us did (Gumperz, 1982; Dabene & Billiez, 1986), that CS for bilinguals is one variety of linguistic means available to speakers for signalling meaning. But we would like to stress the point *that not every occurrence of CS is necessarily rich in pragmatic and rhetoric functions*. CS can also be used to serve only interpersonal functions; in such cases, the switch has its meaning in the bilingual socio-cultural context.

The application of this framework for the case analysed is presented in Figure 1.

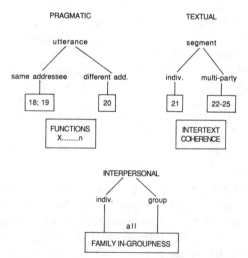

FIGURE 1. *Conversational code-switching: discourse functions* (The numbers refer to examples in the text)

Pragmatic functions

(17) **Mother to Nadav (6):** Nadav, do you want some carrots? NADAV,
ATA ROCE GEZER, GEZER MEVUŠAL? (Nadav, do you want
some carrots, cooked carrots?)

(18) **A mother trying to control the behaviour of her three very noisy boys:**
OK. We are going to sit down now. We're eating now. All right!
MASPIK! (enough) Stop It! DAY!!! (enough)

Reiteration of a message in another code can serve to clarify or
emphasise it (Gumperz 1982). In (17) the repetition of the message in
Hebrew serves as an external modifier (Blum-Kulka *et al.*, in press) to the
control-act encoded in English: the mother, in the best Jewish motherly
tradition, is trying to get the child to eat his carrots, and she uses code-
switching as part of her persuasive efforts. By double coding her message,
she ensures both comprehensibility and a tutoring goal; if her son did not
know until now how to refer to the vegetable offered in one of the two
languages, he can learn the word now.

In (18) in a similar fashion, inserted Hebrew utterances serve to
upgrade and emphasise the control act. The chain of directives in this
example is uttered breathlessly, with a rising pitch level culminating in a yell
(of the word 'day'). Note that the emphasis aimed at is achieved via a
combination of strategies, CS being just one of these. First the message is
repeated twice in English (okay we are going to sit down (to eat)/we are
eating now); then it is formulated in one-word utterances, all four being
synonyms of each other. In running through these four, the mother switches
back and forth, f nding neither language effective enough. This shows that
she is using all the verbal means she has at her disposal, regardless of
whether they are coded in English or in Hebrew.

CS can also be used to differentiate between addressees, as in example
(19).

(19) Parent talking to a guest at dinner:
Father: So we went to this store – – DANY TAFSIK ET ZE (Danny
stop it) and finally got it.

The father in (19) uses CS for a similar pragmatic function; he too is
trying to control the behaviour of a child. But in this case, CS plays a part in
targetting: the main flow of the discourse, addressed at the guest in English,
is self-interrupted in the middle of the sentence for a side sequence
(Jefferson, 1972) (in Hebrew) targetted at the child, to be picked up again
and the sentence completed in English.

(20) 1. **Mother:** I met an interesting guy in Tel-Aviv. Must have been 75 years old.
2. **Rachel (12):** So?
3. **Mother:** He was from Poland and he was all alone and he told how he fought in the Russian army in World War Two.
4. **Rachel:** How did you start talking to him?
5. **Mother:** I was sitting near the beach.
6. **Rachel:** Hmmm!
7. **Mother:** Watching the sunset and we − − am ah—he picked a cute way to start talking. There was this GALSAN (wind-surfer) out in the water. It was already getting dark and he said to me ZE NORA MESUKAN ZE YAXOL LHISAXEF VEZE NORA KAR KVAR, LAMAHU LO NIXNAS, NORA MESUKAN (its terribly dangerous, it can get carried away and its already cold, why doesn't he come back, terribly dangerous) you know and then he said to me ANI YAXOL LAŠEVET (can I sit down). It was so cute cause you know obviously kind of lonely man very very nice, with an accent that mixes Yiddish and Hebrew and (xxx) very interesting guy. He showed me pictures of his family that were wiped out in the ŠOA (holocaust, I think−
8. **Rachel:** = He picked a pretty young girl to start with.[4]

The 'old man on the beach' story (example 20) is a particularly interesting case for illustrating the rhetoric effects achievable by CS.[5] The story is told conversationally, featuring the characteristics of such events: following entrance talk (Polanyi, 1985) that announces the topic and serves as transition to the story-world ('I met an interesting guy in Tel-Aviv'), the teller is being challenged by her daughter to justify the story-worthiness of the topic she had introduced ('so?'). She then plunges into her narrative, helped along with questions for clarification (turn 4) and back-channel signals from her audience. Except for two cases of mixing ('GALŠAN', wind surfer and ŠOA, holocaust), CS is introduced in the narrative to reproduce verbatim the sentences uttered by the old man on the beach. The style of the story is representational rather than reportive; all speech referred to is quoted verbatim. The quotes hence serve an evaluative function (Labov, 1972) which theoretically could have been achieved regardless of the language used. The fact that the teller insists on quoting the old man in Hebrew serves to enhance this effect; it lends the story an air of authenticity and underscores, as it were, the power of direct quotes to *dramatise* the event described (Gumperz, 1982; Weizman, 1984). The quotes in Hebrew allow the teller actually to enact the character she is describing.

The CS used for quotation here helps build up the story in yet another way: it distances the two points of view presented, isolating the old man on the beach, leaving him to worry about the wind-surfer (terribly dangerous, terribly dangerous) while the teller is free to comment metacommunicatively[6] on her reactions to the character she had met ('so cute'/'kind of lonely'/'very very nice').

Distancing also allows for creating a slightly humorous effect; in this respect this story resembles the humorous juxtaposition of Yiddish and English in narrative performance among Jews in Canada described by Kirschenblatt-Gimblett (1971, as quoted in Gumperz, 1982). Not surprisingly, the bilinguals studied by Kirschenblatt-Gimblett were also immigrants; maybe it is the process of acculturation *per se* which develops the kind of sensitivity to language that allows a rich use of the rhetoric potentials embedded in their juxtaposition.

Textual functions

The pragmatic and rhetorical functions of CS are analysed as (potentially) perceived by speakers and receivers alike; but there is a further dimension to the effect of CS, detectable at the level of discourse. At this level, instead of looking at individual speakers, we consider the roles played by code-switching—across different speakers—in building the coherence of larger segments of discourse. The question then becomes: what is the contribution of code-switching to coherence?
Consider the following:

(21) Sara, the observer, is writing down the menu:
    1. **Sara:** Quiche—what—ah—⌈ Squash! ⌉
    2. **Ruth (wife):**   ⌊ Squash ⌋ quich
    3. **Dick (husband):** Quiche quiche [kis kis kisuim] – – KIŠ KIŠUIM
        (squash quiche) =
    4. **Ruth:**   = Oh quiche [kis] is KIŠ [kis].
    5. **Sara:**   ⌈ KIŠ KIŠUIM, ⌉TIRAS, (corn) and
    6. **Jeniffer (8):**   ⌊ KIŠ KIŠUIM ⌋SALAT (salad)
    7. **Dick:**   = and SALAT
    8. **Jason (9):**   = and LEXEM (bread)

If we look at example (21), we can see that one type of contribution to coherence can be purely poetic. Formally, this is a borderline case between switching and mixing, since the alternations concern phrases rather than clauses. But on the level of discourse, the alternations occur both within and across turns, and when the exchange is considered as a whole we feel an element of language play at work: the similarity in sound between squash quiche [skwas kiš] and the equivalent Hebrew KIŠ KIŠUIM [kiš kišuim] serving to create, borrowing a term from Ducrot (1984), a polyphonic code for quiche.

The next two examples (22 and 23) illustrate more subtle ways in which code-switching is triggered off and used in the creation of discourse coherence.

(22) Talking about shelters for battered women:

1. **Mira (13):**   You can't go in (xxx) there are gates and stuff.
2. **Dana (10):**   What do they do there?
3. **Mother:**   The women stay there, they take their clothes and they move into the shelter and there are professionals who help [them]
4. **Dana:**   [MA ZE?] (what's that?)
5. **Mother:**   MIKCOIYIM, ANAŠIM MIKCOIYEN
                    (professionals, professional people)
6. **Mira:**   PSIXOLOGIM VEKOL MINE DEVARIM KAELE
                    (psychologists and stuff like that)
7. **Mother:**   Right. Social workers. You know what a social worker is.
8. **Dana:**   [SOCIALIST] (a socialist)
9. **Mother:**   Mmm
10. **Mira:**   OVDIM SOCIALIYIM (social workers)
11. **Mother:**   And psychologists and just nice, people, who help them and help them.
12. **Dana:**   BANIM? (boys?)
13. **Mother:**   Men and women, sure.../

In (22) the girl, Dana, interrupts her mother in turn 4 with an ambiguous question for clarification. Because the question creates a code-switched situation (Hebrew interruption to English conversation), it can be interpreted both as a metalinguistic query (asking for a translation equivalent of 'professionals' in Hebrew) and as a request for an explanation of the concept. In what follows, the meaning of the concept becomes the focus of the discussion; mother and sister switch back and forth in their, at first, unsuccessful attempt (see turn 8) to clarify the concept of 'social worker' for Dana. The two explainers use whatever means they have at their disposal, in both English and Hebrew, to achieve communicative clarity. Strategy wise, this example would qualify as illustrating the pragmatic function of CS for message clarification. But on the level of discourse, its most striking feature is the intertext coherence (Dabene & Billiez, 1986)[7] served by CS when used both inter and intra turns. Note that while the first switch, in turn 4, is self-announced in being ambiguous between a meta-linguistic question and a concept clarification query, the switches back and forth that follow lack overt marking of the code-switching situation. The speakers show no sign that they are aware of using two different codes; they treat each turn equally, regardless of the language it is encoded in. Thus, turn 6 completes previous turns coded in Hebrew, while both turns 7 and 13 acknowledge in English information provided in Hebrew. Note also that turn 11 continues, via CS, a sentence begun in turn 10, showing that the two languages are used almost as one.

In another segment from the same conversation, it is the girl, Dana, who switches to English for purposes of clarification.

(23) Mother complaining to the observer about her daughter's cooking teacher telling the kids to peel the vegetables:

1. **Mother:**... Isn't that awful?
2. **Dana (10):** LO NAXON! (not true)
3. **Mother:** What *did* she say?
4. **Dana:** She said ŠEULAY GAM ANAŠIM MAŠIRIM (she said that maybe people also leave...)
5. **Mother:** ⎡ What? ⎤
6. **Mira:** ⎣ What? ⎦
7. **Dana:** She said that those that eat vitamins they don't peel the vegetables.

Several points should be noted here. On the level of discourse, CS is introduced by Dana, in turn 2, where she also switches from the role of overhearer to that of active participant (Clark, 1987). In protesting her mother's version of an A-event from her own biography (Labov & Fanshel, 1977). In response to her mother's supportive question ('what did she say?') she switches to English to introduce the 'exact' quotation in Hebrew. But when she perceives the response to her turn as signalling the need for repair work, she switches to English to achieve the repair. Strategically, she manages to use CS for message qualification (Gumperz, 1982), since having two linguistic codes to draw on in case of need entails that they can be distinguished functionally, one used to do repair work on a message encoded in another. Furthermore, it should be noted that the use of CS for quoting verbatim a non-present speaker here is very different in function from the way it was used by the teller in example (20). While the storyteller in (20) code-switches selectively for quotations to dramatise her narrative, the speaker in (23) code-switches the conversation in order to refute her mother's account of the same verbal event; CS for quoting in this instance is for precision, not drama. This point is important because it highlights the need to analyse the functions of code-switching relative to discourse domains and communicative intent.

But the major point which this example illustrates relates to coherence: for the participants present, coherence is achieved intertextually by the use of both languages, regardless of which function is realised in which. This shows that the macro-function of CS in discourse is *its peculiar role in serving intertext coherence*. We can talk of 'intertext coherence' as the situation in which a text derives its coherence from two distinct linguistic codes. This type of coherence is maintained only under conditions of equal comprehensibility by all participants (and overhearers). Viewed from this perspective, all examples considered qualify. In all, CS plays a part in chaining turns of talk and segments of narrative into coherent wholes. This last point is particularly clear in example (24).

(24) A joint effort to fix the date of Dana's haircut:
   1. **Mira (13):** You cut her hair yesterday, Friday.
   2. **Mother:** Friday? Oh, God, it has been many yesterdays.
   3. **Mira:** One, two
   4. **Dana (10):** Two, two!
   5. **Mira:** Today is Monday, Sunday, Saturday, three days ago.
   6. **Dana:** BEYOM ŠABBAT (on Saturday)
   7. **Mira:** Saturday or Friday?
   8. **Dana:** YOM ŠABBAT (Saturday)
   9. **Mira:** ULAY YOM ŠIŠI (Maybe Friday?)
 10. **Dana:** LO, HAYITI BEYOM HULEDET (No, I was at a birthday party)
 11. **Mother:** Oh, right, Saturday morning.
 12. **Dana** YOM ŠABBAT, MA? (Saturday, ah?)
 13. **Mira:** Morning

In this joint effort to establish the day on which Dana's hair had been cut, the two linguistic codes, Hebrew and English are drawn upon freely. Of course, there are personal preferences: the mother uses here only English, Dana mostly but not exclusively Hebrew, and Mira alternates equally between the two. But what characterises this exchange as a discourse unit is that within the bilingual context it is not only perfectly comprehensible and coherent, but this coherence is achieved by a metaphorical suspension of the difference between the two languages. Code-switching here does not signal pragmatic functions; on the contrary, it goes on completely undetected by the participants.

We suspect that the phenomenon exemplified by (24) is quite common in bilingual settings; since speakers can be unaware of the languages used, they can also alternate between them without such alternations necessarily carrying a specific pragmatic or rhetoric function.

The interpersonal function

The interpersonal perspective on CS should help us detect its meaning for different groupings of bilingual participants engaged in CS. If we think of this aspect in terms of individual speakers and addressees, we can delineate certain personal preferences as well as efforts at accommodation. On the other hand, if we think of this aspect in terms of the group of families studied, we can point to one macro interpersonal function, conveyed by the examples analysed and countless others in the data: CS in the American-Israeli families studied communicates a sense of family unity, enhancing a complicity bond of this group's particular version of 'we-ness'.

Conclusion

The particular CM and CS found in our data represents the function and structure of these communicative strategies in a rather unique context of bilingualism, where the relationship between the immigrant language and the local language is quite different from more typical minority–majority settings. In our case, the fact that the 'minority' language enjoys a special status in the hosting community, independently of the immigrant group, enables the rise and development of a special variety of Hebrish (English/ Hebrew mixture) which has in fact become an acceptable and respectable way of speaking among American-Israelis. Thus, Hebrish is commonly used for family interactions even after many years of stay in Israel (up to 19 in our data) and youngsters born in Israel whose Hebrew is their dominant language also become fluent in this special dialect.

Consequently, Hebrish enables the bilingual users of this dialect to take advantage of the resources of a double system—they draw upon Hebrew and English with great ease and within the same discoursal unit. Yet, they seem to have an awareness of the fact that not all family members are equally proficient in both languages and thus parents, whose English is dominant, will accommodate their children by switching to Hebrew and children, whose Hebrew is dominant, will often explain the meanings of Hebrew words and expressions. Furthermore, all members of the family seem to have agreed tacitly that they will make every effort to maintain and promote both languages, although the predominant language spoken in this home is English.

Our findings concerning the phenomena of CM seem to confirm the overall patterns of mixing found in other studies (Poplack, 1978; Pfaff, 1979; Berk-Seligson, 1986; and others), yet we have a strong feeling that much of what we found is affected by the particular group of subjects we investigated and by the special speech event within which the data were collected, namely dinner conversations. It is very possible that the same subjects interacting in other types of conversational encounters would not necessarily adhere to Poplack's boundary constraint, for instance. From another set of data collected during informal English lessons at home among bilingual children from American-Israeli families we have some examples where the guest element (the Hebrew expression) maintains its full morphological formation and receives an English affix added to it, even in cases where there are intricate morphological rules, as in the following two examples:

(25) **Child:** I don't know its...and it MEVALBELs me (it confuses me)

(26) **Child:** I MESIGed him. (I caught up with him)

In these two examples a verbal mix has occurred where the verbal form consists of: the root moneme (Tene, 1969), the Hebrew verb pattern and the masculine present vowel pattern to which in one case the English third person present inflection 's' is added and in the second case the regular past inflection 'ed'.

Our findings with respect to CS also confirm the pragmatic functions discussed by Gumperz in his work. In our study we proposed a distinction between pragmatic, textual and interpersonal functions which were all amply demonstrated by the participants in the recorded interactions. Yet, we must remember the fact, as mentioned earlier, that the Hebrish 'dialect' is really 'Happy Hebrish' which has become legitimate and respectable as well as easily available to American-Israelis and therefore we can expect quite a lot of haphazard switching which does not serve the pragmatic or textual functions discussed in this chapter. Happy Hebrish seems to be the particular interlanguage or dialect developed by the American-Israeli community to serve its needs and aspirations with ease.

Acknowledgement

The research reported was funded by the Binational Science Foundation (Project no. 2977).

Notes to Chapter 4

1. *Transcription notations*
   Regular orthography is used wherever possible, in addition:
   ...   noticeable pause
   [conversational overlap
   =   talk continued with no pause
   (xxx)   unintelligible word
   – –   self interruption
   CAPS   Hebrew (using accepted phonemic transcription unless otherwise specified in the text).

2. All the data were recorded at the family dinner-table of American-Israeli families as part of a large research project investigating cross-cultural differences in interactional styles between Israeli, American and American-Israeli families. (Cross-Cultural Interactional Styles and the Acquisition of Communicative Competence, BSF grant no. 2977, Shoshana Blum-Kulka, in collaboration with David Gordon, Susan Ervin-Tripp and Catherine Snow.) Thirty-four middle to upper middle class Jewish academic families with at least two school-age children participated in the study. Three dinner-table conversations were recorded from each family, one by video and two by audio. One entire dinner-table conversation from each of the American-Israeli families was analysed for the present study.

3. In our data there are also cases of immediate availability of a word in one of the two languages as Grosjean (1982) claims 'Very often a bilingual knows a word in both language x and language y, but the language y word is more available at that moment when speaking language x. He or she may use the word from language y but then later in the conversation use the word from language x' (p. 151). When interviewing our subjects, some claim that they are fully aware of using a Hebrew word when they speak English but that word might be the first that came to mind and in the back of their minds they continue to search for the equivalent English word which will eventually surface.

4. The expression 'to start with' is a transfer from Hebrew ('lehatxil im' literally meaning 'to begin/start with'); we have not analysed so far the specific features of the children's interlanguage (in English) nor the effects of the linguistic environment on the interlanguage of both parents and children at the transition points from one language to another.

5. The full analysis of this narrative is beyond the scope of this chapter; note, however, the use of discourse markers, such as 'you know' (Schiffrin, 1986).

6. For the use of metacommunicative comments in American Oral Narratives see Tannen (1980).

7. The use of the term 'intertext coherence' here is not synonymous with its use by Dabene & Billiez (1986).

References

BERK-SELIGSON, S., 1986, Linguistic constraints on intrasentential code-switching: a study of Spanish/Hebrew bilingualism, *Language in Society*, 15 (3), 313–48.

BLUM-KULKA, S., HOUSE, J. AND KASPER, G. (eds) (in press) *Cross-Cultural Pragmatics: Requests and Apologies.* Norwood, N.J.: Ablex.

CLARK, H., 1987, Four dimensions of language use. In J. VERSCHUEREN & M. BERTUCCELLI-PAPI (eds), *The Pragmatic Perspective*. Amsterdam: John Benjamins.

DABENE, L. and BILLIEZ, J., 1986, Code-switching in the speech of adolescents born of immigrant parents, *Studies in Second Language Acquisition*, 8, 309–25.

DUCROT, O., 1984 *Le dire et le dit*. Paris: Minuit.

FISHMAN, J., 1972, The relationship between micro- and macro-sociolinguistics in the study of who speaks what language to whom and when. In J. B. PRIDE & J. HOLMES (eds), *Sociolinguistics*. Harmondsworth, Middlesex: Penguin Books.

FISHMAN, J., COOPER, R. L. and CONRAD, A. D., 1977, *The Spread of English*. Rowley, Mass.: Newbury House.

GAL, S., 1979, *Language Shift: Social Determinants of Linguistic Change in Bilingual Austria*. New York: Academic Press.

GILES, H., MULAC, A., BRADAC, J. J. and JOHNSON, P., 1987, Speech accommodation theory: the first decade and beyond. In M. L. MCLAUGHLIN (ed.), *Communication Yearbook 10*. Beverly Hills, CA: Sage.

GROSJEAN, F., 1982, *Life with Two Languages*. Cambridge, Mass.: Harvard University Press.

GUMPERZ, J., 1958, Dialect differences and social structure in a north Indian village, *American Anthropologist*, 60, 668–81.

——, 1970, Verbal strategies in multilingual communication. In J. ALATIS (ed.), *Bilingualism and Languages in Contact*. Washington: Georgetown University Press.

——, 1976, The sociolinguistic significance of conversational code-switching. In J. COOK-GUMPERZ & J. GUMPERZ (eds), *Papers on Language and Context*. Working Papers of the Language Behavior Research Laboratory, University of California-Berkeley.

——, 1982, *Discourse Strategies*. Cambridge: Cambridge University Press.

HAUGEN, E., 1956, *Bilingualism in the Americas: a Bibliography and Research Guide*. Tuscaloosa: University of Alabama Press.

——, 1969, *The Norwegian Language in America: a Study of Bilingual Behavior*. Bloomington: Indiana University Press.

JEFFERSON, G., 1972, Side-sequences. In D. SUNDOW (ed.), *Studies in Social Interaction*. New York: Free Press.

LABOV, W., 1972, The transformation of experience in narrative syntax. In W. LABOV (ed.), *Language in the Inner City: Studies in the Black English Vernacular*. Philadelphia: University of Pennsylvania Press.

LABOV, W. and FANSHEL, F., 1977, *Therapeutic Discourse*. London: Academic Press.

PFAFF, C., 1979, Constraints on language mixing: intrasentential code-switching and borrowing in Spanish-English, *Language*, 55, 291–318.

POLANYI, L., 1985, Conversational storytelling. In T. VAN DIJK (ed.), *Handbook of Discourse Analysis Vol. 3, Discourse and Dialogue*. London: Academic Press.

POPLACK, S., 1978, Syntactic structure and social function of code-switching. Centro de Estudios Puertorriquenos. Working Papers 2, 1–32.

RUBIN, J., 1968, *National Bilingualism in Paraguay*. The Hague: Mouton.

SANKOFF, G. 1972, Language use in multilingual societies: some alternative approaches. In J. B. PRIDE & J. HOLMES (eds), *Sociolinguistics*. Harmondsworth, Middlesex: Penguin Books.

SCHIFFRIN, D., 1986, *Discourse Markers*. Cambridge: Cambridge University Press.

SRIDHAR, S. N. and SRIDHAR, K. K., 1980, The syntax and psycholinguistics of bilingual code-mixing, *Canadian Journal of Psychology*, 34, 407–16.

TANNEN, D., 1980, A comparative analysis of oral narrative structures: Athenian Greek and American English. In W. L. CHAFE (ed.), *The Pear Stories*. Norwood, N.J.: Ablex.

TENE, D., 1969, Israeli Hebrew, *Ariel Special issue. The Revival of the Hebrew Language*. Israel: Ministry of Foreign Affairs.

WEIZMAN, E., 1984, Some register characteristics of journalistic language: are they universals? *Applied Linguistics*, 5, 39–50.

5 Communicative inferencing without a common language

JO ANNE KLEIFGEN
Teachers College, Columbia University

'Meaning in conversations is usually jointly produced'
(Gumperz, 1977:195).

Scholars studying conversational interaction have shown that language use and norms for appropriate behaviour vary from culture to culture and from one context to another. Interpretive conventions are generally assumed to be shared by the speakers within a given culture. Increasingly, however, speakers who have little or no linguistic code in common are brought together in communicative situations. Many American classrooms are cases in point, where children coming from non-English speaking homes are present. Children who enter classrooms speaking a native language that is different from the language of instruction face the demand of acquiring social and academic information through the medium of a language that they are only in the process of learning.

How do teachers and children make themselves understood when the children's lexical and grammatical systems in the second language are not completely developed? What kinds of signals are given and received in the process, where the verbal signs are for the most part mutually incomprehensible? In other words, how are messages interpreted? The purpose of this study was to come to a better understanding of the way teachers and limited English proficient pupils negotiate meaning in instructional interaction.

Theoretical framework

In order to take into account the dynamic nature of discourse and to tap the actors' own phenomenological interpretations of the process, a framework was used for the present study that is based on John Gumperz' model (Gumperz, 1982a, 1982b) which he terms 'conversational inference' and defines as 'the situated or context-bound process of interpretation, by means of which participants in an exchange assess the others' intentions, and on which they base their responses' (Gumperz, 1982a:153). Gumperz' approach to the analysis of discourse integrates psychological, sociocultural and contextual elements with linguistic features, and examines their inter-relationship in the interactional process. His model assumes that meaning is created co-operatively through interaction between participants in communicative events.

The instructional communicative inferencing model

Taking this framework into consideration, I will offer here a delineation of the inferencing model that was applied to the present study. The model elaborated here, which I call the 'instructional communicative inferencing model', includes the resources or elements that speakers bring to the communicative act in the classroom, and within which cues to interpretation may be given or received. The elements in the model are as follows.

First, the speakers bring with them into the interaction certain sociocultural components: *values, beliefs* and *attitudes*, including views about schooling, which underlie interactional behaviour (Blom & Gumperz, 1972). These are learned as part of socialisation and experiences with the family in which one is raised. These elements usually operate below the level of consciousness, but they play an important role in the interpretation process.

Next, speakers bring into their interactions a second element, *background knowledge*, which exists internally in the form of knowledge structures (cf. Schank & Abelson, 1977; Minsky, 1975; Rumelhart, 1978) acquired from previous learning and experiences. This background knowledge includes, among other things, factual knowledge about the world, knowledge about social structures, events and roles, and personal histories. As the term is used in this work, background knowledge includes schematic knowledge in the more general sense, which also takes into account factual knowledge that is used as building blocks for learning new concepts in the classroom.

For the purpose of this study, one part of background knowledge was isolated for examination as a more specific component of processing: knowledge of *classroom events, curricula, routines*, that is, 'scripts for school' (Saville-Troike & Kleifgen, 1986), and *discourse structures* for communication (Sinclair & Coulthard, 1975). Classroom knowledge, then, comprises an aspect of meaning that teachers and students make use of during their interactions. All of these elements, sociocultural presuppositions, background knowledge and classroom knowledge, are brought to bear on the actual communicative event between teacher and pupil, permitting an initial assessment, setting up expectations about goals, and then determining what is meant at any point in the interaction.

A fourth element is made up of the generally more perceptible *linguistic* and *nonverbal codes* used in an interaction. These contain signalling mechanisms, which help the speakers to interpret intent. The linguistic and nonverbal codes are the ones that appear to be the most obvious message bearers during an instructional communicative interchange. The participants' utterances are influenced by the sociocultural and knowledge elements, and can in turn trigger those first three sources of information in the course of an interaction. All four elements of meaning are used by interlocutors to varying degrees, consciously or unconsciously, in their efforts to understand their partner's message during a communicative event.

Setting and data collection

The investigation was carried out at an elementary school located in a city (35,000 population) in the Midwest. The school provided a multilingual, multicultural programme designed to serve the needs of non-English speaking children in the community and to enrich the education of the English speaking children in the school. Approximately 40% of the school population came from homes where the mother tongue was not English. Most of the parents from this group were graduate students or university faculty members. The children received native language instruction and English as a second language (ESL) instruction daily on a pull-out basis from the regular classrooms to which they were assigned. This research was centred in the regular classrooms where the children learned subject matter along with their English speaking peers.

The central data collection consisted of two complementary procedures: classroom videotaping and interviews. The first involved videotaping, observing and audiotaping classroom interaction. Three classrooms, a kindergarten, a first grade and a third grade, were selected on the basis of the presence of children who began the school year speaking virtually no English. The focal children wore radio microphones and transmitter units attached to belts. The microphones were clipped close to the children's mouths in order to obtain the best quality of voice data in communication between the child and the teacher, that is, 'interactional' language. The total recorded data base consisted of 40 sessions of instruction in the target classrooms.

The second, complementary procedure was done in order to document the classroom participants' own perceptions of their strategies for successful communication. First, the children were interviewed in their native language; they were asked to view excerpts of the videotaped sessions and to recount what 'was happening'. Every effort was made to keep the questions open-ended and informal, allowing the excerpts from the videotapes to drive the interviews, and probing the children's comments at appropriate points. The pupils were asked probing questions such as: 'What was going on here?' (topic, event); 'How did you know what the teacher said?' (frames, key event components); 'What else helped you to figure it out?' (referents in the physical or linguistic context, background knowledge); 'In general, how do you figure out what the teacher wants you to do?' (other perceived cues or strategies); 'What does your teacher do to help you understand?' (cues, tactics).

The native-speaking assistants who conducted the interviews offered additional ethnographic data after these sessions, on their impressions of the children's understanding. These viewing sessions were audiotaped in order to have an accurate documentation of the children's interpretations. Each interview was made one to two days after the actual events so that it would serve as a stimulated recall rather than a 'creative' interpretation of a forgotten instructional event. Three such interviews were audiotaped for each child, at the beginning, middle and end of the semester.

Documentation was made of the teachers' perceptions of their interactions with the pupils, and of their views with regard to schooling and second language children. In December, the teachers were interviewed during playback sessions using selected excerpts from the videotaped data from various points during that semester. They were first asked to offer their impressions of the focal child's academic, social and linguistic progress as well as that child's ability to participate in classroom activities. Next, they were asked to point out their own accommodation strategies with the focal children. At the discrimination of the teachers, the tape was temporarily halted so that they could interpret the interaction being replayed. If they chose to wait until an excerpt was completed, they were asked then to interpret what they had seen. Finally, they were asked to discuss their techniques for 'getting the children to understand them'. These interviews were audiotaped and transcribed. Information given by the teachers during these interviews was supplemented with their comments made throughout the semester and even after the data were collected, as they continued to report to me on events in their classrooms.

Through interviews with the children's parents in their native language, additional data were gathered on the children's experiential, educational and family background, as well as the children's impressions—as told to their parents—of their classes in English. The parents' educational goals for the children and their participation in the children's schooling were also determined. These interviews provided valuable cultural information at the level of values, beliefs, attitudes and background knowledge. They were conducted with viewings of the same instructional encounters shown to the children and their teachers. Interviews with the parents of the three children, conducted in December, lasted approximately two hours each. These were audiorecorded and transcribed.

Analyses

The recordings were 'scripted', that is, the record included time intervals, interlocutors, verbatim transcriptions including all languages, certain prosodic characteristics, significant aspects of the physical setting and nonverbal signals, and other contextual information. Utterances spoken by children in their native tongues were transcribed and translated by the same Korean and Chinese research assistants who participated in the debriefing interviews with the parents and children. The analysis of communicative inference was taking place during this process, with information to confirm intentionality and understanding such as the participants' subsequent actions and native language information in which the pupils indicated either in private speech or to a native-speaking peer what the teacher meant. This information was stored in computer text files in a word processing mode.

Dyadic instructional encounter

The linguistic analysis gave attention to the interactive nature of teacher—pupil communication and to the participants' interpretation process during the interaction. Following Erickson & Schultz's (1982) requirements that passages studied be self-contained episodes, situations were selected from the data in which incidents occurred that were potentially critical for achieving an educational goal in the classroom. The locus of observation (cf. Merritt & Humphrey, 1980) was a 'Dyadic Instructional Encounter'—an exchange between a teacher and the focal child, initiated either because one of the interactants perceived that the pupil needed help in carrying out an academic task or classroom procedure, or to check the pupil's knowledge or understanding. The exchange could be triggered by:

1. pupil indication of a need for help,
2. teacher-initiated check for knowledge or understanding or
3. child-initiated check of his/her own understanding or request for approval.

The exchange ended when the communicative goal was achieved, was abandoned, or failed.

Interviews

All the recorded interviews conducted with children, parents and teachers were transcribed, translated into English where pertinent and entered into computer files. These interviews totalled 20 hours of taped data. The information therein was categorised according to the elements of meaning used by speakers in making situated interpretations of their partners' intent during the instructional interaction.

The categorised information from the interviews was entered on the transcript next to the dyadic instructional encounters that the interviewees had interpreted. The encounters were then re-examined on videotape for the speakers' application of the various elements in situated interpretations of their partner's intent. Text and context sometimes had to be re-examined outside the encounter itself to confirm either a speaker's intent or a speaker's interpretation of the partner's intent.

The analysis of the interactions between a first grade teacher and one of her pupils will be addressed first, in order to illustrate how communication is achieved when values and knowledge about school appear to be shared. Analyses of interactions in a kindergarten and a third grade classroom will follow, showing what the interactants do to attempt to overcome problems when these elements are not always shared.

Interacting with shared frames

The encounter that will be used for illustration here took place between a Korean girl, Hyun-Joo (HJ),[1] and the first grade teacher, Ms Hanes (T), at the beginning of an instructional event, a maths lesson on telling time. The first graders were seated at their desks in small groups. The video camera was trained on Hyun-Joo's group, consisting of three English speakers, Young-In (YI), another Korean-speaking girl, and Hyun-Joo. Example 1 below is the verbatim transcript of this encounter. Ms Hanes began the lesson by directing the class to clear their desks and take out their clocks made from paper plates (line 1). Hyun-Joo muttered to herself in Korean that she could not understand what the teacher was telling the class (line 2). She then began to comment in Korean about the microphone and to make nonsense sounds into it (lines 3–5). The teacher, hearing the stream of Korean speech and seeing the girls' desks still covered with papers, arrived to issue directives (lines 6–7). As she spoke, she pointed to Hyun-Joo's papers and then gestured toward the inside of her desk. Ms Hanes then continued to check on the other groups (line 8).

Hyun-Joo followed the directive, but could not find her clock in the desk. Hearing Hyun-Joo's dismayed voice as she exclaimed, 'No my clock' (line 9), the teacher returned. When she asked Hyun-Joo where her clock was (line 10), the child replied, 'No', with a negative headshake (line 11). The teacher next asked her whether she took it home, and Hyun-Joo's answer was again in the negative (lines 12–13). The teacher then left to find another paper plate for Hyun-Joo, who in the meantime had retrieved her clock from inside the desk, saying to herself in Korean, 'Oh, here it is' (lines 14–15). The teacher saw Hyun-Joo holding up her clock, and closed the incident with the verbal confirmation that the problem was resolved (lines 16–19).

Example 1

1.	T > ALL	EVERYONE CLEAR EVERYTHING OFF YOUR DESK LIKE TOBEY HAS AND TAKE OUT YOUR CLOCK.
2.	HJ > HJ	SEONSAENGNIM YAEGIREU MOLLA GAZIGO EUNG. AH. 'I did not know what the teacher said.'

(Hyun-Joo then begins to play with sounds in Korean.)

3.	HJ > YI	MWOYA. 'What's this?'

4.   MOLLA.
                'I don't know.'

5.   NAE + GA EODEOHGE ANYA.
                'How do I know?'

(Ms Hanes arrives at Hyun-Joo's group.)

6. T > HJ   HYUN-JOO, CAN YOU PLEASE PUT THIS IN YOUR DESK?

(gesturing toward Hyun-Joo's papers and towards the inside of her desk)

7. T > HJ   AND GET OUT YOUR CLOCK.

(Hyun-Joo begins to clear her desk and look for her clock. Ms Hanes leaves to check the other groups.)

8. T > ALL   EVERYTHING SHOULD BE IN YOUR DESK EXCEPT YOUR CLOCK.

(Hyun-Joo looks up in dismay.)

9. HJ > T   NO MY CLOCK!

(Ms Hanes returns to the scene.)

10. T > HJ   WHERE'S YOUR CLOCK?
11. HJ > T   NO. (shaking head negatively)
12. T > HJ   DID YOU TAKE IT HOME?
13. HJ > T   NO.

(Ms Hanes walks over to the shelf to get a new paper plate for Hyun-Joo. Meanwhile, Hyun-Joo looks in her desk again and finds her clock.)

14. HJ > HJ   AH. *(to herself)*
15. HJ > T   YEOGISSDA AH. *(looking up at Ms Hanes)*
                'Oh, here it is.'
16. T > HJ   HYUN-JOO?
17. *(Hyun-Joo holds up her clock to the teacher.)*
18. T > HJ   OH YOU FOUND YOUR CLOCK.
19.   VERY GOOD, HYUN-JOO.

All four elements for interpreting meaning, from the less perceptible aspects of values, beliefs, attitudes and background knowledge to the directly observable nonverbal and language factors, helped bring this encounter to a satisfactory conclusion. There were the elements that the speakers brought with them to the communicative encounter, beginning with shared educational goals and attitudes. It was well established, through informal meetings and formal interviews with Hyun-Joo, her parents and the teacher, that the attitudes of the interactants towards each other were very positive, and their beliefs about their mutual classroom roles coincided. In Ms Hanes's words, '[Hyun-Joo is] extremely conscientious in her work. I noticed with all the Korean children, as soon as they came back to class ... they'll go right to their desk, pull out their folders, and start working.' According to the teacher, Hyun-Joo was the 'ideal' pupil, always making great efforts to participate, even if nonverbally, in classroom interaction. Moreover, Hyun-Joo told her parents that she liked her teachers, especially Ms Hanes. These beliefs about role relationships and positive attitudes were reflected in this one-to-one instructional encounter, both from the child's appeals for assistance from her teacher and from the teacher's caretaker efforts to avoid or overcome breakdowns in the interaction, attempting to second-guess the child's needs. Teacher and child shared mutual respect and goals of academic achievement. In the above encounter, Hyun-Joo demonstrated her usual desire to participate; Ms Hanes, rather than interpret the misplaced clock as the work of a careless, uninterested pupil, made efforts to replace the missing item.

Painfully, there were analogous situations with some of the American children in which the teacher's interpretation was a negative one, thus cutting off efforts at continued interaction. These contrasting attitudes were occasionally expressed overtly to the researcher. For example, one morning the teacher conducted a classroom discussion with the children about their after-school activities. Afterwards, she made the following remarks, comparing Hyun-Joo with her American classmates:

'You see what she does? She goes home and practices the A-B-C's. You see what most of the Americans do? They watch TV.'

Thus, the perception that there were shared educational goals influenced interpretations in the ensuing interaction.

The second factor that the interactants brought to the encounters and that influenced the success of the communication was shared school knowledge. Sequences of events and structures for communication, such as formulaic expressions marking openings and closings of instructional events, came into play in this interaction. During the playback procedure, Hyun-Joo confirmed the fact that the teacher's general instructions to the whole class (line 1 of Example 1) were difficult for her to understand, saying to her Korean interviewer, 'I heard [the teacher] saying something, but I didn't understand what she was saying'. However, because of Hyun-Joo's familiarity with sequences of classroom events, she said that she was aware that something new was about to begin, and that by watching the other children's actions she would be able to follow suit and act appropriately. She told the Korean interviewer that by watching the teacher's gestures as well as the other children's actions, she figured out that she was supposed to take out her clock.

A second kind of school knowledge further constrained interpretations in this interaction. In the interviews, the teacher recounted a shared classroom experience, or history, that helped her and Hyun-Joo in this situation to work together in order to solve the problem of the missing clock. Ms Hanes explained that from the beginning of the year the Korean pupils had emptied the contents of their desks daily and had taken them home. She permitted this custom, assuming that parents were working with their children at home. By the time of this interaction, the Korean children were beginning to be more selective about what they would take home at the end of each day. Thus, Ms Hane's question, 'Did you take it home?' made sense to both interactants.

Besides using shared educational goals and knowledge as scaffolds for understanding each other's intent, both speakers drew on certain directly observable elements during this encounter in their efforts towards communicative co-operation. The teacher carefully chose linguistic cues. In the interviews, she reported that through her experience with international pupils, she had become aware that children who were beginning to learn English could 'understand long before they can express themselves in English.' Thus, for beginners, the teacher would 'give them the words and just let them say "yes" or "no" in English'. Aware of Hyun-Joo's receptive competence, Ms Hanes repeated key words and phrases and used simple sentences in this encounter. Further, she used simpler question-types. Just as she did in many other situations, Ms Hanes here rephrased a WH-question to form a yes–no type question, so that Hyun-Joo would be able to respond (lines 10,12). Such rephrasings illustrate how she made situated interpretations of Hyun-Joo's need for assistance during the interactional process by monitoring her pupil's reactions. These characteristics of teachers' simplified register were similarly found in earlier work (Kleifgen, 1985). The present research points to the dynamics underlying linguistic accommodation. The skill with which the experienced teacher varied her use of structures and vocabulary is seen here to be linked to the shared frames that constrained possibilities for making communicative inferences.

Hyun-Joo confirmed the teacher's perception of limited English proficient children's ability to understand before they can speak English. After viewing this encounter, she was able to retell in Korean what the teacher said to her in English regarding the missing clock. However, she was unable to produce the equivalent English forms. Hyun-Joo also made use of certain linguistic signals. Her linguistic tactic at the beginning of the year (and illustrated in this interaction) was to vocalise in Korean. This tactic succeeded in attracting Ms Hane's attention toward the two girls, which resulted in the ensuing interaction. Other cues to interpretation of messages included nonverbal signals given by both teacher and pupil, as well as appeals to the physical setting, such as the teacher's gestures accompanying her words, 'Can you please put this in your desk?' (line 6). Wanting for words, Hyun-Joo deictically held up her clock for the teacher to see (line 17).

To summarise, the illustrative example shows that the dyadic instructional encounters reflected the use of a hierarchy of elements to help participants interpret intent. They ranged from those elements usually operating below the level of consciousness, such as values, beliefs and attitudes, to prior school knowledge and the use of directly observable linguistic and nonverbal signals. Both teacher and child co-operated through the use of words, gestures and sounds—interpreted according to the background knowledge and values of each—to convey messages to each other that facilitated their efforts to achieve their respective communicative goals. In other words, because the teacher and the Korean girl shared expectations at higher levels (cultural and experiential), understanding was more likely, despite the absence of common linguistic structures (cf. Saville-Troike, 1987).

Interacting with contrasting frames

The next illustrative encounters show what two experienced teachers did to overcome problems when educational beliefs and attitudes were not entirely shared. Examples from a kindergarten classroom will be presented first, followed by examples from a third grade classroom. Young-Ho (YH) was a five-year-old Korean boy who began his school life in the United States in Sharon Bell's (T) kindergarten. He was confronting the ways of the school subculture for the first time. From the beginning, Young-Ho appeared not to be a co-operative interactant in the classroom: He did not like to respond to the teacher's questions. Politeness and deference towards adults are part of a Korean child's enculturation at home, and are manifested even in Korean language forms. Data from interviews with this boy's parents showed that his behaviour, rather than a sign of rudeness, reflected his culture and family background. Young-Ho's perceptions of his student role manifested themselves in two major ways. He wanted to preserve a certain personal space between himself and his teachers as a signal of respect; he also tried to maintain silence in order to preserve face in situations where he was 'tested' in English. In the retrospective interview with Young-Ho's parents, they noted that upon their arrival in this country, Young-Ho had asked his family to speak only English at home, so that he could have opportunities for practice. The parents explained further that, because of the family's high expectations for educational achievement, any spoken error by Young-Ho in the teacher's presence represented for him a loss of face. They said that Young-Ho wanted to perform well for his teachers, yet he felt strongly that his English was not yet up to his own standards of perfection.

Ms Bell was aware of the high priority that the family put on educational achievement, and she sensed Young-Ho's 'shyness', that is, his desire to show politeness by maintaining social distance, and his preference for silence in situations where he was unsure of his performance in English. In the interview she noted:

> I noticed that when you ask Young-Ho a direct question, he plays with his hair. He's put on the spot, and he's not comfortable with it. But if you can get it out of him another way, he's better. ... So I don't put much pressure on him.

The teacher knew that in many instances Young-Ho may have known the answers to her questions despite his lack of response, and the data verifies her intuitions. In the following encounter (Example 2 below), Ms Bell worked with a group of seven children, who were applying their counting skills during a Halloween art activity. They were to cut out eight spider legs out of black construction paper and attach them to a paper spider-body. The teacher leaned close to him and tried to elicit the word, 'spider' from Young-Ho (lines 1–4), but his reaction was to slide down into his chair (line 3). Joo-Min (JM), a Korean boy who knew some English, told Young-Ho the answer in Korean (line 5) and then answered the teacher in English (lines 6–7), yet Young-Ho still refused to respond, so the teacher closed the encounter with the appropriate response (line 8).

Example 2

1. T > YH   WHAT IS THIS? *(pointing to the paper spider)*
2.   WHAT ARE WE MAKING? *(leaning over his shoulder)*
3. *(Young-Ho slides down his chair)*

4. T > YH   WHAT IS IT?
5. JM > T   SEUPAIDEO-HAE. *(prompting Young-Ho)*
              'Say, "spider."'

(Young-Ho does not respond. Joo-Min answers for him.)

6. JM > T   SPIDER
7.   SPIDER LEGS.

(Young-Ho still does not respond. Ms Bell repeats the answer.)

8. T > YH   SPIDER. *(pointing to the spider)*

Faced with this type of reaction, Ms Bell reported that she consciously tried to be aware of Young-Ho's preference for more personal space. In her words, she 'sensed that he does not like a lot of contact and touching (or) to be enclosed like that.' The classroom data corroborated her claim to attempt to make him more comfortable during these encounters. Moreover, the data showed that she also devised an indirect tactic to elicit language from Young-Ho by directing questions at other children and waiting for Young-Ho to prompt them. In the following encounter (Example 3), the teacher was working with five children at a table as they constructed booklets on the food groups by cutting out pictures from magazines and pasting them on coloured construction paper. Ms Bell asked Mindy (MY), an English speaker, and Shuhong (SU), a Chinese–English bilingual, to name colours (lines 1, 5). Young-Ho provided the answer for each girl (lines 2–3, 6). Once he was able to successfully prompt the two other children in this interaction, he felt confident enough to answer more questions on his own (lines 9–13).

Example 3

1. T > MY   MINDY, WHAT COLOUR? *(pointing to a sheet of construction paper)*

(Young-Ho answers instead, first in Korean, then in English.)

2. YH > T   NORAN. NORAN SAEG.
              'Yellow. Yellow colour.'
3.   YELLOW!
4. T > MY   YOUNG-HO TELLS YOU 'YELLOW'.
5. T > SU   OK, WHAT COLOUR, SHUHONG? *(pointing to another sheet)*

(Young-Ho answers again)

6. YH > T   YELLOW.
7. T > YH   YELLOW?
8.   OK, WHAT'S THIS ONE? *(pointing)*
9. YH > T   RED.
10. T > YH   UM, YOU'RE SO SMART TODAY.
11.   WHAT'S THIS? *(pointing)*
12. YH > T   GREEN.
13. T > YH   OK! THERE'S GREEN.

The teacher was aware of Young-Ho's need to display his knowledge in his own way. In this interaction, she was seated next to him but maintained a comfortable distance. Having observed that Young-Ho would talk when he was sure of the answers (and of his ability to produce them in English), Ms Bell accommodated to him on the interactional level. But her accommodation was also knowledge-based. The vocabulary that she chose to elicit was based on her understanding of Young-Ho's factual knowledge. She reported that she generally elicited words such as colours and numbers that Young-Ho knew in Korean. The parents had told her that Young-Ho could identify colours in Korean before starting kindergarten and that he could count in Korean. The teacher in this and other encounters appealed to prior knowledge learned in the native language in order to associate them with English equivalents. Her skilful use of nonverbal signals and simplified speech (Krashen, 1980) would have had no effect had she not been sensitive to the higher level elements influencing the interaction.

A sharp contrast in sociocultural understandings could be observed in the third grade classroom. Ms Renner (T), who was regarded by the community as an exceptionally gifted educator, was aware of a clash in educational values between herself and Xiaohui (XH), a girl from Shanghai, China. Xiaohui had been schooled in a traditional, whole-group type of classroom instruction, whereas Ms Renner's classroom had a very complex, individualised organisational structure. When students were not participating in small-group learning activities under the supervision of a teacher, they had to budget their free time to carry out tasks in the language, science or listening centres, or complete assignments placed in their individual folders. The teacher's assessment of Xiaohui was that she was confused about the ways of the American classroom, often interpreting her new-found 'freedom' as licence to make several trips to the water fountain, pencil sharpener, bookshelves and supply cabinet. At the same time, Xiaohui was afraid to take the risk of trying something she was not absolutely sure that she could understand. Her difficulty in dealing with uncertainty was evident, not only to the teacher, but also in the videotaped data. She was observed to move about the room, exacting frequent reassurances from classmates and teachers about what was required. In the following example, the teacher had explained to Xiaohui and Yuan (Y), a bilingual speaker, how to complete a task requiring that they write names of things that they were thankful for. Xiaohui became nervous about the assignment and asked Yuan to serve as translator.[2]

Example 4

1. XH > Y   NI3 WEN4 TA1 NENG2 BU4 NENG2 DAI4 DAO4 ZHONG1 WEN2 BAN1?
'Ask her if we can bring this to Chinese class.'

2. Y > XH   WEI4 SHE2 ME NE?
'Why?'

3. XH > Y   YIN1 WEI4 WO3 NA4 GE4 YING1 WEN2 BU2 HUI4 KE3 YI3 WEN4 WEN4 ZHONG1 WEN2 LAO3 SHI1.
'Because I can ask the Chinese teacher about the English I don't know.'

Ms Renner assured Xiaohui that she could do so, and that she could, if she wished, also write in Chinese.

Because of her difficulty in dealing with uncertainty, Xiaohui repeatedly appealed to Ms Renner and to the student-teacher present in the class for detailed directives and approval of her work in progress. Recognising what she termed Xiaohui's over-dependency, Ms Renner reported that she 'tried to decrease the frequency of this by asking [Xiaohui] to complete a certain amount before she shares it with me'. The interaction in Example 5 below took place after a tutorial language lesson. Xiaohui and Ping (PI), another Chinese girl, were directed to return to their places (line 1) to complete a written exercise based on what they had just learned. But Xiaohui was obsessed with knowing all the details of her maths assignment for the day (lines 2, 7–8). The teacher directed her instead to work on her language task (lines 3–6), and asked Ping to explain the instructions to Xiaohui in Chinese (lines 9–11). Xiaohui appeared unsatisfied (lines 12–13) but nevertheless understood the teacher's request (line 14).

Example 5

1. T > XH   AND YOU MAY GO TO YOUR DESK.
2. XH > T   MATH?
3. T > XH   I'LL TALK TO YOU LATER.

4.   LATER.
5.   DO THIS FIRST. *(pointing to the workbook)*
6.   FIRST.
7. XH > T   MATH. *(holding up folder)*
8.   MATH PAGE.

Ms Renner turns to Ping.)

9. T > PI   YOU UNDERSTAND 'FIRST', PING?
10.   WOULD YOU EXPLAIN TO XIAOHUI?
11. PI > XL   YI2 DIN4 YAO4 XIAN1 ZUO4 ZHE4 GE4.
                     'You certainly have to do this first.'
12. XH > PI   ZUO4 ZHE4 ZHANG1. ZAI4 ZUO4 NA3 YI4
                     ZHANG1?
                     'Do this page. Then which page to do?'
13.   ZAI4 ZUO4 NA3 YI2 GE4?
                     'Then which one to do?'

(Xiaohui returns to her desk, whispering to herself.)

14. XH > XH   XIAN1 LA12 UO4 ZHE4 GE4 ... ONE. TWO.
                     'First do this. One. Two.'

Ms Renner worked to inculcate in her pupil independent work habits, whereas the child worked to exact more reassurances that she was proceeding correctly. The teacher was aware of the contrasting values between two cultures: responsibility for learning residing in the teacher vs. responsibility for learning resting primarily with the child (cf. Spindler & Spindler, 1987). She wanted Xiaohui to become more independent in her decision-making, so she created situations that gently nudged the girl 'to stretch a bit and to go on hunches at times...'.

In this encounter, communication was made clear through the use of the child's native language. Aware of the conflicting frames, the teacher held frequent conferences with the parents and used native language interpreters to attempt to bring the pupil gradually into conformity with the new ways of schooling. Ms Renner perceived that Xiaohui's ambivalence in the classroom could not be attributed to the 'language barrier' alone.[3] She thus provided a delicate balance between encouraging risk-taking and encouraging the use of the native language as a scaffold for understanding. The teacher's insight about Xiaohui's behaviour enabled her to guide the Chinese student through the transitional period from an overtly rigid whole-class instructional approach in China to varied participation structures in her new school in the US.

Discussion and conclusions

The key to successful communication resided mainly in two things that the teachers in this study did. They exerted great efforts to make sense of the students' speech and behaviour, and they appealed to the non-linguistic elements of culture and background knowledge in order to better interpret what was happening. The examination of sociocultural components for this work focused on their manifestations in the educational domain, that is, goals in the classroom founded on the participants' educational values, beliefs and attitudes. To the degree that the teachers perceived that they shared the same educational goals as the international children and their families, such common underlying assumptions paved the way for inferring what was going to be said during the dyadic instructional encounters. Without agreement that both interactants were willing to make special efforts to negotiate meaning without a common language, communicative co-operation was more likely to fail than in other, 'ordinary' circumstances.

The notion of teacher expectations (Anyon, 1981; Rosenthal & Jacobson, 1968) is related to this element in the negotiation of meaning. All the teachers in this study *expected* the international children to do well in school, or at least to attempt to do so, because, they explained, the limited English speakers were very 'motivated' and, unlike most of their American classmates, the children came from more affluent and highly educated family backgrounds. The teachers also perceived that there was more involvement and support from the international parents than from their American counterparts. In one teacher's words:

> Fortunately, at our school these [international] children are highly motivated to learn, and they catch on very quickly. I'm not sure children would be as easily accepted if they had discipline problems. ... We found the international parents are much more appreciative. ... So I think that at the school we have a very good attitude.

These shared expectations at higher levels laid the necessary groundwork for understanding, with the result that communication was often successful even in the absence of common linguistic structures.

To summarise, with examination and interpretive analysis of the videotaped instructional encounters and with the help of the participants themselves, some of the inferencing processes employed during the interactions were reconstructed. Participants appeared to draw on a combination of elements to infer the intent of their partners: (1) sociocultural—attitudes, beliefs and values; (2) prior knowledge and experience; (3) knowledge of classroom events, routines and discourse structures, and (4) linguistic and nonverbal code. These four elements together had a bearing on the success or failure of an interaction. With sociocultural and knowledge-based elements of meaning providing a basis for inferring what was intended, teachers in speaking with the children accommodated linguistic forms according to their judgements of the pupils' understanding. Pupils in turn used certain attention-getting and nonverbal tactics that served as signals for their teachers. A complete theory of second language communication, then, should take into account the non-linguistic factors that interact with linguistic forms and functions, recognising the variation in interpretive frames across cultures and contexts.

Notes to Chapter 5

1. Names of persons in this research are pseudonymous.
2. Interactions in Chinese are transcribed in pinyin, with tones indicated by numbers.
3. In contrast, the third grade student-teacher misinterpreted Xiaohui's behaviour. For a more detailed description of student-teachers' failure to draw on sociocultural and experiential elements in order to construct meaning, see Kleifgen (1986, 1988).

References

ANYON, J., 1981, Social class and school knowledge, *Curriculum Inquiry*, 11:1, 3–42.

BLOM, J-P. and GUMPERZ, J., 1972, Social meaning in linguistic structures. In J. GUMPERZ & D. HYMES (eds), *Directions in Sociolinguistics*. New York: Holt, Rinehart & Winston.

ERICKSON, F. and SCHULTZ, J., 1982, *The Counselor as Gatekeeper*. New York: Academic Press.

GUMPERZ, J., 1977, Sociocultural knowledge in conversational inference. In M. SAVILLE-TROIKE (ed.), *Georgetown University Roundtable in Languages and Linguistics, 1977*. Washington, DC: Georgetown University Press.

——, 1982a, *Discourse Strategies*. Cambridge: Cambridge University Press.

——, (ed.), 1982b, *Language and Social Identity*. Cambridge: Cambridge University Press.

KLEIFGEN, J., 1985, Skilled variation in a kindergarten teacher's use of foreigner talk. In S. GASS & C. MADDEN (eds), *Input in Second Language Acquisition*. Rowley, MA: Newbury House.

——, 1986, *Communicative Inferencing between Classroom Teachers and Limited English Proficient International Children*. (Ph.D. Dissertation, University of Illinois at Urbana-Champaign). *Dissertation Abstracts International*, 47–9A, 333–8A. (University Microfilms No. 87-01, 533).

——, 1988, Learning from student-teachers' cross-cultural communicative failures, *Anthropology and Education Quarterly*, 19, 218–34.

KRASHEN, S., 1980, The theoretical and practical relevance of simple codes in second language acquisition. In R. SCARCELLA & S. KRASHEN (eds), *Research in Second Language Acquisition*. Rowley, MA: Newbury House.

MERRITT, M. and HUMPHREY, F., 1980, *Service-Like Events During Individual Work Time and their Contribution to the Nature of Communication in Primary Classrooms*. (Contract No. NIE G-78-0159.) Washington, DC: National Institute of Education.

MINSKY, M., 1975, A framework for representing knowledge. In P. WINSTON (ed.), *The Psychology of Computer Vision*. New York: McGraw Hill.

ROSENTHAL, R. and JACOBSON, L., 1968, *Pygmalion in the Classroom*. New York: Holt, Rinehart & Winston.

RUMELHART, D., 1978, Schemata: The building blocks of cognition. In R. SPIRO, B. BURCE, & W. BREWER (eds), *Theoretical Issues in Reading Comprehension*. Hillsdale, NJ: Lawrence Erlbaum.

SAVILLE-TROIKE, M., 1987, Dilingual discourse: Communication without a common language, *Linguistics*, 25, 81–106.

SAVILLE-TROIKE, M. and KLEIFGEN, J., 1986, Scripts for school: Cross-cultural communication in elementary classrooms, *Text*, 6(2), 207–21.

SCHANK, R. and ABELSON, R., 1977, *Scripts, Plans, Goals, and Understanding*. Hillsdale, NJ: Lawrence Erlbaum.

SINCLAIR, J. and COULTHARD, M., 1975, *Towards an Analysis of Discourse: The English Used by Teachers and Pupils*. Oxford: Oxford University Press.

SPINDLER, G. and SPINDLER, L., 1987, Cultural dialogue and schooling in Schoenhausen and Roseville: A comparative analysis, *Anthropology and Education Quarterly*, 18, 3–16.

6 Do you have a bag?: Social status and patterned variation in second language acquisition[1]

LESLIE M. BEEBE
TOMOKO TAKAHASHI
Teachers College, Columbia University

Introduction

Recently, at Dan Tempura, a local country-style Japanese sushi bar and tempura restaurant on the West Side of Manhattan, I sat impatiently waiting to catch the waiter's eye after a hard day at the office. All I wanted was my bargain 'sushi regular' and a glass of Kirin beer with typical Japanese prompt and efficient service. But on this day, I simply could not seem to catch the waiter's eye, even though I had the impression he realised I was ready to order. He was talking to another waiter and looking in the direction of the two thirtyish, middle class women sitting to my left. The women were clearly quite oblivious, being deeply involved in their conversation, and not seeking the waiter's attention. A moment later, I watched with interest as the waiter walked up and said to the women, 'Do you have a bag?' First they stared blankly at the waiter. Next they looked in dismay at each other. Then one of them turned to me (the tables were so close, we were practically sitting together) and her facial expression said, 'What in God's name does this man mean?' I had not seen a thing prior to the waiter's arrival, but having researched Japanese English vs. American English speech acts over the last three years, I knew instantly what the waiter was trying to do. So, without a moment's hesitation, I butted in and said, 'That is a Japanese warning that someone is trying to steal your purse'. They both looked down aghast, and on the floor, one woman's wallet, credit cards, and chequebook were strewn about two feet away from her pocketbook. Two men, sitting at a table next to them, calmly, but quickly, got up and left the restaurant. [LMB field notes]

This story serves to reinforce two stereotypes: (1) New York is full of thieves, (2) Japanese people are inscrutably indirect. The fact is that New York has one of the lowest crime rates of the large American cities. And Japanese people (like other people in the world) can be mercilessly direct. They can indeed be extremely indirect as well. The picture becomes clearer when we realise that the situations in which both Japanese and Americans choose to be direct or indirect depend to a great extent on the relative social status of the interlocutors. Japanese, however, attend to factors that Americans do not hold to be particularly important. And Americans simply are not sensitised to all of these social nuances that, for Japanese, are involved in the decision to speak directly or indirectly. This is not to say that Americans speaking English are insensitive to social factors. Nevertheless, over and over again in our data, we have found Japanese asking questions like, 'Do you have a bag?' to accomplish a speech act (in this case, a warning) that Americans would approach more explicitly and directly. And over and over again we have noticed the preponderance of this type of hinting behaviour showing up in data involving lower status people speaking to higher status interlocutors. The seemingly factual question has shown up in our data on face-threatening acts—disagreement, chastisement, correction, and giving embarrassing information. In most, not all cases, it has been a strategy that a lower status Japanese used in English to avoid telling something face-threatening to a higher status person. The seemingly factual question is part of a hinting strategy designed to promote self discovery by the higher status person, thereby letting the lower status person off the hook for telling them something they don't want to hear.

In this chapter, we investigate American and Japanese performance on two face-threatening acts in English—disagreement and giving embarrassing information.[2] Brown & Levinson (1978) argue that there exist universal strategies in performing face-threatening acts. At the same time, we are aware of crosscultural differences in the realisation of speech acts. In fact, we believe that a lot of international incidents could be avoided if the speakers were aware of the differences in the culturally specific usage of politeness strategies (see Nagai & Rosovsky, 1973; Takahashi & Beebe, 1987, for examples of such incidents).

Another central concern of this chapter is how Japanese ESL speakers vs. American English speakers perform face-threatening speech acts with *status unequals*. That is, how does each group respond to a higher vs. a lower status interlocutor, and how do Japanese compare to Americans speaking English? It is generally believed that Japanese people are extremely status conscious (see Condon, 1984; Deutsch, 1983; Goldstein & Tamura, 1975; Nakane, 1972, 1974; Sakamoto & Naotsuka, 1982). It seems that the Japanese tend to transfer this status consciousness into English. In our previous studies on refusals, we found that Japanese often differed from Americans in the frequency of certain semantic formulas they used (e.g. Beebe *et al.*, in press). For instance, in the situation where an employee had to refuse the boss's request to stay late at the office, Japanese speakers (both in Japanese and English) said 'I'm sorry' much more frequently than Americans. What is more interesting, however, is that Japanese speakers displayed noticeable style shifting in frequency of regret/apology formulas between status unequals, whereas Americans did not. In other words, Japanese said 'I'm sorry' much more frequently when talking to a lower status person. Thus, in general, it appears that Japanese subjects can be particularly sensitive to high vs. low status.

The Japanese are stereotyped as people who apologise all the time (see, for example, Condon, 1984). In fact, we find much discussion and many anecdotal descriptions of the overuse of apology expressions by the Japanese both in Japanese and in English (e.g. Coulmas, 1981; Deutsch, 1983; Takahashi, 1984). We are also aware of stereotypes about differences between Americans and Japanese people: Americans are more direct than Japanese. Americans are more explicit than Japanese. Japanese do not make critical remarks to someone else's face. They avoid disagreement and avoid telling you anything that you don't want to hear. These are stereotypes which many Americans and Japanese alike subscribe to. The stereotypes are claimed to apply to Japanese both when they speak their own native language and when they speak English as a second language. The work on comparative culture and the Japanese language seem to support these views (e.g. Barnlund, 1974; Condon & Yousef, 1975; Doi, 1974; Kunihiro, 1973; Passin, 1980; Seward, 1968).

Our initial investigation of face-threatening acts leads us to question whether or not such stereotypes hold true in different situations—particularly situations with different status relations. What we have done is to compare Japanese vs. American performance of face-threatening acts in English in two status-unequal situations: a lower status person talking to someone of higher status (such as an employee talking to the boss) and a higher status person talking to someone of a lower status (such as a boss to an assistant).

It is reasonable to expect that there would be major differences between American native and Japanese ESL speakers' rules for sociolinguistically appropriate behaviour and that these differences would be tied to the relative status of the interlocutors. Based on our preliminary data, we wish to make three very general claims. (1) Japanese speaking English differ from native Americans speaking their own language, not only in the linguistic form but especially in the semantic content, of what they say. And our Japanese subjects have different social rules of speaking (i.e. rules of sociolinguistic appropriateness) than the Americans they were compared to. (2) The Japanese speaking English frequently break stereotypes about their social and linguistic behaviour—stereotypes that are widely held by Japanese and English speakers alike and that are commonly written up in books comparing Japanese and American culture. The stereotypes are based on behaviour in Japanese and an assumption that characteristics of Japanese transfer into English. We cannot begin to understand where our characterisations hold true and where they are unfortunate overgeneralisations if we do not examine Japanese ESL behaviour in the light of the relative social status of the two interlocutors. (3) Both Japanese ESL speakers and American native speakers linguistically style shift according to the status of the interlocutor.

It is not surprising that we have found data to substantiate such general claims. Many of the actual differences that we find between Japanese ESL and American native speakers, however, are not at all obvious; nor are they easy to describe and categorise. What *does* turn out to be surprising is the number of times the data contradict prevailing stereotypes about the two languages and cultures.

Method

In order to study American native vs. Japanese ESL face-threatening acts, we used two data collection procedures. (1) We kept a notebook on naturally occurring instances of face-threatening acts—particularly disagreement, chastisement, correction of others' statements and giving others information they will find embarrassing. We also recorded natural examples given to us by graduate students in TESOL and Applied Linguistics at Columbia University Teachers College and by other language professionals with experience in this type of research. (2) We collected 30 discourse completion tests (DCTs) from 15 native Americans and 15 advanced

Japanese ESL speakers using English. All subjects were college graduates. For the Japanese, there were eight females and seven males with an average age of 33. For the Americans, there were eleven females and four males, also with an average age of 33. The discourse completion test was a role play questionnaire containing 12 situations in which the subject was asked to write what they would say or indicate if they would say nothing—i.e. they were allowed to 'opt out' if they wished to do so (see Bonikowska, 1985). The questionnaire contained two situations each for disagreement, chastisement, correction, giving embarrassing information and two other speech acts as controls. In this chapter, we shall discuss only disagreement and giving embarrassing information. One situation in each pair involved a higher status person responding to a lower status person. A second situation involved just the reverse—a lower status person responding to a higher status person. All situations were presented in random order on the questionnaire.

All the responses were analysed as consisting of a sequence of 'semantic formulas' or slots of meaning such as the apology, excuse or expression of regret (see Olshtain & Cohen, 1983). For instance, a typical disagreement might include a positive remark ('That's an interesting idea') plus a criticism ('... but I think it's impractical'). For each of the subject groups (American and Japanese), the total number of semantic formulas of any kind used for each situation was obtained. In a few cases, some subjects described what they would do instead of indicating precisely what they would say, e.g. 'I will go over the plan with him'. Such responses were excluded from the data, which explains why some of the descriptive statistics are based on 13 or 14 subjects instead of 15.

The data for this chapter are presented descriptively. The natural data we have do not permit statistical analysis. Descriptive statistics are used on the questionnaire data, but the primary purpose of this chapter is to describe the content of the responses—i.e. to give the flavour of the Japanese ESL vs. the American responses when speaking to a higher or lower status interlocutor.

Results

Disagreement

From our natural data we have examples of a distinctively Japanese questioning strategy which was used in face-threatening speech acts, including disagreement. In one naturally occurring situation, an American professor hired a Japanese student to act as editor on her research. On one occasion the student disagreed with the professor, but did not explicitly say so. Instead, he asked seemingly factual questions, getting the professor to go over her argument repeatedly in detail—**four** times in succession. After the fourth time, the desired self-discovery **occurred**—the professor finally heard the flaws in her own reasoning. She began to realise that the student was indirectly expressing disagreement. But after repeating her arguments four times in a row, she felt foolish. She felt 'nailed'. She wouldn't have been uncomfortable, however, if the student had expressed disagreement according to the 'American' rules of speaking: 'I see what you mean, but ...' or 'I like the idea that X, but don't you think possibly Y?' What the American professor found embarrassing was that she had said something illogical four times in a row, getting more and more explicit every time, thinking that clarification was being directly requested, not disagreement being indirectly suggested. And then she had to begin a questioning routine to find out the student's arguments because she still didn't have any idea what they were.

LoCastro (1986) captures the essence of a typical American pattern in the title of her paper on disagreement: 'I agree with you, but ...'. We often preface our face-threatening speech acts with a statement of the exact opposite of what we mean to say. Similarly, based on his American data, Sacks (1973) reports the same phenomenon, where speakers tend to twist their utterances in order to hide disagreement by responding to a preceding utterance with 'Yes, but ...' (cited in Brown & Levinson, 1978:119). We say 'I agree with you, but ...' as a 'token agreement' (Brown & Levinson, 1978; Levinson, 1983) just before we disagree with an opinion. We say, 'That was a great report, but ...' just before we correct the student for giving the wrong date. So it is perhaps dangerous to stereotype American responses as 'direct' while claiming that Japanese responses are 'indirect'.[3]

Still, Americans continue to complain that Japanese are so indirect that they don't understand what Japanese are saying, and Japanese continue to lament that Americans have to spell everything out *ad nauseam* when certain things would be better left unsaid. The Japanese use of the question as an expression of disagreement or a statement of opinion is a frequent source of misunderstanding. In another of our naturally occurring examples, an American professor was giving doctoral advice to a Japanese student doing his dissertation. The professor made a suggestion that the student did not think it advisable to follow. The student indicated this by an extended series of questions about the reasoning behind the suggestion. Finally the professor decided her suggestion was not such a great idea after all, and the student was relieved that he did not have to take advice he didn't agree with. The problem was that the American professor felt that her time had been wasted. She would have considered it much simpler if the Japanese student had told her he thought another approach might be better. Also, the more the professor elaborated, the more she felt she had dug her own grave and made herself appear foolish. The very strategy that the Japanese used to help the American professor save face is the very strategy that made the professor feel that she had lost it.

It is well known that Americans and Japanese have different strategies for expressing disagreement, but there is very little research explaining what exactly the differences are. As mentioned above, the stereotype is that Japanese are indirect and Americans are direct. Deutsch (1983:182), for instance, advises the following to Americans doing business with the Japanese:

> It is not appropriate, according to Japanese custom, to criticize someone openly, thus causing him to lose face; embarrassment should be avoided whenever possible by refraining from negative or combative statements that will make the Japanese look wrong or foolish.

It is, however, an oversimplification to think that the Japanese are always indirect. Tatsuya Komatsu, one of the most famous simultaneous interpreters in Japan, explains that in talking to their superiors, Japanese would try to avoid disagreement—not saying they disagree, saying nothing if possible, or if forced to state some disagreement, toning it down. They would seek harmony with equals. But with their status inferiors, they would essentially say, 'I disagree. You are wrong' (Komatsu, personal communication).

Now let us turn to the questionnaire data.

Disagreement Situation I (higher to lower status): You are a corporate executive. Your assistant submits a proposal for reassignment of secretarial duties in your division. Your assistant describes the benefits of this new plan, but you believe it will not work.

Disagreement is always a face-threatening act. In this situation we are dealing with disagreement by someone of higher status (a corporate executive) with someone of lower status (an assistant). The question is: do Japanese ESL speakers handle the situation differently from American native speakers? Are they blunter and more direct in a situation where they are in a higher status than their interlocutor? From our preliminary data, it seems that Komatsu is right. Japanese ESL speakers, playing the part of the corporate executive, were much more likely to state an explicit criticism of their assistant's proposal. Eleven out of 13 Japanese (85%) criticised the lower status person's plan, whereas only 7 out of 14 Americans (50%) did so. One Japanese gave two explicit criticisms: 'I don't think that's a good idea; besides what you said about X doesn't seem to be making any sense here'. Another one actually used the words 'don't agree' (which American native speakers never did), saying: 'I don't agree with you. I don't think your plan will work well'. These examples can be explained in terms of the power or authority the speaker has. That is, the speaker with greater power chooses to assert his/her authority over the addressee (Thomas, 1984) and to go 'on record' (Brown & Levinson, 1978) with the disagreement.

In this higher to lower status situation, many Japanese felt it appropriate to state criticism outright—that the plan would not work. They used softeners in every case of criticism, just as Americans did (in every case but one). Still, their responses did not sound as gentle to the 'American ear' as the native American ones did.[4] For one thing, what we coded as softeners were mostly just expressions (or 'hedges') like 'I (don't) think', 'I believe', 'I think it's kind of doubtful' (see Brown & Levinson, 1978:276–8). And some of the intended softeners weren't particularly soft, such as 'I'm afraid ...' and 'I hate to tell you that ...'.

More importantly, the things that really soften disagreement the most in American English are other semantic formulas that we coded as positive remarks or expressions of gratitude. Five Americans (33%) expressed appreciation or gratitude at receiving the proposal from the lower status person, whereas only two Japanese (15%) did. This is not significant quantitatively, but qualitatively there seems to be a big difference. Americans said things like, 'Thank you for your concern and efforts to ...' or 'I really appreciate your giving so much thought to this matter ...'. The two Japanese said, 'Thank you for giving me your proposal' and 'Thank you very much for your proposal'. Thus, the Japanese said a rather formulaic thank you, whereas the Americans integrated positive remarks and tried to sound original in their statements of gratitude. Loveday (1982) supports this point, arguing that Japanese speakers of English are likely to transfer ceremonial formulas for thanks and other speech acts into English. He explains that in the Japanese community 'politeness is closely connected with the use of ceremonial-like formulae which are unhesitantly used, without fear of sounding unoriginal' (Loveday, 1982:83). The same point is made by Coulmas (1981:84) as follows.

> ... the Japanese are very particular about using the appropriate form in the appropriate context. There is not so much demand for originality as in Western cultures, and no fear of repeating the same formula others have just used. In many situations the choice of possible locutions is very limited.

Americans, on the other hand, seem to prefer 'a "formless" personal touch' (Goldstein & Tamura, 1975:90) to a standard form. (See Condon, 1984; Fukushima & Iwata, 1985; Sakamoto & Naotsuka, 1982, for similar views.)

Eight out of 14 Americans (57%) used a positive remark to accompany their criticism, whereas not one Japanese ESL speaker used a strictly positive remark. Japanese occasionally used gratitude (2/13) and occasionally used a statement of empathy (2/13), such as 'I recognise your concern'. But despite these expressions which admittedly have a softening effect, Japanese ESL responses did not sound gentle. Here are some typical Japanese statements that have no prefacing gratitude or empathy: (1) 'I think it will not work. Think it over again'. (2) 'I'm sorry, but I'm afraid this won't work'. (3) 'Well, it doesn't seem to work to me because ...' When there is a prefacing formula, such as a statement of empathy, it sounds a bit short, and perhaps perfunctory or even condescending to the American ear: 'I appreciate your concern. But I hate to tell you that I don't think it will work'.

A major difference between American and Japanese responses was that Americans frequently made a suggestion or request to talk further, reconsider, rethink, etc. Nine out of 14 Americans (64%) decided to go 'off record' (Brown & Levinson, 1978) and used this strategy with the lower status interlocutor, whereas only 2 out of 13 Japanese ESL speakers (15%) made suggestions. And when the Americans made suggestions, they seemed to be avoiding direct disagreement. When the Japanese made suggestions, they seemed to express disagreement. Americans typically said things like: 'I think you've put a lot of thought in this plan and I appreciate that. I have a few ideas that I'd like to toss out as well, so let's set aside some time to go through this'. Another said, 'Thanks for your concern and efforts to streamline things but I think you and I ought to sit down and give this proposal thorough scrutiny before we implement the plan'. These suggestions to talk or rethink are quite different from Japanese ESL answers. Japanese responses were shorter and blunter—more likely to criticise (also see Porter, 1986). One Japanese ESL speaker said, 'Frankly speaking, I don't think it is fine. I will submit my plan better than this'. Contrary to prevailing stereotypes, it is the Americans who sound indirect and the Japanese who take the disagreement with the lower status person head on. (See Table 1 for a summary of the data for the above situation.)

A second disagreement situation in the questionnaire read as follows:

Disagreement Situation II (lower to higher status): You work in a corporation. Your boss presents you with a plan for reorganisation of the department that you are convinced will not work. Your boss says: 'Isn't this a great plan?'

TABLE 1.　*Use of major semantic formulas in the Disagreement Situation I (higher to lower status)*

Semantic formulas	Groups*	
	Japanese (n = 13) (%)	American (n = 14) (%)
Criticism	85	50
Suggestion	15	64
Positive remark	—	57
Gratitude	15	33
Empathy	15	—

* Two Japanese and one American were excluded from the subject pool because they described what they would do instead of specifying what they would say.

In this situation the disagreement is expressed from the lower status employee to his/her boss. According to the stereotype that many Americans and Japanese have of Japanese disagreement, it should be very polite, hesitant and indirect, even in English. Or it shouldn't be expressed at all. The data did not seem to confirm the stereotype, or at least not as completely as we might expect.

It was true that in this situation where disagreement would have to be from the lower status person to the higher status person, 5 out of 15 (33%) of the Japanese ESL speakers said 'yes' that the boss's plan was wonderful. All then proceeded to say, 'but ...' and promptly criticised it or suggested doing something else. This could lead us to say that they were indirect, but that may not be a proper analysis. Three out of 15 Japanese responded with an explicit 'no' and then criticised the plan. American native speakers never once used an explicit 'no' and only once used an explicit 'yes'. So they never resorted to the ultimate directness.

Beyond the question of saying an explicit 'yes' or 'no', Japanese responses simply sounded harsher and more direct. When the boss said, 'Isn't this a great plan?', one Japanese ESL speaker said, 'No, it isn't, I'm afraid'. Another said, 'No, I don't think it's a great plan.' However, this type of minimalist answer, which sounds very blunt, is characteristic of ESL learners (Porter, 1986), not just Japanese speakers. It reflects lack of fluency and lack of proficiency in the target language social rules of speaking. Therefore, we cannot simply assume that in this case it stems from native Japanese sociolinguistic transfer (see Takahashi & Beebe, 1987).

The major generalisations that we can make are that the Americans used more positive remarks, more softeners, and most importantly, fewer explicit criticisms to a higher status interlocutor. Ten out of 15 (67%) of the Japanese made an explicit criticism in English, whereas only 5 out of 15 (33%) of the Americans did. So, at least on written role play data, Japanese felt they could criticise, even a higher status person. This last finding is quite surprising. Is it true of natural situations as well? Or, is it an artifact of the data collection method? Questionnaires are known to favour shorter, less elaborated answers that give less attention to the psycho-social dynamics of the situation than natural speech does (see Beebe & Cummings, 1985). Does it reflect Japanese native language transfer, or is it a function of limited second language proficiency? It could also be an accurate reflection of the Japanese ESL speakers' American personas. We are repeatedly told by Japanese people in the United States that EFL classes in Japan stress the need for Japanese to be more direct and explicit in English as a second language than they are in Japanese. Thus, some of their directness may be a transfer of training (Selinker, 1972). At this point, we know *what* the subjects did, but we do not yet know *why* they did it. (See the Conclusion of this chapter for a discussion of 'why' and Table 2 for a summary of the data.)

Both groups generally chose between making positive remarks and criticisms. The very common American pattern of making a positive remark and then a subsequent criticism, which we saw in higher to lower status interaction, did not show up in this situation, where a lower status employee spoke to a higher status person—the boss. Instead, Americans used very lukewarm positive remarks (e.g. 'It has potential' or 'It has possibilities') or

TABLE 2. *Use of major semantic formulas in the Disagreement Situation II (lower to higher status)*

Semantic formulas	Groups	
	Japanese (n = 15) (%)	American (n = 15) (%)
Criticism	67	33
Suggestion	20	33
Positive remark	40	47
Token agreement ('Yes')	33	7

they followed up their positive remark with a suggestion or request that looked very much like avoidance of direct disagreement. For instance, one American said, 'It looks interesting. If you really want my opinion, I'd like to look it over more carefully, and maybe ask a few questions.' Another said, 'I really haven't had much time to look through it yet. Maybe we could sit down and talk about if after I've had a chance to look through it.' These responses contain hedging and postponing tactics.

It was mentioned earlier that Japanese ESL speakers use a questioning strategy to show disagreement and that American native speakers often fail to pick up the pragmatic intent of the questions. Interestingly, one Japanese respondent wrote after her response to the boss's enthusiasm about his own plan: 'I'll keep asking questions to convince him that there are things to be revised in the plan.' It is helpful to have a Japanese explicitly state that she uses this strategy. However, we must be careful not to claim that the questioning strategy is totally alien to American culture. One American responded, 'Uh. How do you see this being carried out? How do you think it will work?' But after that, he explicitly stated, 'I guess I see problems ...' Another American said, 'You put a lot of time into this. Do you think it will really work?' So Americans also use questions to express doubts and disagreements, and they, too, can be very indirect. The question is: what are the differences between American and Japanese use of questioning to express disagreement?

One crucial difference may be that Japanese use a repeated questioning strategy when they fail to get results. Americans may resort to the statement of opinion (in this case, disagreement) when their initial questioning does not seem to work. Another difference may be that the Japanese question appears designed to solicit facts. The Americans who asked questions said, 'Do you think it will really work?' The use of 'think' clues the American listener that an opinion is being solicited, and the use of 'really' suggests that there is some scepticism.

Giving embarrassing information

Some of the same themes and linguistic patterns show up in the study of giving others embarrassing information as in the investigation of disagreement.

> **Embarrassing Information Situation I (higher to lower status):** You are a corporation executive talking to your assistant. Your assistant, who will be greeting some important guests arriving soon, has some spinach in his/her teeth.

To our surprise, no Japanese ESL speakers opted out and said nothing in this situation, and only two Americans did. Other differences did not seem so surprising. Nine out of 15 Americans (60%) specifically told the assistant that there was something caught in the assistant's teeth, whereas only 4 out of 15 Japanese (27%) did the same. But we should not jump to stereotypes here about explicitness, because 6 of the 9 Americans used the word 'something'. Japanese used the word 'spinach'. Of course, spinach is a clichéd example in American English, so it is not surprising that Americans didn't like to name it.

One of the main differences between Japanese and American respondents in the higher to lower status situation is that there were only three suggestions (e.g. to go to the bathroom) used by American native speakers, whereas Japanese ESL speakers made 12 such suggestions (by seven speakers). It is somewhat reminiscent of the questioning strategy used to express disagreement, in that the goal is to lead the other person to self discovery. By suggesting that the interlocutor look in the mirror or go to the ladies room, the Japanese ESL speaker never actually says that the assistant has spinach in his/her teeth.

There is also a quantitative difference in hints between the two groups. Japanese gave more hints than Americans. More interestingly, their hints were qualitatively different from American hints. One Japanese said, 'Did you have quiche for your lunch?' All the Americans we have interviewed claim that they would not get this hint. They found other Japanese hints sarcastic, almost mean sounding, but Japanese informants feel that the Japanese hints are meant to reduce, not increase, embarrassment by introducing levity into the conversation. One Japanese wrote, 'By the way, how do you use spinach in your teeth in negotiating your guests?' Another said, 'Did you have lunch with Popeye?' Still another remarked, 'You don't need to be Popeye to greet your guests.' There was only one example like this in the American data ('You'll want to finish your lunch before you see the big boys'.) (See Table 3 for a summary of the data.)

The hints Japanese use in English to convey embarrassing information are quite distinctive. In fact, the Japanese belief that it may be helpful to joke to people about food on their face may not be shared by Americans. In a naturally occurring example, one Japanese who had been living in the United States for about ten years told her American friend that she had something on her cheek. (It was a black spot of something.) Her friend was terribly embarrassed and ran to the bathroom to wash it away when a couple of attempts failed to get rid of it without a mirror. When she came out of the ladies room, her Japanese friend tried to make light of the whole matter to make her feel less embarrassed. She said, 'So it wasn't a mole? It

TABLE 3.   *Use of major semantic formulas in the Embarrassing Information Situation I (higher to lower status)*

Semantic formulas	Groups	
	Japanese (n = 15) (%)	American (n = 15) (%)
Inform fact		
'you have spinach ...'	27	20
'you have something ...'	—	40
	27	60
Suggestion	47	20
Hint	27	13
Opt out	—	13

didn't grow out over night?' Although Americans love to make jokes about hypothetical spinach in their own or someone else's teeth, this use of a joke directly to the person's face at the time of the embarrassment was not well received, and Americans queried about the joke winced upon hearing it. It seems then that what is helpfully funny and perhaps even face-saving for a Japanese can be very embarrassing to many Americans.

Embarrassing Information Situation II (lower to higher status): You are a student, speaking with your professor to prepare for a three-way meeting you have with the Dean of the College. Your professor has some mustard on his cheek from lunch and you are aware of it.

Japanese ESL respondents did not opt out in the previous situation where it was the higher status person talking to the lower status person, but here, where it is the student talking to the professor, several Japanese said they would not say anything. In our natural data, we found that a Japanese middle manager in a school told an American female teacher she needed to put on some lipstick. It doesn't seem likely that the teacher would tell her superior to put on lipstick.

In the questionnaire situation, Japanese ESL speakers named the offending food more often than their American counterparts when addressing the higher status interlocutor. Six Japanese actually referred to 'mustard', whereas only one said 'something'. As for Americans, only four said 'mustard' and seven found another word to describe it—usually 'something', but also 'yellow' and two other expressions. In future research we shall try to determine whether these differences might be due to native language transfer. Perhaps Japanese do not mind naming the offending food even in Japanese. Another explanation is that second language speakers in general, i.e. from any country, are not fully sensitive to the force of words in the non-native tongue. Witness, for example, our ability to repeat obscene words in a foreign language without the embarrassment that we would feel saying them in our native language. It is also noticeable how much ESL speakers (not just those from Japan) tend to copy the wording of their interlocutor's written or spoken questions. This is a common ESL phenomenon. (See Table 4 for a summary of the data.)

Again, in the lower to higher status comments, the verbal hints used by Japanese ESL speakers were the most interesting part of the data. Only one American hinted, using the nonverbal tactic of wiping his/her own face to hint that the other person had something on his cheek. But there were several verbal hints in Japanese ESL responses: (1) 'Excuse me professor, but don't tell me you want to make such a hot and sour discussion with the Dean of the College as your mustard on your cheek'. (2) 'By the way, did you have nice sandwiches in lunch?' (3) 'Professor, where did you eat your lunch? You must have gone to Callahan's. I like their hotdogs, too'. When questioned, a group of American native English speakers said that they would not understand the Japanese hints. Perhaps the Japanese reputation

TABLE 4. *Use of major semantic formulas in the Embarrassing Information Situation II (lower to higher status)*

Semantic formulas	Groups	
	Japanese (n = 15) (%)	American (n = 15) (%)
Inform fact		
'you have mustard ...'	40	27
'you have something ...'	7	47
	47	74
Hint		
Verbal hint	20	—
Nonverbal hint	13	7
	33	7
Opt out	20	13

for indirectness comes in part from their more frequent use of hints, and their use of hints which Americans don't follow. It surely does not come from some of their typical responses, such as, 'You have mustard on your cheek' or 'Excuse me, Sir. You have mustard on your cheek'.

Americans tend to think that hints won't work. It is not yet clear how efficacious Japanese think their hints are. The Japanese who told the assistant, 'You don't need to be Popeye to greet your guests' shrugged when questioned about the assistant's reply, saying that the assistant might not get the point. On the other hand, the Japanese who wrote, 'By the way, did you have nice sandwiches in lunch?' also wrote that the professor would respond, 'Oh, thank you very much'. This shows that he definitely thought the professor would get the hint. An American woman married to a Japanese man reports that their biggest communication problem as a couple is that he sees hints (and acts on them!) where she means off-hand statements. At first glance, it appears that Japanese people have more faith in hints than Americans (see Sakamoto & Naotsuka, 1982, for similar episodes; Tannen, 1981, for similar examples from Greek and American crosscultural communication).

Conclusion

This research has been both an eye-opener and a 'stereotype-buster'. With respect to how Americans and Japanese speak the English language, we have the following conclusions:

1. Americans are not always more direct than Japanese.
2. Americans are not always more explicit than Japanese.
3. Japanese do not always avoid disagreement.
4. Japanese do not always avoid critical remarks, especially when speaking to someone of lower status.
5. Japanese and Americans can both use questions to function as warning, correction, disagreement, chastisement and embarrassing information, but the questions they use can be significantly different in tone and content.
6. Americans use positive remarks (compliments/praise) more frequently and in more places than Japanese.

We do not yet know why Japanese ESL speakers act as they do. First, we must investigate to what extent the characteristics of Japanese ESL described here are due to transfer from the native language. Our previous research has demonstrated a great deal of sociolinguistic transfer from the native language in Japanese ESL refusals (Beebe *et al.*, in press). It is possible that transfer (sociolinguistic or otherwise) is a major explanation for the data we now have. We are currently gathering data on native Japanese face-threatening acts to determine if this is so.

Another possible explanation for the data is that the directness described here is partly a function of the fact that the Japanese are using a second language in which they do not have full native-like proficiency. Takahashi & Beebe (1987) found that higher proficiency Japanese ESL speakers were more indirect in their refusals than lower proficiency Japanese who tended more frequently to say bluntly, 'I can't'. We have further evidence that ESL speakers from countries other than Japan sound blunt and direct (Takahashi & Beebe, unpublished data on international ESL refusals) apparently due to lack of native speaker competence in the social rules of speaking.

Besides the native language transfer and the limited proficiency explanations, there is the possibility, especially with advanced and relatively assimilated ESL speakers, that their directness and explicitness is an instance of psychological convergence (see Thakerar *et al.*, 1982). Psychological convergence occurs when speakers want and intend to converge linguistically, but somehow go too far, and instead of succeeding in convergence (i.e. getting close to the interlocutor), they end up diverging from (i.e. moving farther away from) the listener. In this case, the directness would be explained by an attempt to converge toward the stereotype or what is perceived to be the native American English norm—that is, a great deal of directness. In attempting to converge psychologically, the non-native speaker 'overshoots the mark', ending up diverging in actual linguistic terms.[5] This could be called 'stereotype-induced error'. In some instances, as discussed above, the student was formally taught the stereotype—e.g. 'Americans are very direct, so be direct when talking to them'. In this case, we have psychological convergence, but it is also triggered by 'transfer of training' (Selinker, 1972) and constitutes a 'teacher-induced error' (Stenson, 1974). Many Japanese ESL learners have reported to us that they were, in fact, taught by their Japanese teachers of English to 'be direct when using English'. And since this stereotype is probably wrong for certain situations, these students may, at times, be shooting for a false goal.

There are other explanations for the data which lead us to avoid hypothesising that transfer is the only answer. For one thing, stereotypes are overgeneralisations, but they are not always *completely* false. Japanese ESL speakers may not be transferring native Japanese directness, or 'overshooting the mark' of American directness, but rather overgeneralising accurately perceived American directness from the situation where it does apply to another where it does not. Or they may have wrongly concluded that softeners and politeness indicators are often not needed in English because they have not yet seen the American English counterparts to Japanese honorifics, particles, lexical selections, and formula choices. Of course, this latter explanation is a kind of transfer in the sense that it is a type of cross-linguistic influence. In addition to these explanations, there is always the possibility that Japanese ESL speakers simply made errors because they focused uniquely on their own message: directness, politeness and affect on others were not even in their minds.

Finally, before any hard and fast conclusions can be drawn about either the findings themselves or the theoretical explanations for them, we need to amass more data on what Japanese and Americans do in natural conversation. Beebe & Cummings (1985) have shown that written role play data can be extremely useful in creating an initial classification of semantic formulas used in natural speech and in studying the perceived requirements for a socially appropriate speech act. However, the data do not always reflect the full range of formulas or even the length of the response. They do not adequately show the depth of emotion, the amount of repetition, or the degree of elaboration. Consequently, we need more natural data.

We have, however, found problems with natural data. They are biased by the linguistic preferences of our friends, relatives and associates. They are also biased in favour of short exchanges, because long ones are impossible to get down word for word in a notebook. And they are biased to ones that the researcher finds especially typical, especially atypical, or especially non-native sounding. It is much harder to notice a native-like ESL example than a distinctively non-native one. Moreover, natural data give us lots of examples that are not at all comparable in terms of speakers, hearers and social situations, unless one or two situations are selected, and this poses other limitations.

Despite the unknowns and limitations of this selected study, we believe we have strong evidence that: (1) Japanese and Americans are substantially different in the way they go about accomplishing face-threatening acts in English. (2) Japanese ESL speakers often do not conform to prevalent stereotypes about their indirectness and their inexplicitness. (3) Both Japanese and Americans style shift in English according to the status of the interlocutor. (4) Japanese using English as a second language can be extremely skilful at style shifting according to the status of their interlocutor. And, in some instances, they display more socially attuned variation than native speakers.

Notes to Chapter 6

1. We would like to acknowledge that this paper overlaps in the discussion of disagreement with our paper 'Sociolinguistic variation in face threatening speech acts: chastisement and disagreement', to appear in M. Eisenstein (ed.), *Variation and Second Language Acquisition: An Empirical View*, New York: Plenum Publishing Corporation. We would also like to express our appreciation to Shoshana Blum-Kulka, Elite Olshtain, Albert Valdman, and the editors of this volume, whose comments were extremely helpful. We also wish to thank a large number of students in the TESOL and Applied Linguistics programmes at Columbia University Teachers College who gave us many helpful suggestions. Special mention also goes to Patrick Aquilina of the American Language Program at Columbia University for his assistance in data collection, and all those who gave their time to answer the discourse completion questionnaire for the present research.

2. Research has been done on a number of face-threatening speech acts—e.g. on apologies (Blum-Kulka & Olshtain, 1984, 1986; Blum-Kulka *et al.*, in press; Borkin & Reinhart, 1978; Cohen & Olshtain, 1981, 1985; Coulmas, 1981; Godard, 1977; Olshtain, 1983; Olshtain & Cohen, 1983) requests (Blum-Kulka, 1982, 1987; Blum-Kulka & Olshtain, 1984, 1986; Blum-Kulka *et al.*, in press; Tanaka & Kawade, 1982); refusals (Beebe & Cummings, 1985; Beebe *et al.*, in press; Takahashi & Beebe, 1986, 1987); complaints (Bonikowska, 1985; Olshtain & Weinbach, 1986); disagreement (LoCastro, 1986; Pomerantz, 1984); and expressions of disapproval (D'Amico-Reisner, 1983). It is, however, quite problematic to determine which speech acts are face threatening as well as whose face (the speaker's or hearer's) is being threatened. According to Brown and Levinson, for instance, expressing thanks can be face threatening because in this act the speaker 'accepts a debt [and] humbles his own face' (1978:72). Compliments can also be face threatening, predicting 'some desire of S [the speaker] toward H [the addressee] or H's goods, giving H reason to think that he may have to take action to protect the object of S's desire, or give it to S' (Brown & Levinson, 1978:71). Scollon and Scollon are thus quite right in stating that 'any act of communication is a threat to face, that is, to the public self-image that a person seeks to maintain' (1981:171). We may thus add to the list studies on compliments (Holmes & Brown, 1987; Manes, 1983; Manes & Wolfson, 1981; Wolfson, 1981, 1983, 1984) and expressions of gratitude (Eisenstein & Bodman, 1986). In this chapter we will focus on inherently face-threatening acts such as disagreement and giving embarrassing information.

3. The study of directness/indirectness is a vast field where a great deal of work has been done. However, a great deal of work needs to be done even in defining the concepts. We are aware of definitional and other problems in the study of directness/indirectness, but they are beyond the scope of this chapter. Readers should see Blum-Kulka (1987) and Blum-Kulka & Olshtain (1984, 1986) for references on directness/indirectness.

4. We realise that there is no one subjective reaction to any English statement that all the speakers of American English would share. We use the somewhat vague term 'American ear' to reflect the fact that we have checked the response of many American native speakers to the data in this chapter, and we do find a commonality in their responses. We have asked graduate students in TESOL and

Applied Linguistics at Columbia University Teachers College. We have also asked friends, acquaintances, relatives, and even a few strangers, for their reactions. Their is a pattern in their responses (the details are not reported here) which gives us some empirical ground for saying the 'American ear'. We realise, however, it is an overgeneralisation and an oversimplification.

Furthermore, the analysis presented in this study represents an examination of interlanguage, but it is not purely interlanguage analysis in the sense advocated by Selinker (1972) or Corder (1967, 1971). It compares Japanese ESL responses to American responses and gives American reactions to the interlanguage data. We do not attempt to discuss the interlanguage data in terms of the individual's interlanguage pragmatic system. We feel it is premature to do so at this stage of investigation.

5. Outside the speech accommodation framework, this phenomenon has been described as exaggerating the difference between the NL and the TL (see Gass, 1984; Gass & Ard, 1984; Obler, 1982).

References

BARNLUND, D. C., 1974, The public self and the private self in Japan and the United States. In J. C. CONDON & M. SAITO (eds), *Intercultural Encounters with Japan*. Tokyo: Simul Press.

BEEBE, L. and CUMMINGS, M., 1985, Speech act performance: A function of the data collection procedure? Paper presented at TESOL '85, New York, April 1985.

BEEBE, L., TAKAHASHI, T. and ULISS-WELTZ, R. (in press) Pragmatic transfer in ESL refusals. In R. C. SCARCELLA, E. ANDERSEN & S. D. KRASHEN (eds), *Developing Communicative Competence in a Second Language*. Cambridge, MA: Newbury House.

BLUM-KULKA, S., 1982, Learning to say what you mean in a second language: A study of the speech act performance of learners of Hebrew as a second language, *Applied Linguistics*, 3, 29–59.

——, 1987, Indirectness and politeness in requests: same or different? *Journal of Pragmatics*, 11, 131–46.

BLUM-KULKA, S. and OLSHTAIN, E., 1984, Requests and apologies: A cross-cultural study of speech act realization patterns (CCSARP), *Applied Linguistics*, 5, 196–213.

——, 1986, Too many words: Length of utterance and pragmatic failure, *Studies in Second Language Acquisition*, 8, 165–79.

BLUM-KULKA, S., HOUSE, J. and KASPER, G. (eds) (in press) *Cross-Cultural Pragmatics: Requests and Apologies*. Norwood, NJ: Ablex.

BONIKOWSKA, M., 1985, Opting out from performing speech acts–pragmatic domain? Manuscript, University of Warsaw, Poland.

BORKIN, A. and REINHART, S. M., 1978, Excuse me and I'm sorry, *TESOL Quarterly*, 12, 57–70.

BROWN, P. and LEVINSON, S., 1978, Universals in language usage: Politeness phenomena. In E. N. GOODY (ed.), *Questions and Politeness*. Cambridge: Cambridge University Press.

COHEN, A. and OLSHTAIN, E., 1981, Developing a measure of sociocultural competence: The case of apology, *Language Learning*, 31, 113–34.

——, 1985, Comparing apologies across languages. In K. R. JANIKOWSKY (ed.), *Scientific and Humanistic Dimensions of Language*. Amsterdam: John Benjamins.

CORDER, S., 1967, The significance of learners' errors, *International Review of Applied Linguistics (IRAL)*, 5, 161–9.

——, 1971, Idiosyncratic dialects and error analysis, *International Review of Applied Linguistics*, 9, 149–59.

CONDON, J. C., 1984, *With Respect to the Japanese*. Tokyo: Yohan Publications.

CONDON, J. C. and YOUSEF, F., 1975, *An Introduction to Intercultural Communication*. Indianapolis, IN: Bobbs-Merrill Educational Publishing.

COULMAS, F., 1981, 'Poison to your soul': Thanks and apologies contrastively viewed. In F. COULMAS (ed.), *Conversational Routines*. The Hague: Mouton.

D'AMICO-REISNER, L., 1983, An analysis of the surface structure of disapproval exchanges. In N. WOLFSON & E. JUDD, (eds), *Sociolinguistics and Language Acquisition*. Rowley, MA: Newbury House.

DEUTSCH, M. F., 1983, *Doing Business with the Japanese*. New York: New American Library.

DOI, T., 1974, Some psychological themes in Japanese human relationships. In J. C. CONDON & M. SAITO (eds), *Intercultural Encounters with Japan*. Tokyo: Simul Press.

EISENSTEIN, M. and BODMAN, J., 1986, 'I very appreciate': expressions of gratitude by native and non-native speakers of American English, *Applied Linguistics*, 7, 167–85.

FUKUSHIMA, S. and IWATA, Y., 1985, Politeness in English, *JALT Journal*, 7, 1–14.

GASS, S., 1984, Development of speech perception and speech production abilities in adult second language learners, *Applied Psycholinguistics*, 5, 51–74.

GASS, S. and ARD, J., 1984, Second language acquisition and the ontology of language universals. In W. RUTHERFORD (ed.), *Language Universals and Second Language Acquisition. Typological Studies in Language*, Vol. 5. Amsterdam: John Benjamins.

GODARD, D., 1977, Same settings, different norms: phone call beginnings in France and the United States, *Language in Society*, 5, 257–314.

GOLDSTEIN, B. Z. and TAMURA, K., 1975, *Japan and America: A Comparative Study in Language and Culture*. Tokyo: Charles E. Tuttle Company.

HOLMES, J. and BROWN, D. R., 1987, Teachers and students learning about compliments, *TESOL Quarterly*, 21, 523–46.

KUNIHIRO, M., 1973, Nihon-teki komyunikeeshon-no heisasei [Closedness in Japanese communication]. In Y. NAGAI & H. ROSOVSKY (eds), *Nichibei komyunikeeshon gyappu*. Tokyo: Simul Press.

LEVINSON, S. 1983, *Pragmatics*. Cambridge: Cambridge University Press.

LOCASTRO, V., 1986, I agree with you, but ... Paper presented at JALT '86 Conference, Hamamatsu, Japan, November 1986.

LOVEDAY, L., 1982, *The Sociolinguistics of Learning and Using a Non-Native Language*. Oxford: Pergamon Press.

MANES, J., 1983, Compliments: A mirror of cultural values. In N. WOLFSON & E. JUDD (eds), *Sociolinguistics and Language Acquisition*. Rowley, MA: Newbury House.

MANES, J. and WOLFSON, N., 1981, The compliment formula. In F. COULMAS (ed.), *Conversational Routines*. The Hague: Mouton.

NAGAI, Y. and ROSOVSKY, H., 1973, *Nichibei Komyunikeeshon Gyappu* [Communication Gap between Japan and the United States]. Tokyo: Simul Press.

NAKANE, C., 1972, *Japanese Society*. Berkeley, CA: University of California Press.
——, 1974, The social system reflected in interpersonal communication. In J. C. CONDON & M. SAITO (eds), *Intercultural Encounters with Japan*. Tokyo: Simul Press.
OBLER, E., 1982, The parsimonious bilingual. In L. OBLER & L. MENN (eds), *Exceptional Language and Linguistics*. New York: Academic Press.
OLSHTAIN, E., 1983, Sociocultural competence and language transfer: The case of apology. In S. GASS & L. SELINKER (eds), *Language Transfer in Language Learning*. Rowley, MA: Newbury House.
OLSHTAIN, E. and COHEN, A., 1983, Apology: A speech-act set. In N. WOLFSON & E. JUDD (eds), *Sociolinguistics and Language Acquisition*. Rowley, MA: Newbury House.
OLSHTAIN, E. and WEINBACH, L., 1986, Complaints—A study of speech act behavior among native and nonnative speakers of Hebrew. In M. B. PAPI & J. VERSCHUEREN (eds), *The Pragmatic Perspective: Selected Papers from the 1985 International Pragmatic Conference*. Amsterdam: John Benjamins.
PASSIN, H., 1980, *Japanese and the Japanese: Language and Culture Change*. Tokyo: Kinseido.
POMERANTZ, A., 1984, Agreeing and disagreeing with assessments: Some features of preferred/dispreferred twin shapes. In J. MAXWELL ATKINSON & J. HERITAGE (eds), *Structures in Social Action*. Cambridge: Cambridge University Press.
PORTER, P., 1986, How learners talk to each other: Input and interaction in task-centred discussions. In R. DAY (ed.), *Talking to Learn: Conversation in Second Language Acquisition*. Rowley, MA: Newbury House.
SACKS, H., 1973, Lecture notes. LSA Summer Institute, Ann Arbor, Michigan.
SAKAMOTO, N. and NAOTSUKA, R., 1982, *Polite Fictions: Why Japanese and Americans Seem Rude to Each Other*. Tokyo: Kinseido.
SCOLLON, R. and SCOLLON, B., 1981, *Narrative, Literacy and Face in Interethnic Communication*. Norwood, NJ: Ablex.
SELINKER, L., 1972, Interlanguage, *International Review of Applied Linguistics*, 10, 209–30.
SEWARD, J., 1968, *Japanese in Action*. New York: Weatherhill.
STENSON, N., 1974, Induced errors. In J. SCHUMANN & N. STENSON (eds), *New Frontiers of Second Language Learning*. Rowley, MA: Newbury House.
TAKAHASHI, T., 1984, *A Study on Lexico-Semantic Transfer*. Unpublished doctoral dissertation, Teachers College, Columbia University.
TAKAHASHI, T. and BEEBE, L., 1986, ESL teachers' evaluation of pragmatic vs. grammatical errors, *CUNY Forum*, 12, 172–203.
——, 1987, The development of pragmatic competence by Japanese learners of English, *JALT Journal*, 8, 131–55.
TANAKA, S. and KAWADE, S., 1982, Politeness strategies and second language acquisition, *Studies in Second Language Acquisition*, 5, 18–33.
TANNEN, D., 1981, Indirectness in discourse: Ethnicity as conversational style, *Discourse Processes*, 4, 221–38.
THAKERAR, J. N., GILES, H. and CHESHIRE, J., 1982, Psychological and linguistic parameters of speech accommodation theory. In C. FRASER & K. R. SCHERER (eds), *Advances in Social Psychology of Language*. Cambridge: Cambridge University Press.
THOMAS, J., 1984, Cross-cultural discourse as 'unequal encounter': Towards a pragmatic analysis, *Applied Linguistics*, 5, 226–35.

WOLFSON, N., 1981, Compliments in cross-cultural perspective, *TESOL Quarterly*, 15, 117–24.

——, 1983, An empirically based analysis of complimenting in American English. In N. WOLFSON & E. JUDD (eds), *Sociolinguistics and Language Acquisition*. Rowley, MA: Newbury House.

——, 1984, Pretty is as pretty does: A speech act view of sex roles, *Applied Linguistics*, 5, 236–44.

Section Four:
Text and Conversation

7 Variation in modal use by Alaskan Eskimo student writers

CHARLOTTE BASHAM
PATRICIA KWACHKA
University of Alaska, Fairbanks

It is well documented that people speaking or writing a language which is not their mother tongue or which is not the indigenous language of their community tend to produce variant forms of that language. The degree of variation depends on a number of factors, including the amount of contact with native speakers, the situations in which the language is used, and the extent to which language serves to mark one's ethnic identity. Likewise, the stability of variant forms over time may depend on similar factors. Some are relatively transitory: second language learners, for example, are known to create forms which reflect current, intermediate stages in learning. Other varieties of interlanguage appear to be more tenacious, where certain forms become 'fossilised'.

That these varieties are systematic, operating with a fair degree of regularity, has been widely demonstrated, both for second language acquisition (Tarone, 1982) and for emerging dialects of English (Bailey & Görlach, 1983). Moreover, just as regional and social dialects can serve as badges of identity, emerging varieties may do so as well (Beebe, 1985; Zuengler, 1987).

In correlating language and sociocultural variables such as ethnicity and ethnic identity, scholars have relied primarily on discrete linguistic features, frequently phonological, following the trend set by Labov (1972), sometimes syntactic (Wolfram *et al.*, 1979), and occasionally pragmatic (Olshtain, 1983); relatively few, however, have dealt with extensive written discourse.

Our research focuses on the varieties of English which appear in the writing of Alaska native students.[1] In general, we have found that these students systematically exploit specific aspects of English grammar to encode their own distinct social values and pragmatic perspectives. We believe that this strategy contributes, on the one hand, to the continuity of culture and the maintenance of ethnic identity but, on the other, to academic difficulties in the university discourse community.

In this chapter we describe a feature we have found to be unique, persistent and systematic in the writing of Eskimo students: the proliferation of a limited set of modal auxiliary verbs, specifically *will, would, can* and *could*. We argue that the use of these modals, while similar to interlanguage phenomena (Selinker, 1972), exemplifies a natural process of language change, and we provide a preliminary analysis of modals which separates primarily syntactic from primarily pragmatic functions, clarifying both standard and nonstandard usage.

The students whose written work we are describing were born and raised in Alaskan Eskimo communities, either Yup'ik or Inupiaq.[2] These communities, like all Alaska Native communities, are quite small with populations averaging around 300 individuals, and with varying degrees of native language retention.[3] Some of the students are bilingual, but most speak English only, although many have passive competence in Eskimo. The isolation of these communities is extreme: many are hundreds of miles from each other, sometimes thousands of miles from small, regional centres, and unconnected by either road or rail. Exit and access are possible via small aircraft only, causing travel to be prohibitively expensive and relatively infrequent. With reference to our topic, this isolation has an extremely important consequence: the opportunity to interact with speakers of other varieties of English is limited. Thus localised patterns of English have developed. These patterns are not only influenced by the area's first language (Jacobson, 1984), but also exhibit an attenuated range of lexical, syntactic, rhetorical and social levels of elaboration. Finally, language in these communities is traditionally and primarily oral; reading and writing may be learned in local schools but are rarely used outside that setting. As a result of these and other factors, students typically arrive at the university without college level literacy skills.

From the point of view of the university community, these students' relative inexperience with either literacy or standard English is compounded by differences in conventions for oral discourse. Discourse patterns in Eskimo villages can be related to the values found in many small, isolated communities oriented primarily to subsistence hunting and gathering. The values emphasise consensual decision-making on topics considered to be within the collective purview, that is topics touching on the common weal; in all other matters a high degree of individual autonomy and responsibility is expected and respected. (See, for example, Hensel *et al.*, 1983.)

These values result in a pervasive circumspection of assertion. In other words, it is permissible to speak with relative definiteness on topics which are known to everyone in the community, topics which have, through literally centuries of accretion, gathered a 'group viewpoint'. It is impermissible to assert or speculate about other topics, either because personal opinion is relatively unimportant or because the speaker might be mistaken and, in a small community, responsibility for the truth value of a statement is strict: idle speculation cannot be indulged because of the relative fragility of social relationships and the necessity, in an arctic environment, for harmony and co-operation. Thus, if the topic is one about which one cannot be certain, assertion must be backed with varying degrees of qualification.[4]

The difference between these conventions and those of successful academic discourse is strikingly clear. In the university community, speakers frequently adopt exaggerated or even ridiculous positions just 'for the sake of argument'; a critical, rather than a consensual, posture is rewarded. Qualification and equivocation are considered the mark of a mediocre mind, while rapid opinions and decisions are admired; and, because discussion is abstract and theoretical, the speaker is not necessarily accountable in casual debate for erroneous conclusions, since 'it's all rhetorical, anyway'. In fact, a coherent, fallacious argument may receive a more positive evaluation than a disorganised, but accurate presentation.

In academic communities writing typically requires a greater degree of circumspection than speaking, since authors are held responsible for their claims. Modals, along with other hedging devices, serve the important function of allowing writers a degree of both flexibility and precision in making statements (Rounds, 1982; Huckin & Olsen, 1983). However, overuse of modals can give an impression of 'fuzzy' thinking. Eskimo student writers, unlike their non-native counterparts learning to write for academic purposes, must not only learn the subtle rules of expressing evidentiality in both spoken and written English, but also determine the differences between these rules and their own system of evidentials (see Chafe, 1986).

Finally, students with different ideas about language and literacy may not only have difficulty with the conventions of western rhetoric but may well have different attitudes toward the end product itself, the text. No matter how accountable one's culture requires one to be with regard to the use of words, spoken language is nevertheless more ephemeral than written. The permanent character of writing and the unknowable nature of the audience must certainly increase the students' already cautious habits.

The data discussed in this chapter were gathered over a four-year period from first drafts of essays written by Alaska natives (AN) and a comparison group of general freshmen (GE) all of whom were enrolled in freshman level writing classes. Entire essays were read, and various linguistic features were coded and then collected by computer.

While some of these features may be classified as developmental or transfer errors,[5] other features must be attributed to a process we are terming *sociolinguistic extension*, a process by which Standard English forms are used to express Eskimo functions. Specifically, a general characteristic of Eskimo student writing which fulfils an important Eskimo pragmatic function is a pervasive circumspection of assertion achieved by a variety of qualifying devices, among which modals are perhaps the most complex. (See Kwachka & Basham, 1987, for extended discussion of qualification and other features of Eskimo student writing.)

Below is a sample text to provide the reader with the general 'flavour' of Eskimo student writing and to illustrate a number of qualifying devices besides modals. (Please note that in this and all examples original spelling and grammar have been maintained.)

My village is located on the Yukon River. During the winter, people would go across the river to go hunting, trapping, and way down southwest to go fishing.

During the summers, the majority of the people would go fish camping. They don't go for one night, but for a few weeks, or a month, then come home for the weekend, and go back to camp within a couple of days or so. Some people commercial fish, some subsistence fish and maybe some of the others do both. They usually fish for King, Silver, and Chum Salmons. Some of the other fish they get for themselves are Pike and White fish. They would also fish for humpies for their dogs, if they have any dogs.

Some of the recreational activities they do at (my village) are Eskimo dances, which are usually held during the winter. The older folks would like to have the younger people start dancing. Some of the young people have already started to Eskimo dance. I think they enjoy it, but some of the other young people are to embarassed too dance, although they aren't scared to dance at a white-mans dance. I sure don't see why they should be afraid to Eskimo dance, because I started to Eskimo dance when I was a little girl, and it is a lot of fun. I'm not going to be able to dance this year, because I'm attending college. (213–E–D).

In the second sentence of this sample text, the student, who is describing typical, ongoing activities in her village, uses the modal *would* in a way which, if read as 'standard' implies a past habitual modality. We discuss this usage in detail in a later section of this chapter. In addition, note the use of other qualifying expressions: 'a couple of days *or so*' and '*maybe* some of the others do both'.

Two further types of qualification will be briefly noted here. First is the use of adverbial and adjectival modifiers in contexts where qualification is, at best, redundant and frequently incongruous. For example, 'usually' in the third sentence from the end of the second paragraph: 'They usually fish for King, Silver, and Chum Salmons' is actually misleading, since they 'always' fish for these varieties. An example from another essay is more widely recognisable as incongruous:

> When the village men go out to hunt, they would be on a look out for the breakup, which *usually* happens during the spring. (103.E–C)

If 'breakup', the going out of the winter ice, did not occur in the spring, we would be moving into the next ice age; the absolute certainty, from a western perspective, of breakup makes inappropriate even the use of 'always' in this context.

A second type of qualification, unfortunately not illustrated in the sample essay, is the use of 'doubles':

> They *all or most of them* are eating. ... (N)

Neither of these patterns of qualification can be straightforwardly explained as transfer, since no similar structures or processes can be found in Eskimo.

Modals in American English

The semantic functions of modal auxiliaries have been extensively studied, particularly in British English (Halliday, 1976; Leech, 1971; Lyons, 1977; Palmer, 1979). Because our study of Eskimo use of modals in written discourse depends at least in part on a comparison with a standard, and because none of the existing analyses addresses pragmatic functions, we found it necessary to develop our own framework for analysing the English modals that appear most frequently in the writing of our students: *will, would, can* and *could*.

It seems to us that the most sensible means of distinguishing broadly between the various functions of modals, and a means which takes into account their pragmatic ramifications, is to categorise them according to whether the speaker or the subject has the active role with regard to the predicate. For example, if a doctor were to say, 'Natasha *will* take her medicine now', the pragmatic force lies beyond the internal grammar of the discourse unit, and is external to the potential agent, Natasha. The power to influence social outcomes is in the speaker, in this case the doctor. If, on the other hand, we say, 'Natasha *will* not take her medicine', it is obvious that agency and control reside in the sentential subject and the sentence, moreover, is amenable to internal analysis without necessary reference to the non-linguistic universe.

The distinction between internal and external reference becomes particularly useful for disambiguation. For example: 'Natasha *could* have skinned that beaver' can be interpreted from the speaker/active perspective as a possible event; 'It is possible that Natasha skinned the beaver'; or from the subject/active perspective as ability: 'Natasha is/was capable of skinning that beaver'. In the outline below, the distinction between these two perspectives is marked as 'A' and 'B'. Included within each of these categories are the traditional semantic notions (obligation, permission, possibility, and so forth) which are attached to the various expressions.

Each subcategory contains example sentences, constructed to illustrate each notion, as well as sample sentences from the data. Those numbered 100 and 200 are Eskimo writers; 300 are from the comparison group of freshman English writers. Note that we have separated out 'tense' and 'aspect'. While we recognise that these categories must be included in an account of modal auxiliaries, we felt that such distinctions lie outside the pragmatic range we have defined: that is, what is included in this category is more a matter of linguistic marking than of pragmatic force.

In considering these examples and data, two caveats must be borne in mind. The first results from the very fact that makes modals so interesting; that is, their dependence on pragmatic considerations which causes them to be particularly difficult to separate from their social or textual source as we have attempted to do here. Secondly, in our exploration of the literature we have come to appreciate the variation in modal usage that exists among dialects of English, not only between British and American usage, but within regions of the United States as well. In our following analysis we have relied, in the traditional fashion of our profession, on our versions of 'standard' American English (SAE).

MODAL OUTLINE

A. Speaker (or designated speaker) Active; Circumstance external to sentence grammar: OBLIGATION/PERMISSION

1. Obligation (will/would, could):
   a. **She *WILL* take the medicine (said the doctor).**
      — No examples in any group
   b. [+ Polite]: *Would* **you like to/*could* you take your medicine now?**
      (1) Larry hollerd Ron *could* you head up the hill with the truck to pick up our guests. (262–E–N–4)

2. Permission (can/could):
   a. **She *can* take the medicine now (said the doctor).**
      (1) My dad ... said I *could* not go out hunting by myself anymore. (100–E–N–9)
      (2) Dr. Wheeler said he *couldn't* go home until the infection had gone ... (307–N–9)
   b. [+ Polite]: **Could she take the medicine now?**
      — No examples in the data

3. Possibility (Can)
   a. **This medicine *can* cause serious side effects.**
      (1) I said 'about' because you *can't* measure the miles from an imaginary line. (5K–E–D)
      (2) How *can* a place of happiness be lonely? (308–D)

B. Subject Active; Circumstance internal to sentence grammar:

1. Volition (will/would):
   a. **She *will/won't* take the medicine.**
      (insists/refuses) even though we've told her (to/not to)
      (1) I started getting scared because the boys *wouldn't* wait for me. (261–E–N–4)
      (2) I *would* not wear it because the wrinkles still showed. (306–2)
   b. [+ Polite] (would/could): **She *would* like to/*could* take her medicine now**
      (1) The older folks *would* like to have the younger people start dancing. (213–E–D)

2. Ability (can/could)
   a. General and physical: **She *can* take the pills.**
      (She doesn't have to have an injection)

     (1) He told me he *could* not hear anything on his right ear. (100–E–N)

     (2) He knew it so well he *could* read along with me by memorization. (307–N)

  b. Perceptual and sensory: **She *could* see the medicine on the shelf**.

     (1) To the south I *could* see the bay ... (2K–E–D–3)

     (2) As I walked outside, I *could* feel the sun already beginning to warm my skin. (307–D)

  c. Mental: **She *can* remember taking the medicine**.

     (1) How *can* anyone in the world know for a fact of the number of Caribou in Alaska? (1K–E–A)

     (2) I *can* remember being able to skateboard all the way ... (307–D–3)

3. Conditional and Hypothetical

  a. Conditional: **If she improves, she *can* stop taking her medicine/ will not have to etc.**

     (1) In town, the people usually have three or four wheelers that are used all year long. They *can* travel out of town to another village, if the ice is safe enough to travel on. (203–E–C–1)

  b. Hypothetical: **If she improved, she *could* stop taking her medicine/would not have to etc.**

     (1) Just think of how things *would* be if you had no idea what time it was ... (203–E–Df)

     (2) He gave her [a dog] to me, and she immediately shook nervously, as a caged animal *would*. (302)

C. Tense/Aspect

  1. Will/Would

    a. [+ Future, – Past]: **He will take the medicine tomorrow**

     (1) ... maybe a road *will* be built in years to come. (203–E–C–3)

     (2) Even if I never do go diving again, I *will* be glad I took the class. (304–N)

    b. [+ Future + Past/Punctual]: **He decided he *would* take the medicine after he ate.**

     (1) I even thought that the police *would* pick me up for shooting someone by accident. (100–E–N–6)

     (2) We drove off into the sun, and into town, where she *would* adjust to her new home with me. (300)

   c. [+ Past, Habitual]: **He** *would* **(usually/always) take the medicine after he ate.**
     (1) During the early years it *would* almost flood. (3K–E–D–2)
     (2) Our garden was 20′ by 30′. ... We *would* till this up every May and prepare the ground for seeding. (302–D)
   d. [+ Past, Distributive]: **She would occasionally take medicine.**
     (1) ... as if Jim and I were traveling in a black hole, at times my boat *would* hit gravel and I *would* veer sharply ... (262–E–N)

  2. Can/Could
   a. [+ past]: **I could take the medicine yesterday (but can't today)**
     (1) He wanted to believe me, but *couldn't*. (300)

The examples and the sample sentences from the data demonstrate that both groups of students, the Eskimo and the freshman English students, use modals proficiently in standard ways. What is not obvious from the sample is that the model accounts for virtually *all* of the modal uses of the GE students while the Eskimo students use the modals in a variety of ways not found in the outline.

Types of extensions

There are in the data a number of instances of modal use that we attribute to logical extensions of existing linguistic or semantic properties of SAE modals. These extensions were found *only* in the Eskimo student writing, not in the writing of other first-year English students.[6] The first type of logical extension we have labelled 'conditional with omission of premise'. Frequently in SAE, the premise of a conditional statement can be omitted when the context is both shared and obvious (Palmer, 1979:31). For example, in discussing the possibility of an outing, where the premise 'if we go' is understood, one might say, 'We *could* take the old highway', omitting explicit mention of the premise. However, speakers and writers must continually assess the degree of shared knowledge and experience in determining when such premises can be assumed. The problem for Eskimo students in dealing with university culture is determining the extent to which their assumptions and experiences are sufficiently different from those of the SAE culture that the premise must be stated. Examples 1(a) to 1(c) below illustrate the Eskimo students' tendency to overestimate social commonality; that is, they have omitted information they consider self-evident.

1(a) I actually hated my own sister. That *would* be too mean and I was not about to cause any trouble. (100–E–N–12)

1(b) They just installed telephone poles around the village so that every household *could* have a phone ... (216–E–D–1)

1(c) First of all many students are broke and they can't go somewhere (e.g. off-campus) to eat. That *would* cause a mini starvation to students. (2K–E–A–2)

What is omitted in 1(a) is the premise that expressing sibling hatred would be socially unacceptable in the extreme. Sibling rivalry and friction are not routinely expected in Eskimo society. In 1(b), 'could' in this context seems to carry the premise 'if they wish', emphasising individual choice. Although 'could' is acceptable, a more likely SAE construct would be 'can' in the sense of 'now has the capability'. In 1(c), the understood premise is 'if they could not eat on campus', reflecting the student's assumption that the general public is familiar with the details of student life, including campus food service.

The second type of logical extension is the habitual past extended to include habitual present circumstances. In SAE one of the functions of *would* is to mark a past habitual activity, usually in the context of a narrative. For example, 'He would usually take the medicine after he ate'. However, there are numerous instances in the data when this narrative function appears to be extended to describe habitual activities that are on-going in the present, i.e. activities that would be described in SAE by using the simple present. In examples 2(a) to 2(d) below, the students are clearly referring to current, repetitive or customary events, rather than recalling the past.

2(a) The experienced sewers which usually is the older ladies, *would* all meet (SAE: meet) in the captain's house usually around 8:00 a.m. (103–E–C–1)

2(b) My dad and my brothers usually do the job in getting the fish, but at times I *would* help them in getting it also. (212–E–R)

2(c) Our family *would* always have our own Thanksgiving or Christmas Dinner ... (210–E–R)

2(d) My dad *would* hunt for caribou and moose way out into the hills. Some other people are always hunting and picking berries too, so we get to visit other people ... (258–E–D)

Example 2(a) above refers to the making of walrus skin boats used for whaling in Point Hope, an activity that is as much a part of the subsistence cycle now as it was in the past. In 2(b), the initial clause establishes a mood of present habitual: '... usually do the job', so that we expect the second clause to be '... I help them ...'. However, the student has chosen instead to qualify that assertion with the modal *would*. Likewise 2(c) and 2(d) set up expectations for the present habitual.[7]

A third type of logical extension is the use of *would* as past distributive without a distributive adverbial (e.g. *now and then, occasionally*). A standard use of this structure, combining the past habitual *would* with a distributive adverb or implied distributive action, is illustrated in the following sentence from the data:

3(a) ... as if Jim and I were traveling in a black hole, *at times* my boat *would* hit gravel and I *would* veer sharply ... (262–E–N)

Note the use of *at times* in 3(a). Examples 3(b) to 3(c) below illustrate the tendency of Eskimo students to use the distributive form *would* without the adverbials.

3(b) I looked all around me to see if any ducks were approaching me. I *would* rest on a place where the grass was dry and sit for a few minutes. (101–E–N–1) (SAE: now and then I would rest)

3(c) Because they are so white like the snow they [rabbits] are very hard to see. I *would* shoot a couple of times at them but never did hit any ... (261–E–N–2) (SAE: I would occasionally shoot)

3(d) The branches *would* sting our legs, hands, and faces as we tried to make our way through them. (260–E–N–5) (SAE: The branches would frequently sting)

A fourth type of logical extension is the use of *can* to emphasise choice and personal autonomy within the parameters of expected behaviour. The following sentence is an example:

4. If there is some left overs from the feast, people who want to take some home *can*. (259–E–D–1) (SAE: If there are leftovers, people usually take them home.) Note, in addition, the careful qualification of 'people', that is, only those 'who want to'.

In addition to *logical* extensions, a second category of nonstandard modal use, much less coherent in its boundaries, cannot be explained as linguistic/semantic extension; they appear to be simply an over-reliance on modals, because they represent a more cautious and responsible way of presenting and organising statements, clearly an Eskimo culture-related value.

Example 5(a) below is an example of the first type of over-reliance on modals. Here we see an alternation of tense and modals to mark a rhetorical shift.

5(a) The trainer then *picks* the best long lasting runners, for any planned dog races in the future. Each dog *would run* it's own pace, the trainer *would keep* the fast, untireable dog's up front, slower dogs, that get tire easily on the back ... During the winter, the villages around the lower Kuskokwim region, *hold up* carnivals, which *consists* of Dog races, Men's basketball tournaments, and games of all shorts. The main events *would be* the dog races, and the women, boys and girls *would have* there own catagories of races. The men's races *would last* three days. All three days score's *would be combined* and that *would be* the total. ... [etc. with additional descriptive details and continued use of 'would'] Dog racing *is* very fun, tireing but fab! If you *like* competing, then dog racing *is* the sports. (204–E–C–1)

Note that the first sentence in the example above includes a present tense verb form, 'picks'. That statement is followed by several statements which include the modal *would*. If we take the first statement to be a generalisation, then the following sentences can be seen as examples. In the sixth line of the essay, when the topic shifts from picking dogs to the role of dog races in winter carnival, you will note that once again the present tense is used: 'During the winter the villages ... hold up carnivals', and once again that statement is followed by a series of statements with *would*, and those statements supply details about the carnival. Examples 5(b) and 5(c) below illustrate a similar pattern:

5(b) Winter festival *had just begun* in the early 1970's, and the main purpose for this festival *was* for the villages to get together and perform eskimo dances. The surrounding villages, Scammon Bay, Hooper Bay, and Newtok dancers *would* provide (SAE: provided) their own transportation by snow machine. (207–E–C–1)

5(c) Then the 14–17 year-olds *would* race about 4 miles. Then the racers from 18 on up *would* race for 17 miles.

    After the races *are* over the people *would* go home and start getting food together ... (210–E–R–3, 4)

    A second example of over-reliance is the substitution of 'would' for 'will' in cases that call for either the volitional or future.

6. They told stories of the past what they learned from there grandfathers or grandmothers. So the stories are going down generations of natives to the younger generations so the customs *wouldn't* be forgotten. (204–E–CC–2) (SAE: won't be forgotten)

This type falls into the category of a general softening of assertion mentioned earlier.

A third category of over-reliance is the use of 'would' for simple past:

7(a) There songs were all different not the same songs like the other dancers. Like they *would* have more meanings, telling stories of so many hunt's, family life, traveling ... (204–E–CC–3)

The writer was describing a single event, a dance festival during which two sets of dancers performed.

7(b) Whenever my parents went out I would follow. They *would* (SAE: did) not understand why I feared her so. (101–E–N–3)

The final example of over-reliance is the use of 'would' instead of 'was going to':

8.   My dad talk and told me what *would* happen. He said I could not go out hunting by myself anymore. (100–E–N–9)

Although this could be explained as an instance of future in the past, it seems to us that the force of the situation (the writer was being disciplined) would be stronger with: 'My dad told me what was going to happen'. Again, note the caution of expression.

On the basis of our analysis of these extensions, we propose that the unique uses of modals in the writing of Eskimo students derive from an inherent property of modals, their intersection with that aspect of social relationships regulating the expression of personal autonomy and accountability. They therefore represent the logical locus in English grammar for the translation and maintenance of these extremely important Eskimo social concepts. Moreover, we suspect that modals, both diachronically and synchronically, are 'leaky' interstices between the logic and intention of speakers and the dictates of English grammar. They are therefore particularly prone to pragmatic extension and exploitation.

Notes to Chapter 7

1. This work comprises only a small portion of a much larger research effort to document and describe the nature of the oral and written Englishes developing in Alaska as a result of bilingualism and language shift. Although this larger work includes Athabaskans, Tlingits and Aleuts, as well as Eskimos, our discussion here is limited to the *writing* of Eskimo students.

2. See Damas (1984) for general ethnographic and linguistic information on Eskimo society and culture.

3. See Kwachka (1985) for general discussion of native language maintenance in Alaska.

4. See Morrow (1987) for discussion.

5. Some authors (e.g. Wolfram, 1984) argue that features such as nonstandard tense usage are motivated by transfer of L1 patterns; in the case of nonstandard tense, habitual aspect has been proposed as the responsible structure.

6. Although the GE students made a variety of other errors, their modal use was completely standard.

7. Extension in this case may be reinforced by L1 patterns; Yup'ik Eskimo marks habitual aspect but does not necessarily mark tense distinctions in running discourse.

References

BAILEY, R. W. and GORLACH, M., 1983, *English as a World Language*. Ann Arbor: University of Michigan Press.

BEEBE, L. M., 1985, Input: choosing the right stuff. In S. M. GASS & C. G. MADDEN (eds), *Input in Second Language Acquisition*. Rowley, MA: Newbury House.

CHAFE, W., 1986, Evidentiality in English conversation and academic writing. In W. CHAFE & J. NICHOLS (eds), *Evidentiality: The Linguistic Coding of Epistemology*. Norwood, N.J.: Ablex.

DAMAS, D. (ed.), 1984, *Handbook of North American Indians*, Vol. 5. Washington, D.C.: Smithsonian Institution.

HALLIDAY, M. A. K., 1976, Modality and modulation in English. In G. KRESS (ed.), *Halliday: System and Function in Language*. London: Oxford University Press.

HENSEL, C., BLANCHETT, M., ALEXIE, I. and MORROW, P., 1983, *Qaneryaurci Yup'igtun, An Introductory Course in Yup'ik Eskimo for Non-Speakers*. Bethel: Yup'ik Language Center, Kuskokwim Community College.

HUCKIN, T. N. and OLSEN, L., 1983, *English for Science and Technology: A Handbook for Nonnative Speakers*. New York: McGraw-Hill, Inc.

JACOBSON, S., 1984, *Central Yup'ik and the Schools*. Juneau, AK: Department of Education, Bilingual/Bicultural Program.

KWACHKA, P., 1985, Perspectives on the viability of Native language in Alaska, *The Laurentian Review*, 18(2), 105–16.

KWACHKA, P. and BASHAM, C., 1987, Literacy acts and cultural artifacts. Paper presented to the International Pragmatics Association. Antwerp, August.

LABOV, W., 1972, *Language in the Inner City: Studies in the Black English Vernacular*. Philadelphia: University of Pennsylvania Press.

LEECH, G. N., 1971, *Meaning and the English Verb*. London: Longman.

LYONS, J., 1977, *Semantics*. 2 vols. Cambridge: Cambridge University Press.

MORROW, P., 1987, *Making the Best of Two Worlds: An Anthropological Approach to the Development of Bilingual Education Materials in Southwestern Alaska*. PhD Dissertation. Cornell University.

OLSHTAIN, E., 1983, Sociocultural competence and language transfer: the case of apology. In S. GASS & L. SELINKER (eds), *Language Transfer in Language Learning*. Rowley, MA: Newbury House.

PALMER, F. R., 1979, *Modality and the English Modals*. London: Longman.

ROUNDS, P., 1982, Hedging in written academic discourse: precision and flexibility. Unpublished paper. The University of Michigan.

SELINKER, L., 1972, Interlanguage, *International Review of Applied Linguistics*, 10, 209–31.

TARONE, E., 1982, Systematicity and attention in interlanguage, *Language Learning*, 32, 69–82.

WOLFRAM, W., 1984, Unmarked tense in American Indian English. *American Speech*, 59: 1, 31–509.

WOLFRAM, W., CHRISTIAN, D., LEAP, W. and POTTER, L., 1979, *Variability in the English of Two Indian Communities and its Effect on Reading and Writing*. Arlington, VA: Center for Applied Linguistics.

ZUENGLER, J., 1987, Identity and IL development and use. Paper presented at the 21st Annual TESOL Conference, Miami.

8 The acquisition of rhetorical strategies in introductory paragraphs in written academic English: A comparison of NNSs and NSs

JACQUELINE W. STALKER
JAMES C. STALKER
Michigan State University

A basic premise of this chapter is that there are no native 'speakers' of academic written English. Based on our study of five second language learners (two Chinese, one each Cypriot, Greek and Tunisian) and five native speakers of American English in a developmental freshman English writing class, it appears that with regard to both sentence level errors and discourse organisation, native and non-native speakers follow the same developmental patterns and are influenced by the same developmental factors. Our research supports Mohan & Lo's (1985) conclusions that negative transfer from L1, specifically 'interference from a preference for "indirectness" in the language and culture of Chinese', did not seem significant. Mohan & Lo's study suggests that for all writers rhetorical organisation develops late, a pattern which accords with our experience of teaching native American student writers.

This study was undertaken because the papers produced by native and non-native speakers in a developmental writing class contained sentence level errors which on casual inspection did not seem to distinguish the native writers from the non-native. We expected this impression to be proved wrong because of the assumptions embodied in Kaplan's oft reprinted essay (1966) on the influence of native rhetorical style on learning American rhetorical styles and institutionalised in the widespread practice of separating native from advanced fluency non-native speakers in freshman composition courses. However, we found that a count revealed that native and non-native speakers produced the same kinds and numbers of sentence level errors. A greater surprise was that the non-native speakers produced essays which more nearly followed the rhetorical structure being taught for the introductory paragraph of the argumentative, academic essay than the native students did.

The ten students whose papers provide the data for this study were in a developmental writing class in a large midwestern university. All NNS students who were enrolled in and passed out of the intensive English programme are automatically placed in the developmental class. American students who have low SAT (scholastic aptitude test) or ACT (American College testing) scores and NNS students who supply proof of sufficient English fluency upon admission to the university are placed in this class on the basis of a writing sample which indicates that the student will not be able to profit from the faster pace and greater reading demands of the regular writing classes. The developmental classes are smaller than regular freshman English classes and meet five days a week instead of three. The emphasis is on writing instruction, as opposed to the regular classes in which there is a greater emphasis on reading and discussing literary and historical texts. The developmental classes also de-emphasise in-class impromptu writing and emphasise the discussion of writing strategies and peer-editing. There were twenty-six students in the class—six NNSs and twenty NSs. Sixteen papers were excluded because they were at the extreme ends of the writing proficiency in this class, i.e. they either showed very few rhetorical or sentential problems, or they had a great many, complex problems. The one excluded NNS was in the most proficient group.

During the course of the term, students read five short stories, wrote four papers, all of which were edited at least twice, and kept a reading journal. A key principle which the students were required to keep in mind when editing their own and other students' papers was that they were writing for a reader; they edited with questions which probed the effectiveness of the writing from a reader's point of view. The data presented here are from third, edited drafts of papers written for an assignment asking the students to write about the aspect of the characters or theme or events of the story that seemed most interesting or important to them as readers. All the students in these ten papers argue that the father in F. Scott Fitzgerald's story 'Babylon Revisited' should or should not regain custody of his

---

Non-native speakers

NNS1 Chinese
No unusual preposition selection.

NNS2 Cypriot
He is now a reformed alcoholic, and is ready to accept responsibility *of* his daughter, and be her provider. (for)

NNS3 Chinese
Richard seemed to have lost interest *for* Joan, because there was no intimacy between them. (in)

NNS4 Greek
No unusual preposition selection.

NNS5 Tunisian
Apparently, Joan and Richard will not reconcilate because ø Richard's affair, the maturity of the children, house emprevement and also because of the fact that Joan seems to accept the seperation so easily and help him do it. (of)

Native speakers

NS1
No unusual preposition selection.

NS2
This story about Charles Wales took place in 1931, ø Paris France, two years *previous to* the stock market crash. (in, before)

He back-tracked to Paris *for* the custody of his daughter, Honoria. (to get)

Charles Babylon (*or*, 'Fame for Luxury') took toll in the failure of the things he lost in the 'boom'. (in)

NS3
NS4
No unusual preposition selection.

NS5
All this shows evidence that Charlie is now taking responsibility *of* his life and deserves to get Honoria back. (for)

Before the crash of 1929, Charlie threw money away *such as*; giving the bellhop a 100 Franc note, just for getting him a cab. (by)

---

daughter, or that the husband and wife in John Updyke's 'Separating' will or will not divorce.

A brief look at prepositions will illustrate why we turned to discourse level analysis in search of features which might distinguish native speakers from non-native speakers. Table 1 lists examples of preposition choices in the first and second paragraphs of the ten essays. Both groups show unusual preposition choices, but the non-native choices do not appear to be substantially different in kind from the native choices. Other sentence level features (article deletion, lexical selection, punctuation choice) also do not distinguish native from non-native writers (Stalker & Stalker, 1988).

Given our failure to find sentence level features that distinguished native from non-native speakers, we turned to an analysis of the discourse level to determine whether rhetorical structure separated the two groups. Among other discourse possibilities, we analysed the structure of the first paragraph to determine whether it showed any evidence of the structure for introductions that was being modelled for them. The students were asked to follow a model for the introductory paragraph which contained a sentence or two establishing the context of the writing by naming the essay or story being discussed, giving the author's name, and stating the character or topic to be discussed in the essay. Most important, the paragraph should also contain a thesis sentence stating the main argument or opinion about the character or topic which would then be supported by examples. The thesis sentence was not to be a description of events or characters or simply a statement of the obvious conflicts. It was to use very specific language to state the proposed argument or opinion. A thesis sentence should then be generally recognisable because it would take the form of a prefatory clause followed by an overt statement of the thesis; for example, 'This paper will prove that...', 'I believe that...', or be a direct, positive statement such as '(Some event) should or will happen'. The writer could also include a statement of *why* the event should or will happen.

The format for the introductory paragraph was defined quite narrowly in an attempt to aid the students in coping with the rather common problem or stating a clear supportable thesis rather than with the intent of presenting one model as 'the' model. The expectation was that the students could, and would, revise their initial formulations toward this model, at least to the extent that they would produce a clear thesis statement within the first paragraph.

Even with this very prescriptive, definite model, we found that of the ten papers analysed three of the native speakers did not have a clear thesis statement in the first paragraph, even though the essays were third drafts.

One of these three had a thesis statement, but it appeared late in the paper. This finding for the native speakers was quite reasonable because the placement of thesis statements late in the essay is quite typical of early drafts, especially for novice writers. Writers have to write their way to what they want to argue. In later, improved, drafts of shorter essays they typically move the thesis to the first paragraph for brief essays. This pattern of 'discovering' their thesis in the last paragraph of early drafts and then moving the thesis to an initial paragraph position in late and final drafts represents two developmental steps in the acquisition of first paragraph thesis placement for NSs. These three writers clearly had not acquired the second step of this process.

In contrast to the three native speakers, only one non-native student had no clear thesis statement in the first paragraph. This student was different from the other NNSs in other ways as well. He had an unusually large number of sentence level errors. It is worth noting that this student, a Greek immigrant, attended high school in a large midwestern city, and thus came to the university with a longer period of immersion language use than the other non-native students in this study. Because his native language was not English, and because he had begun the study of English relatively late, we classified him as a non-native speaker, but as the only NNS who was unable to produce the rhetorical structures presented in the class, he looks more like a NS than a NNS.

The fact that only one of the non-native students did not produce a thesis statement in the first paragraph was surprising. We expected these students to show various influences from their native languages, influences which would result in rhetorical structures not congruent with this traditional American, academic, edited English format. However, the non-native writers all followed the format for the introductory paragraph given by the instructor. In the sense that they were able to acquire this structure and use it in their final drafts, they were more 'normal', more proficient in using the required rhetorical structure, than were the native writers.

Only one of the non-natives provided possible evidence of rhetorical 'interference' from his native language. He was an Arabic–French speaker, a Tunisian, who persisted in beginning his essay with a quotation and then focusing his essay on the metaphors, conflicts or symbols embodied in the quotation. His essays were quite long and detailed, certainly much longer than the average, native or non-native. When questioned, he said that he was taught to write his essays in this form by his French masters. We presume that he was taught to follow the style of close textual analysis found in French literary criticism. The more important point here is not that he used a particular rhetorical style from his native language, but that he *chose* not to use the American style. He was quite conscious of his options.

Not only were the L1 and L2 writers very different in their ability to follow the set rhetorical pattern, they showed differences in another acquisitional feature as well. We expected writers in both groups to use a summarising statement of the conflict in the story instead of a clear thesis statement arguing for a specific resolution of the conflict. The summarising statement would probably be the only attempt at a thesis statement or would appear in the first paragraph while the actual thesis would appear late in the essay. Because this is a common trait in novice native writers, L1 freshman writing teachers and freshman writing texts almost universally set up paradigms and exercises to help students distinguish between descriptive and argumentative statements. We expected that the non-native speakers would have less well developed thesis statements, not only because they were developing writers, but also because there would be interference from native rhetorical styles.

We found that three native speakers restated the conflict and used this sentence in the first paragraph where we would expect to find the thesis statement. However, only one non-native followed this pattern, and again, this student was the one who had attended an American high school. (Table 2 lists the sentences which were to function as thesis statements, for both groups.) If language or cultural communication interference had been operative for the five non-native writers, the number of non-natives who were unable to produce an initial paragraph or statement that they could defend should have been greater. In fact, the non-natives performed better at this rhetorical task than the natives.

In our opinion, this particular analysis raises more questions than it answers. Because the purpose of this study was not to analyse the editing process, we did not analyse the series of drafts to determine whether the non-native writers followed the same developmental pattern we find in native writers (i.e. producing summarising statements, then editing them appropriately) or whether they produced appropriate thesis statements in first or early drafts. Experience suggests that non-natives do follow the native pattern, but this question needs further research to establish that the pattern does in fact exist.

Although more data need to be gathered from a larger sample, we can establish some working hypotheses on the basis of these data. Natives and non-natives at this level of writing fluency make similar kinds of intra-sentential 'errors'. The writing will not be readily discernible as native or non-native on the basis of preposition choice, for example. At the discourse

TABLE 2. *(Thesis statements are marked (T). Summarising statements are marked (S). Errors are the students'.)*

Non-native speakers

NNS1
In my opion, Charlie should be given Honoria. (T)

NNS2
In the story 'Babylon Revisited', Charlie J. Wales should be given custody of his daughter Honoria. (T)

NNS3
The mian concern of Richard and Joan were their children, the family that they had built up together, so it was definite they would not want a separation, but a reconiliation of their marriage. (T)

NNS4
After the summer there is two different paths that their marriage could sway to; one way is that the marriage ending in devorce of they could reconcile. (S)

NNS5
Apparently, Joan and Richard will not reconcilate because Richard's affair the maturity of the children, house emprevement and also because of the fact that Joan seems to accept the seperation so easily and help him do it. (T)

Native speakers

NS1
Although Charlie seems reformed because he has a good job and is not drinking, Marion's grudge may cause Charlie to not get his daughter back. (S)

NS2
Although Charles seems responsible because he has a good job and isn't drinking anymore—Charles may never get custody of his daughter because Marion, his sister-in-law still holds him to blame for her sister's death. (S)

NS3
Although Charlie seems reformed and rehabilitated because he has a good job and stop drinking Charlie may never get custody of his daughter Honoria because Marian still blames him for the death of her sister and his wife, Helen. (S)

NS4

Although Marian blames Charlie, he has truly changed and should be allowed to have his daughter, Honoria. (T)

NS5

All this shows evidence that Charlie is now taking responsibility of his life and deserves to get Honoria back. (T)

---

level, there is no apparent unconscious transfer of non-native rhetorical structures or styles. Where we found transfer, it was a conscious decision on the part of the writer. On the contrary, non-natives more successfully learned and used the argumentative structure presented than the natives did.

The causes of this particular effect need further study, although those causes may be quite difficult to ferret out. It is possible that the non-native writers are more skilled language learners and therefore discern and adopt the expected patterns more readily than the native writers (Hakuta, 1986). It is also possible that non-native speakers who come to the US to study have been exposed to American rhetorical structures through their English study at home, and are not naive learners; their educational background favours the acquisition of edited written American English. Kaplan (1987) suggests that his 1966 position is too strong, and that rhetorical styles are not peculiar to particular cultures, but may simply be more favoured. Perhaps the previous education (or lack of it) of the native writers causes difficulty in acquiring the structures of academic written English because they have read little academic register prose and so have had little opportunity to acquire its rules, or because their native dialects are relatively far from the academic register.

More research needs to be done which follows the editing process of native and non-native speakers writing on the same subjects in the same class to determine if both are following the same developmental pattern. These data indicate that they do, but the data are not clearly enough focused on the editing process itself to make that claim with surety.

In any case, the assumption that native and non-native speakers need to be separated into writing classes which deal with them differently is not supported by these data. Both can learn the same rhetorical structures in the same class. On the contrary, one pedagogical interpretation of these data is that non-native students at a fairly high level of proficiency in English may profit more from instruction intended for native speakers than the native speakers do. One sure conclusion is that 'impressions' of non-nativeness must be examined very carefully. Close analysis of this set of texts indicates that the distinction between natives and non-natives may be the result of factors other than the sentence or discourse level features which the essays contain.

References

HAKUTA, K., 1986, *The Mirror of Language: The Debate on Bilingualism.* New York: Basic Books.

KAPLAN, R. B., 1966, Cultural thought patterns in intercultural education. *Language Learning*, 16, 1–20.

——, 1987, Cultural thought patterns revisited. In U. CONNER & R. B. KAPLAN (eds), *Writing Across Languages: Analysis of L2 Text.* Reading, Massachusetts: Addison-Wesley.

MOHAN, B. A. and LO, W. A., 1985, Academic writing and Chinese students: transfer and development factors. *TESOL Quarterly*, 19, 515–34.

STALKER, J. and STALKER, J., 1988, A comparison of pragmatic accommodation of NNSs and NSs in written English. *World Englishes*, 7(2) 119–28.

9 Pronoun copies, pronominal anaphora and zero anaphora in second language production

JESSICA WILLIAMS
University of Illinois, Chicago

Introduction

There is a wide variety of referential devices in English, among them, pronouns, nouns, pronoun copies and zero anaphora. In some contexts, given devices may be considered prescriptively correct, while in others, they may be found in spontaneous oral production despite the fact that they are considered prescriptively incorrect. There is wide variation in the use of these devices, among both native speakers (NSs) and second language learners (SLLs). In NS English, pronouns are introduced and nouns are repeated, in order to keep track of referents, and at the same time to maintain discourse economy and cohesion. There is an extensive body of rules which both prescribe and describe this usage. In some cases, the choice between a repeated full noun or a pronoun is a stylistic one; in others, it is obligatory (Halliday & Hassan, 1976; Kuno, 1975; Rinehart, 1976). The rules for pronominalisation are complex and beyond the scope of this study, but in general, a pronoun can only be used successfully if its referent can be found in the preceding discourse or in the context of the speech situation. Another option, when referring to a previously mentioned NP or exophoric referent, is zero anaphora. According to NS prescriptive rules, zero anaphora in the subject position is only permitted in the second clause of co-ordinate constructions where the subject NPs are co-referential and the structure of the two clauses is parallel (Quirk *et al.*, 1985). However, in informal spoken production, NSs sometimes also omit subject pronouns if

(a) two clauses stand in a co-ordinate relationship but are not actually joined by a co-ordinating conjunction (*and, or, but*) or a conjunctive adverb (*yet, so*) or, (b) the exophoric referent is clear from context (Quirk *et al.*, 1985).

> (a) He just walked into the crossfire. ø Never knew what hit him. [1]
> (b) (at a lecture) ø Sure knows his stuff.

Zero anaphora is frequently found in the production of non-native speakers (NNSs) (Felix, 1980; Schumann, 1984; Zobl, 1984).

(1) *They* make you run round and round and round until you can't take it. You sit down and you know you are giddy, but the *fellows* still push you, ø say, 'I give you another ten more second to do the—the circle—to do again.' That kind of torture you know. And ø ask you to carry rifle overhead and do duck walk. (SE5–336)

(2) *My friend*$_1$ have many problem. *His wife*$_2$ have another baby, ø$_2$ cannot work. ø$_1$ always ask me to help him. (SL6–224)

In general, neither pronominal nor zero anaphora is used to introduce non-exophoric referents; this is usually done with a full noun or, sometimes, especially in spoken discourse, a noun followed by a co-referential subject pronoun. This latter form, which will be referred to as a *pronoun copy* here, is often considered to be nonstandard. It is frequently found in the production of non-native speakers.

(3) **P:** You mean when you're with girls, you pretend?
    A: Usually when you're with girls –– *Most people they* pretend when they are with the opposite sex, you know. (SE3–594)

(4) **M:** Why you buy pass?
    A: Just to come to school because––
    M: ––ah your husband––
    A: ––use the car in the morning.
    M: You only have one. Maybe some day you gonna buy yours. *Your brother he* has car?
    A: No. (SLL1–509)

Were these instances of pronoun omission and pronoun copy found only in the speech of NNSs, they might be attributed to first language (L1) influence or to acquisition strategies or processes. However, they are not limited to learner varieties. The following excerpts are examples of NS speech.

(5) I seen her twice after *she* came into the store to buy––get bracelets for her girlfriends. I was making them bracelets with the names. *She*

wanted them for her girlfriends. I called her up after. ø never came
back. But see–see I think that's the guilt. (NS6–126)

(6) **A:**   That was a friend of mine. That's all he put on the title. He was an
old friend from the neighborhood.
J: Who?
A: Mike Pound his name is. *His wife she* died at 39. She died with five
kids. (NS3–573)

The analysis below examines whether the use of these devices differs
substantially across or within speaker groups, and if so, if there is any
functional explanation for this variation. The view taken here basically
follows that of Kumpf (1984:132), in what she calls a discourse–functional
approach, that is, 'grammatical form(s) appear to fulfill a function in the
discourse: it is the discourse context which creates the conditions under
which the forms appear, and in order to explain the forms, it is necessary to
refer to the context'.

Past research

Continuity of reference

All the devices named above are used to introduce and/or maintain
reference in discourse. The question of their specific function in NNS
production is therefore bound up in the issue of continuity of topics and
referents. Givón (1983, 1984) has proposed a continuum of topicality, or
predictability of topic, which he claims is universal. This continuum is in
contrast to earlier formulations of the notion *topic* as a single, discrete
entity (Li & Thompson, 1976). According to Givón, the ease with which a
topic may be identified and, by implication, processed, can be used to
predict the likelihood of the production of the surface forms listed below
(Givón, 1984:112). For example, if a topic is highly predictable, the
probability of finding a surface form from the top of this list is high.
Conversely, surprising topics will most likely be marked by devices found at
the bottom of this list. The items in boldface will be considered in the
present discussion.

most continuous/predictable

zero anaphora
clitic/unstressed/agreement pronoun
independent/stressed **pronoun**
Right dislocated definite NPs or comment-topic word order
simple definite NPs in neutral word order

Left dislocated definite NPs or topic-comment word order

least continuous/predictable

Givón arrived at this tentative discourse universal by taking a number of quantitative measurements from large amounts of cross-linguistic data. The three factors involved in Givón's measurement of topic continuity/predictability are as follows.

(a) Referential distance

This measure assesses the distance to the left in terms of number of clauses, or how far back in the discourse the last mention of the topic or referent which is associated with the referential device can be found.

(7) So $Eddie_1$ turned around, he_2 said, 'yous got a problem?' 'Yeah, we want you,' they say. So––, $ø_3$ walked right up to them and they just pulled him down. (NS6–353)

In this example, *Eddie, he*, and ø all mark the same referent. To calculate referential distance for 2, one must count back to 1. The referential distance is 1; counting back from 3 to 2, there is a referential distance of 2.

(b) Potential ambiguity

This measure refers to the presence of other referents in the immediately preceding discourse which are semantically compatible with the referent being measured, and as such, are a potential source of confusion with that topic or referent.

(8) L: When did you see $Andy_1$? You saw $Andy_1$ with *Uncle Vinny₂*?
 A: Yea, Saturday.
 L: Where—at *Uncle Vinny₂*'s?
 A: Yea.
 L: You know, *he*? called me. I meant to tell you. (NS5–195)

In this example, there is potential ambiguity between the two semantically compatible referents, *Andy* and *Uncle Vinny*. The potential ambiguity score for *he* is 2.

(c) Persistence or decay

This measure indicates how long the topic survives, that is, how far to the right the reference to that topic persists in subsequent discourse. This is more properly a measure of the importance or thematic nature of a referent or topic, rather than of its predictability or ease of identification.

(9) Me and Sean and Phil was in the park and we're having a real good time. And *these three guys* started with us. You know, *they* start saying something. I figured maybe *they*'re just kids cruising around. *They* thought we were out—you know—somebody from out of the neighborhood. It really made me think. (NS4–345)

In the above example, the referent *these three guys* has a topic persistence value of 4.

Givón concludes from his cross-linguistic data that some general discourse universals may be inferred. As the devices cited above move from more to less predictable, or from less to more continuous, they become longer, more complex, and tend to occupy initial position. In terms of amount of marking material, zero anaphora rates high on the scale of continuity, whereas pronoun copies come out considerably lower, and repetition of full noun and pronominal anaphora, somewhere between these two extremes. Givón (1984:126) has called this principle the *Quantity Universal*:

> More continuous, predictable, non-disruptive topics will be marked by *less marking material*; while less continuous, unpredictable/surprising, or disruptive topics will be marked by *more marking material*. [emphasis in original]

A number of researchers have tested the Quantity Universal (QU) against their own data. Huebner (1985) found it to hold true for referential definite NPs in his longitudinal study of a Hmong SLL of English. Zero anaphora showed very low scores for referential distance. However, arguments of zero anaphors were far more persistent in the discourse than the QU would predict—in fact the figures for topic persistence were relatively high. Huebner suggests that this may be due to the fact that, in conversation, the speaker does not always have complete control over the fate of the topics and references he or she introduces. This is especially true in the case of NS–NNS interaction, where topic nominations and shifts are frequent and often abrupt.

Zero anaphora and subject pronoun omission

Pronoun omission and zero anaphora have been noted frequently throughout the second language acquisition literature (for example, Huebner, 1985; Butterworth & Hatch, 1978; Schumann, 1984). It is important to distinguish between these two terms. Pronoun *omission* indicates the absence of a pronoun in what is usually considered to be an obligatory context in the target language. *Omission* suggests that, in order for the utterance to be grammatically correct, the pronoun should have been supplied. Another view of the non-use of subject pronouns is implied in the term *zero anaphora*. In fact, these two terms may be used to describe exactly the same data, but imply different interpretations. Unlike *pronoun omission*, the term *zero anaphora* carries no judgement of grammaticality. Another important difference between the two terms is that pronoun *omission* does not indicate anything about its functional role as an anaphor. In other words, *zero anaphora*, as a subset of ellipsis, implies that the referent is recoverable either from prior discourse, the context of the discourse, or general knowledge, while *pronoun omission* indicates nothing about recoverability.

In English, permissible contexts for zero anaphora are very restricted. Specifically, subject pronouns may be deleted in the second clause of parallel co-ordinate constructions.

(10) She went to the store and ø bought apples.

The actual use of zero anaphora by NSs of English as in (5) is certainly more widespread than in the contexts in which it is considered grammatical by prescriptive standards. There are other contexts in which zero anaphora is used by both NSs and NNSs, but it is important to situate these contexts within discourse. Analysis of sentences in isolation, such as (11) would obscure any referential role of zero anaphora, making it difficult to determine how often instances of pronoun omission are also instances of zero anaphora.

(11a) ø eat with the daun pisang. (= banana leaf)

(11b) Last time when *we* were young, *we* used to––I mean *we* are not invited, you know––then *we* used to go and eat also. ø eat with the daun pisang. (SE1–240)

Although the omission of pronouns is noted repeatedly in the second language acquisition literature, it is unclear how many of these omitted pronouns found in SLL data may have been recoverable in the immediately preceding discourse. If the referents are recoverable, it may be that repeated explicit reference is considered redundant by the speaker. If the speaker's production is already constrained by limited proficiency, omission of redundant elements can be an attractive short cut. In an effort to keep production as economical as possible, constituents such as pronouns may simply be omitted with little loss of meaning. These findings are not limited to SLLs of English. Dittmar (1984:258) found that pidginised learner varieties of German often lacked the obligatory subject pronouns: 'apart from *ich* and *du* (*I* and *you*)—if new statements are made about people, objects, or affairs which have already been mentioned once, their referential identity is not verbally secured'. In his subjects' production, reference was maintained discoursally, rather than syntactically.

The influence of transfer on expressions of anaphoric reference has been explored in several studies. Gundel & Tarone (1983) and Gundel *et al.* (1984) focused on the interaction of L1 influence and markedness criteria. They looked at the use of zero anaphora by SLLs of English. Their *L1–L2 Facilitation Hypothesis* states that such facilitation (positive transfer) is guaranteed if a certain feature, such as a permissible context for pronominal anaphora, is shared by all languages. If, on the other hand, the L1 and L2 share the property or feature, but it is *not* a universal feature, transfer may occur, but facilitation is not necessarily guaranteed. They attribute the use of zero anaphora in positions which would be ungrammatical in both the source and target languages to the strength of this constraint. One of the tasks in the Gundel *et al.* study was a free conversation; however, no mention is made of the discourse history of the referents in these data. It is possible that, once again, the omission of subject pronouns is related to their recoverability from discourse, in addition to first language influence.

The most recent research on pronoun omission has been within the framework of universal grammar (UG), in particular, the setting and resetting of parameters during the process of language learning. In these studies the phenomenon has generally been referred to as *pro-drop*. While UG, L1 influence, or other factors may be adequate to explain the absolute occurrence of *pro-drop* in the production of second language learners, a discourse-functional approach may be more appropriate to account for variation in *pro-drop*. Within a UG framework, variation can be viewed in two ways: first, it may be regarded as a part of pragmatic performance, rather than a manifestation of syntactic competence, and as such, not a focus of investigation; second, because the process of second language acquisition is viewed as a setting or resetting of parameters, variation is seen as a no man's land between parametric values—a mixture of the old and new systems, presumably starting with a greater concentration of the former and proceeding to a greater concentration of the latter. There are a number of problems with this view. Most importantly, it fails to account for the fact that not all variation is developmental. On the contrary, there is significant variation in *pro-drop* even in the production of NSs, in spite of the fact that their *pro-drop* parameter has presumably not been activated.

In one study of *pro-drop*, White (1985) proposes that this usage in the L2 is due to the activation of the *pro-drop* parameter which is carried over from the speakers' L1s. In a study of Spanish L1 (*pro-drop*) and French L1 (*non-pro-drop*) learners of English, White found that there was some evidence of the activated parameter in her L1 Spanish subjects' performance on grammatical judgement tasks. The *pro-drop* parameter is thought by some to include a cluster of constructions, of which subject pronoun omission is only one. Also included are alternative VS order in declarative sentences and the *that-trace* effect. White found only limited evidence that the three were connected in the interlanguage (IL) grammars of her subjects.

In another study of the effect of the *pro-drop* parameters on IL development, Hilles (1986) connects the omission of subject pronouns with the acquisition of non-referential *it* and the emergence of lexically realised AUX. According to Hilles, for learners with a *pro-drop* L1, in the process of acquiring a *non-pro-drop* L2, the development of lexical material in AUX and non-referential *it* should be inversely proportional to the frequency of pronoun omission. In this view, non-referential *it* acts as a trigger by forcing the learner to restructure INFL (inflection), where AUX is located, and hence to re-evaluate English as a *non-pro-drop* language. Unlike White, Hilles uses some connected discourse in her analysis. However, she does not report on the discourse history of the omitted referents, so it is difficult to judge what role it might play in an explanation of pronoun (non-)production. Again, while UG may account for the absolute phenomenon of pronominal omission in the L2 data here, it does little to explain either the NS data or the regular variation in pronoun omission in the L2 data. All variation within this model is developmental, that is, in terms of movement away from the native language toward the target. Hilles, quoting Hyams (1983:234), describes this as the 'parameter wavering between two values'. Because the aim of these UG studies has generally been to examine linguistic (= syntactic) competence, discourse function plays little role, and no explanation is provided for the distribution of omitted pronouns. Thus, while parameter setting may be responsible for a speaker's basic choice to use or omit pronouns, discourse constraints could provide the fine tuning for their distribution.

There have been some functional studies of zero anaphora. Fakhri (1984) found that an English L1 (subject pronouns required) SLL of Moroccan Arabic (subject pronouns not required) developed some novel, non-NS-like uses for subject pronouns and zero anaphora. The subject used these two devices in such a way as to compensate for her lack of proficiency in the use of verbal inflections. She introduced participants into narratives with a noun or pronoun, but in subsequent references, the pronoun was dropped, even though the accuracy of her verb endings was variable. However, where there was any potential ambiguity in the reference of this zero anaphor, caused by the introduction of a new character into the narrative, the pronoun was retained. When she used a pronoun, the subject's accuracy in verb inflections fell, in contrast to the instances of pronoun omission, when her accuracy rose. These results suggest that the wide variation in the use of pronouns, which is seen in these and other data, may be linked to their function in discourse.

Pronouns and pronominal anaphora

Pronominal anaphora has received less attention in the second language acquisition literature than zero anaphora because, while the latter is only grammatical in English in certain co-ordinate structures, the former has a much wider range of grammatical contexts and thus is less often the focus as a learner error. The decision to use a pronoun instead of a full noun (as opposed to the pronoun/zero choice) is often based on stylistic rather than grammatical constraints. Pronominal anaphora exhibits a continuity and persistence that the Quantity Universal does not predict. Givón (1983:354) has proposed an explanation for this apparent anomaly. He suggests that the unexpected topic persistence of pronouns may be due to the fact that the category *pronoun* actually consists of two kinds of pronouns, with two separate functions in discourse: (i) 'purely anaphoric unstressed pronouns with referential distance values essentially the same as for zero anaphora' and (ii) 'a significant subcategory of stressed, contrastive topic changing pronouns, with a characteristic referential distance of 2–3 or more clauses to the left.' In an effort to break apart these two categories, Givón divided pronouns with a referential distance of one from those with a referential distance of two or more. He found that these two groups corresponded to minor and major discourse junctures. Minor junctures are those across which a sequence of action continues, while major junctures represent a break in continuity. This distinction indicates that pronouns may indeed function anaphorically as well as contrastively.

Pronoun copies

Most of the research on pronominal copies in second language acquisition has centred around the pronoun retention in relative clauses. In contrast to the extensive literature on these resumptive pronouns, pronoun copies out of the subject position in non-relative clauses have not been treated fully. Indeed, they have rarely been noted at all. Duskova (1969) reports both subject pronoun omission and subject pronoun copies in her study of L1 Czech learners of English. Both Givón (1976, 1983) and Gundel & Tarone (1983) regard this usage as commonplace in English. Givón sees it as a discourse marker of topic shift. In Gundel & Tarone's study (1983:287) sentences such as *That boy, he's smart* are not starred as ungrammatical.

Another possible explanation for the use of subject pronoun copies is that they are a special case of the topic-comment construction. Superficially, they resemble the *double subject* construction which is so characteristic of topic-prominent languages (Li & Thompson, 1976). In the case of pronoun copying, however, the two 'subjects' are co-referential, whereas in topic-prominent languages, the first 'subject' is actually the topic, and the second might be called the subject of the comment, as in the classic example:

(12) That tree, the leaves are big. (Li & Thompson, 1976:468)

The comparison of pronoun copies to the double subject construction is worth noting, however. According to Huebner (1983:79), this latter construction is a relatively infrequent one, even in topic-prominent languages, because the requirements for its use are somewhat restrictive. Huebner states, 'when one considers from a functional point of view the contexts of such constructions, one realises that at least two conditions must be met for the double subject construction to be grammatical. First, *it is only used when there is a shift in topic*. Second, the topic in question would have to have no grammatical relation with the verb of the comment predicate' (emphasis mine). In his own data, Huebner found that pronoun copies were sometimes used to reintroduce topics where there had been two competing referents, thus performing a disambiguating function.

Pronoun copying, sometimes called left dislocation, has also been reported in the production of NSs. The term 'pronoun copy' will be maintained in this study, rather than left dislocation, as there is no evidence in the present data that any movement has taken place. Givón (1983) found that, except for hesitation phenomena, left-dislocated NPs (LDs) yielded the highest figures for referential distance of any referential device. LDs also proved to be highly persistent in the subsequent discourse. These two characteristics suggest that LD is a common way of introducing new topics. Givón maintains that LDs are a special device for *reintroducing* topics or referents. Prince (1981) concurs. According to her analysis, LD will only be used when the referent can already be located in the preceding discourse, though probably not in the immediately preceding discourse. Montgomery

(1983), in contrast, in a study of NS oral discourse, contends that LDs (of which subject pronoun copies are a subset, according to his definition) are a discourse device which establish a conversational theme. They reintroduce topics which have been absent from the discourse, but can also introduce new ones, creating what Montgomery calls *oral paragraphs*, often in the form of anaphoric chains.

The study

Many explanations have been put forward for variation in the use of pronouns and zero anaphora by NSs and SLLs. It is argued here that there is frequently a functional explanation of this variation. This study examines this phenomenon in the production of three groups of subjects.

The task

Production data were gathered from three speaker groups: NSs of American English, SLLs of English living in the United States, and speakers of Singapore English (SingE), an institutionalised regional second language variety of English. The task was an *unguided* (see Perdue, 1984) conversation between two subjects. These conversations occurred between six pairs of previously acquainted speakers from each of the three groups. Six subjects were recruited and then asked to select a partner of his or her own choice to complete the task. Each pair spoke for forty-five minutes in free conversations. The subjects were given no prior instruction as to the content or direction of their conversation, nor was there any monitoring of the conversations by the researcher (other than through the tape recorder). Age ranged from 18 to 45. Except in the case of the NSs, none of the pairs shared a first language or dialect.

Subjects: characteristics and method of selection

The first group consists of speakers of an institutionalised non-native variety of English spoken in the Republic of Singapore. The English language in Singapore is both an intra- and inter-ethnic lingua franca. It is widely spoken, especially among those who have completed secondary education, and the level of proficiency is extremely high. While English is chronologically the first language of very few speakers in Singapore, it is often the dominant language. For many Singaporeans who have been through English-medium education, English is the language in which they claim to be the most proficient (Lim, 1980). Thus, certain SingE speakers can be thought of as somewhere between first and second language speakers of English. English, as it is spoken in Singapore, exhibits a number of differences from NS varieties. Some of these differences resemble features which are thought typical of individuals ILs, but have now become institutionalised and are widely recognised by Singaporeans as characteristic of their own variety of English (Williams, 1987). As regards second language acquisition research, SingE is particularly interesting because of its stability. In the speech of the SingE subjects, there is little variation due to development (Ritchie, 1986).

The range of competence in English in Singapore may be represented in terms of a continuum or cline (Kachru, 1981; Platt & Weber, 1980), ranging from rudimentary language use by speakers for whom English is clearly a foreign language, to a variety of English which is virtually indistinguishable from Received Pronunciation. The population chosen for this study is taken from the middle of this cline of proficiency. They are English medium educated, and have the equivalent of high school diplomas. This group of English-dominant speakers is an appropriate choice because their speech is less likely to exhibit heavy NS influence, as speakers higher up on the cline, with their greater exposure to NS varieties, might; nor do they use English as a foreign language, as those farther down on the cline would be likely to do. The production of speakers from the middle of this cline shows the influence of a variety of L1s but, at the same time, shows a number of common features which are characteristic of the production of all speakers of SingE, regardless of their primary language. First languages in the SingE group consist of Malay, Tamil, and four dialects of Chinese.

The selection of SLL subjects was based on the same selection criteria for the subjects in the SingE group, described above. An attempt was made to choose SLL subjects of the same general educational and occupational background as the SingE subjects. However, meeting the criteria which had been set up for subject selection in the SingE group, including the ability to execute the necessary task, proved problematic in the case of this speaker group. It was almost impossible to locate subjects who were accustomed to conversing in English, who met the other, primarily educational, requirements for inclusion in the study. In addition, because there is normally no SLL speech community to speak of, except in the case of a shared L1, it was not possible to find an intermediary from within the speech community who could set up previously acquainted pairs. In contrast to the SingE and NS subject selection procedure, the intermediaries in the case of the SLLs were, of necessity, the subjects' teachers. The length of residence in the

United States of these subjects ranged from three to ten years. All had had both formal and informal exposure to English. First languages include Mandarin, Cantonese, Malay, Korean, Russian, Mende (Sierra Leone), Kikongo (Angola) and Vietnamese.

The final group of subjects in this study are NSs of American English, again matched as closely as possible to the SingE speakers for educational and occupational status and age. All subjects in this group had high school diplomas but minimal, if any, tertiary education. Their occupations were similar to those of the Singaporeans. As in the case of the SingE speakers, a field assistant from within the speech community was employed to locate the first six subjects and to set up conversational pairs.

Method of analysis

The analysis examines those devices which act as subjects of main verbs. It is limited to referential devices in the third person. Specifically, these devices are the focus in an effort to determine their function in relation to the preceding discourse rather than to participants in the speech event. Excluded from the data are interrogatives, since it has been shown elsewhere that subject pronouns may be deleted in questions for reasons quite independent of the discourse functions under consideration here (Meisel, 1983; Williams, in press; Zobl, 1984). There is one further exclusion from the analysis—those utterances containing non-referring *it*, which appears frequently in the production of all subjects (13).

(13) **J**: I'm talking about moving—buying.
    N: I thought you meant rent.
    J: ø doesn't make no sense to rent—to me. (NS4–018)

There is evidence that non-referential pronouns should be treated differently from referential pronouns (Hilles, 1986; Gundel, 1978). In addition, the measures described above are meaningless in relation to non-referential pronouns. For these reasons, only the latter are included here.

Within the category of zero anaphora, both grammatical and ungrammatical examples are examined. Levels of grammaticality in production are categorised in the following way:

(i) Native speaker-prescriptive (NSP): those instances of zero anaphora which meet prescriptive standards of grammaticality

(ii) Native speaker-descriptive (NSD): those zero anaphors which, in addition to appearing in the production of the SingE speakers and

SLLs, can also be found in the speech of the NSs in this study, yet do not meet prescriptive standards

(iii) Non-target-like (NTL): those zero anaphors which are ungrammatical by both prescriptive and the descriptive standards of NSs in this study; that is, they are found only in the production of the SingE speakers and SLLs.

Structurally, the category of zero anaphora is subdivided into three types.

(a) *Overtly co-ordinate structures.* These are utterances which contain a co-ordinating conjunction. These zero anaphors are grammatical by NSP norms.

(b) *Functionally co-ordinate structures.* In these cases, the co-ordinating conjunction (usually *and*) may be missing, but if it were inserted, an NSP utterance, such as in (a), would result. This means that the same referent continues as the grammatical subject into the next clause and the relationship between the two clauses is co-ordinate. Semantic role is also conserved.

(c) *Non-coordinate structures.* In these utterances, the zero anaphor does not have parallel links with the subject of the previous clause. Any one of the following conditions may hold: (i) the referent appears in a non-subject position in the previous clause; or (ii) the referent is separated from the zero anaphor by more than one clause; or (iii) the two clauses are connected by subordination rather than by co-ordination. The insertion of a co-ordinating conjunction will not produce a grammatical utterance by any standard in these instances.

Examples of these three contexts for zero anaphora come from data from all three speaker groups.

A

(14) M: Ken is supposed to either just get us tickets or––there's no guest list. *He* just went there at lunch time and ø found out. I knew he would. (NS3–081)

(15) Then this *boy* this afternoon come in and ø tell me, the fa––the parent of this––this missing girl uh—sort of break up. (SE4–207)

B

(16) J: Oh listen, *they*'re gonna need a month just to relax and forget *they* were even over here. But I think *they* really miss him.

    A: mmm.

J: ø miss the baby because *they*'re so––*they* raised him, you know. (NS3–169)

(17) I scared about the fighting. I really hate it. But I saw a lot of *Vietnam*(ese). *They* are just 5′2″, you know ø fight with the black people. *They* really fight. (SLL3–151)

C

(18) **M:** My husband were in jail before coming here.
A: Yeah? Why?
M: Because he was politician. He was against the *government*, so ø put him in jail for one year. (SLL1–268) (type (i))

(19) **M:** Well, what are you now? Waiter? Like is there––is there like a head waiter?
C: No, there's just two of us. Me and *Tony*.
M: Through the whole place?
C: Yeah—it's a––it's only a small place.
M: ø told me it was three floors.
C: *He* meant the disco on the top floor. (NS1–665) (type (ii))

(20) Then *my friend* put down the phone like that. *She* was very happy because ø thought *she* is the winner. (SE1–675) (type (iii))

In order to determine the function of these devices within discourse, the three basic measures—referential distance, potential ambiguity and topic persistence—were made. A figure for referential distance was obtained by finding the closest reference to the left whose referent was identical to that of the device in question. The distance was then counted in number of clauses. The traditional definition of clause was used, that is, a group of words forming a grammatical unit which contains a finite verb. However, in addition to those utterances which contained finite verbs, utterances without a (finite) verb, but which were bounded by pauses, were also included in the analysis. This practice was limited to those turns containing content words and excludes back channel cues such as *mmhm* and *really*.

So far, this discussion has focused on the role of these devices in referring to NPs in the previous discourse. However, some of them may also be used to introduce new topics and referents. When a device is found in an utterance which is topic-initiating, naturally no referent will be found in the discourse to the left, or it will be located so far back in the discourse as to be the functional equivalent. For this reason, Givón sets an arbitrary limit of 20 clauses to the left in calculating referential distance. Figures for referential distance then will vary between 1 and 20.

Topic persistence to the right, also calculated in terms of average number of clauses, was determined for the four devices. The values for topic persistence, or decay, begin at 0.0. If the referent disappeared immediately, that is, it did not recur in the next clause, a value of 0.0 was assigned. Otherwise, the number of consecutive clauses in which the referent, or at least arguments of that referent, appeared was the assigned value. These figures begin at 0.0 and have no upper bound. This measure has a serious weakness, however. If a referent is introduced, but is then separated from the next reference by an intervening but non-anaphoric clause, the second instance becomes, in effect, a new referent or in any event cannot be calculated with the method of measurement described above. This problem is illustrated in example (21). The clauses which appear in italics separate the anaphoric device from its previous referent. Furthermore, there is a new referent, the speaker himself. Strictly speaking, then, it cannot be said that the persistence of the referent, *some guy*, is X number of clauses, since a reference to it does not appear in every clause.

(21) The other day, some guy he$_i$ was impressing his girlfriend, *and a friend of mine and I were walking and he*$_i$ *wanted to trip me because I was small—I look small.* $\emptyset_i$ *says 'motha fo, what's your problem?'* So, I cursed him out a little bit, so $\emptyset_i$ gets up and says, 'hey little kid, what are you gonna do about it?' (SLL3–160)

As a result of this problem, the measure was modified. The figures given in the next section include any intervening clauses, and all counts continue until the final reference within the space of 20 clauses. The topic persistence figure for the above example (21) would, therefore, be seven.

Finally, potential ambiguity is defined by Givón as the average number of semantically compatible, competing referents in the immediately preceding discourse (up to three clauses to the left). Semantically compatible in this case means referents with the same number, gender, and $+/-$ animate/human feature. In general, a device is given either a score of 0.0, meaning there are no competing referents, or 1.0, meaning that there are.

Two-way analyses of variance (ANOVA) were performed on these means to determine the significance of the differences among them. Because the figures obtained by the Givón analysis are the result of averaging, some characteristics of these devices may be obscured. A referent may disappear from the discourse for a short time and then reappear. Other references occur in chains, with some sort of marking in almost every clause. Any determination of exactly how long a referent must be absent for it to disappear from the listener's consciousness is impossible to determine empirically in the context of spontaneous conversation. However, a referent which reappears after two clauses cannot be lumped together with one which reappears after twelve clauses. For this reason, instances of zero anaphora were placed into three groups: (1) topic-introducing: those anaphors with no referents or referents at least 20 clauses back; (2) topic-reinstating: those anaphors with referents less than 20 but more than eight clauses back; and finally, (3) topic-continuing: anaphors with a referential distance of eight clauses or less.

Before the results are presented, a brief word should be said about terminology. The following analysis hinges basically on determining what is considered *new* and what is considered *old* or *given* information. The definitions of these terms have a long history of controversy. Chafe (1976) has defined them as a function of what the speaker believes to be either in or out of the addressee's consciousness. Prince (1981) prefers to see these characteristics as part of a taxonomy of *assumed familiarity*, which includes several kinds of *given* and as many kinds of *new* information. Both Gundel (1978) and Halliday & Hassan (1976) conclude that there are actually two dichotomies rather than one. Gundel calls them *activated/inactivated* and *topic/comment*, while Halliday & Hassan describe them as *recoverable/non-recoverable* and *theme/rheme*. The first terms in each set are listener-oriented, or at least what the speaker thinks the listener knows, while the second term in each set is speaker-oriented, that is, what the speaker wants to talk about. It is the interaction of these distinctions with pronominalisation (or zeroing) which is crucial in this analysis. According to Kuno (1975), pronominalisation, and by extrapolation, zeroing, can only occur if references are clear from the preceding discourse. Gundel (1978) claims that it is activation of a referent in the listener's consciousness which is vital in pronominalisation. According to her *Condition on Successful Pronominalisation*, a noun phrase must both be activated and have no competing referents in order to be successfully pronominalised.

There are several problems with the above approach in the present data-based analysis. First, there is the difficulty of measuring what has been a successful pronominalisation (or zeroing). In some instances, miscommunication is obvious, but this is not always the case. Second, it is almost impossible to demonstrate empirically, outside an experimental setting, what is activated or in the listener's consciousness. Even more problematic is the task of determining what the speaker *thinks* is activated in the addressee's consciousness. In addition, NNSs may omit elements even if they do not believe their listener holds them in his or her consciousness, simply because the production task is too taxing (Klein, 1986). For these reasons, only those references which actually appear in the discourse will be counted in this analysis. This explicitly excludes pronominal or unmarked references to general knowledge or to shared experiences prior to the present conversation. For instance, an utterance such as *So, did you see him*? where *him* has no prior referent in the conversation, would be excluded. In this way, activation can be operationalised and measured quantitatively in terms of *last mention*, rather than as active or inactive.

Results

Global measures of topic/referent continuity

The figures for referential distance are seen in Table 1. The means are displayed graphically in Figure 1.

(i) Referential distance

The trend for all three speaker groups is quite similar. Pronoun copies and definite nouns have high values relative to pronominal and zero anaphora. This is consistent across speaker groups. In a two-way ANOVA to determine the effect of (a) referential device and (b) speaker group, the results of Table 2 show that the first is significant, while the second is not.

The selection of a particular grammatical device has a strong effect on referential distance. It appears that pronoun copies can extend far back into

TABLE 1. *Referential distance means*

	Pronoun copy	Definite noun	Pronominal	Zero
SingE:				
Mean	15.06	8.24	4.24	3.19
sd	5.14	6.29	4.72	3.66
N	53	200	200	124
NS				
Mean	13.96	9.62	3.46	1.88
sd	5.02	5.62	3.77	1.48
N	56	200	200	52
SLL				
Mean	12.41	7.35	3.12	3.52
sd	5.52	4.61	3.50	3.59
N	86	200	200	46

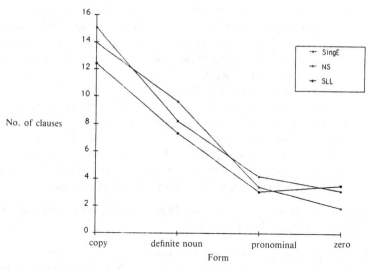

FIGURE 1. *Referential distance*

TABLE 2. *Referential distance ANOVA*

Source	S.S.	d.f.	MS	F
Between groups:				
a. Referential device	19,743.63	3	6,581.21	143.61*
b. Speaker group	115.01	2	57.95	1.26†
a × b	866.26	6	144.38	3.15*
Within groups	73,644.44	1,605		
Total	94,369.34	1,616		

* $p < 0.01$ † n.s.

the discourse to connect with a referent, as in example (22) from SingE, below. The high figure for standard deviation also indicates that some pronoun copies have even higher values for referential distance. A figure of 20 means that the device is introducing a referent for the first time, as in example (23) from a NS. This double role of introducing and reintroducing referents may account for the variability of this measure.

(22) C: Last time, I play with *my friend*, you know. We play in the classroom. There was—after our exams, so we were very free, lah, so a few of us, our gang, is planning to play this. After that, we play, then we invited already. We say, you know, we say, 'What

do you see, uh, Mr Coin?' or whatever. 'Mr Coin, spirit of the coin, can you please come out?' We repeat so many times, and our fingers put on the coin. After that, it came out, you see? So, we tried to ask questions, uh? So it will move, you see? Actually, I just don't believe it, lah. Really, I don't.

S: But then your finger was there.

C: Maybe I push or I don't know what, I'm not so sure. So, our teacher came in, you see, so she ask us to stop the game, you know. We say, 'I'm sorry, Mrs Koh, we can't, you see? This is the spirit.' 'I don't bother whether this is the spirit of the coin or whatever, you better stop the game.' After that, *my friend she* ask the spirit of the coin to go back to the home, lah. (SE1–315)

(23) (new referent) *The guy next door Pete, he* sold his bike for a lot more than he bought it for. (NS2–115)

If the referent can be found a relatively short distance into the preceding discourse, all speakers are more likely to use a shorter form, either a pronoun (24) or nothing at all (25).

(24) You know what happen, Eddie? *Singhs* are the *Sikh people.* When *they* take off the turban, that means *they* are becoming modern. *They* are naughty buggers. *They* smoke. *They* take off their turban because *they* no more holy. (SE4–292)

(25) While I was eating my lunch, he scream, 'I want my lunch!' It was so funny. I throw the rice to the people. The *teacher* just come in. the bell was just rang and the *teacher* look at me, 'what's going on?' ø look at the floor. You know there was all the rice on the floor and the table. (SLL4–240)

Although the results of the ANOVA show that there is a significant difference in referential distance depending on device, the differences between pronominal and zero anaphora for the SingE speakers and SLLs seem small. In order to determine whether they are different enough to infer some distinct referential functions, a t-test was performed. There is a substantial difference in the way NSs use these two devices ($t = 4.7$ $p < 0.001$). NSs' use of zero anaphora is very restricted; it is only used when the referent can be located in the immediately preceding discourse, and even then in restricted contexts. Pronouns have a much wider freedom of occurrence. SingE speakers also differentiate between the two devices, although the trend is not as strong ($t = 2.24$ $p < 0.05$) as for NSs. SingE speakers' use of zero anaphora is less limited and closer to that of pronominal anaphora. The SLLs, on the other hand, use zero anaphora in virtually the same contexts as they use subject pronouns; a t-test yielded no significant difference in the use of these two devices.

(ii) Potential ambiguity

The figures for potential ambiguity shown in Table 3 indicate that choice of form is far more important than speaker group. The trend can also be seen in Figure 2. For NSs and SingE speakers, there is a clear

TABLE 3. *Potential ambiguity means*

	Pronoun copy	Definite noun	Pronominal	Zero
SingE:				
Mean	1.49	1.30	1.17	1.13
sd	0.54	0.52	0.39	0.34
N	53	200	200	124
NS				
Mean	1.54	1.35	1.19	1.10
sd	0.60	0.52	0.41	0.30
N	56	200	200	52
SLL				
Mean	1.42	1.39	1.25	1.26
sd	0.55	0.92	0.49	0.44
N	86	200	200	46

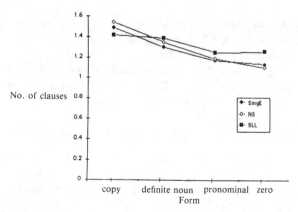

FIGURE 2. *Potential ambiguity*

TABLE 4. *Potential ambiguity ANOVA*

Source	S.S.	d.f.	MS	F
Between groups:				
a. Referential device	17.06	3	5.69	8.44*
b. Speaker group	2.41	2	1.20	1.79†
a × b	0.28	6	0.05	0.66†
Within groups	1,056.78	1,605		
Total	1,076.53	1,616		

* $p < 0.01$ † n.s.

inclination to use forms with more marking material in contexts where there are semantically compatible referents. This is true to a lesser extent for SLLs, who do not differentiate as much among the four forms. Example (22) given above for referential distance remains a valid illustration of the power of pronoun copies to counteract potential ambiguity. *My friend* and *Mrs Koh* are semantically compatible, and thus competing referents. While a simple NP would be sufficient to differentiate them, the additional pronoun copy highlights the change in referent. The use of pronoun copies and other devices seems to be substantially the same across speaker groups. The results of a two-way ANOVA are seen in Table 4.

All speakers tend to use pronoun copies and definite nouns in potentially ambiguous contexts, and conversely, they generally use pronouns where there are no referents which might cause confusion, and the repetition of the full noun could be considered redundant, as in this NS example:

(26) **B**: Aunt Cassie$_1$ brings all her kids$_2$—all over on holidays and they$_2$ all party at Uncle Charlie's$_3$ house.
   L: They$_2$ all drunk too—the kids?
   B: Yeah, all of them. The whole bunch of them drinkers. They$_2$ used to come and spend the weekends. He$_3$'d give them a case of beer, bottle of booze. He$_3$'s a goody two shoes.
   L: Does she$_1$ know that?
   B: Yeah, she$_1$ used to bring them over. (NS6–141)

In the above example, in no case would there be any confusion among the three referents. Among the SingE speakers and SLLs, pronouns are sometimes used in contexts where misreference is a possibility, as in (27). There is similar usage, but to a lesser extent, in the production of NSs, causing the ambiguity which can be seen in example (28).

(27) **P:** You called up my office, right? You said you——I was supposed to call you. Do you know about this? *Anthony* pass me the message and *Lou* was there and *your brother* was there. *He*? said 'I said I'm going to call him back.' (SE5–464)

(28) **H:** *Carolyn* came down, didn't *she*?

    T: Something to do with that night. *She* had gone to see Jackie and Chris's team play and then somebody asked her if *she* was going to go out afterwards. And *she* said, 'Well, I'm going out, but not——I'm going down South Philly.' And before that, it was something about going to the game, well, if it's going to be there, do you think it would be all right? You know and *Judy* kind of resented that. You know it was something that ticked her off and *she*? had to say something to her. And *she* said it and——

    H: *Judy* had something to say to *Carolyn*? (NS2–360)

It was shown in the previous section that in terms of cohesion with referents in preceding discourse, zero and pronominal anaphora have different functions. Zero anaphora is the more continuous of the two devices. In differentiating between potentially ambiguous referents, there is, however, no difference between the two in the production of any of the speakers in this study, including the NSs. T-tests to measure the differences between the mean values for potential ambiguity reveal that they are not significant for NSs or NNSs. This finding is not surprising when the definition of this property is examined. In order to be potentially ambiguous, two referents must be semantically compatible. If this is the case, a pronoun has little more power to disambiguate between them than a zero anaphor. Neither can pinpoint a specific referent. The insertion of *he* would not resolve the ambiguity, since it could still refer either to *this fellow* or *Singh* as in (29).

(29) **E:** So, this afternoon, *this fellow* come in and talk to me, you know. Talk, talk, talk. Before *he* could talk to me, *he* call *Singh*, because *Singh* is his friend, or bloody relative. So, ø call me in the office, you know, I was not in. (SE4–189)

(iii) Topic persistence

The findings for topic persistence are somewhat more difficult to interpret. It is the most problematic of all three measures since it takes into account not what has gone before the referent, but what comes after a part of the discourse over which the speaker has far less control. As a result, it is not always clear whether the figure for topic persistence can be taken as a measure of topic/referent importance. For instance, a referent introduced

TABLE 5. *Topic persistence means*

	Pronoun copy	*Definite noun*	*Pronominal*	*Zero*
SingE:				
Mean	6.32	4.08	2.30	1.00
sd	4.03	2.88	1.74	0.85
N	47	75	50	15
NS				
Mean	4.57	5.52	2.15	3.00
sd	4.03	2.88	1.74	0.85
N	49	106	34	1
SLL				
Mean	6.07	4.44	2.13	1.11
sd	3.73	3.24	1.50	0.78
N	61	54	30	9

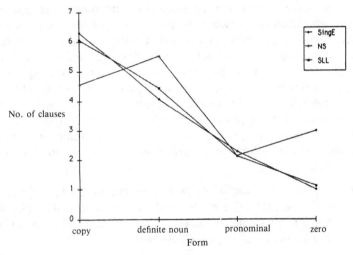

FIGURE 3. *Topic persistence*

by one speaker may be continued or dropped by the other. It is, therefore, difficult to say conclusively to what extent it is the form of the initial reference which indicates its importance in discourse. The means shown in Table 5 show that, as in the other measures, there is a general trend towards the use of discontinuous devices to mark persistent topics and continuous devices to mark less important ones. However, Figure 3 shows that the

TABLE 6.   *Topic persistence ANOVA*

Source	S.S.	d.f.	MS	F
Between groups:				
a. Referential device	1.11	3	0.37	0.02†
b. Speaker group	53.80	2	26.90	1.34†
a × b	1,248.15	6	208.02	10.38*
Within groups	10,403.39	519		
Total	11,706.45	530		

* $p < 0.01$ † n.s.

pattern is not nearly as regular as in the first two measures. In fact, the descending order of the means for all three speaker groups is somewhat misleading, as can be seen from the results of the ANOVA presented in Table 6.

The greatest part of the variance in this case is within, rather than between, groups. Particularly among the NNSs, the use of these devices is inconsistent as regards the maintenance of topics. Arguments of both pronoun copies (30) and zero anaphors (31) may persist, representing both ends of the continuum.

(30) *This guy,* he's a classmate—grade four, grade five, something. He moved to here, in New York Chinatown. When I know him in Hong Kong, grade four, grade five, you know—still a kid. *He* don't know anything, right? But two years later, *he* come back Hong Kong. You know *he* told me—what *he*—*he* said is that, 'I kill a person in Chinatown, so I got to come back here, you know. The police is looking for me.' I don't believe it. And then after a few weeks, Hong Kong's police catch *him*. (SLL3–213)

(31) Third story is bad enough. You break your bone, break your neck, you're finished man. ø take poison also. Foot lotion. My batch, there was one guy took lotion and died. We have to send *them* to the funeral and all this, go to bury *them*--have the full military I don't know what. (SE5–364)

These results indicate that, as far as topic persistence or importance is concerned, the different speaker groups do not use these devices in the same ways. Nor is it clear that the marking of important topics is consistent across the referential devices in this study. One possible explanation for this variability is that topic persistence is more sensitive to genre than the other two measures. For instance, in narratives, the discourse theme may persist for long stretches with little in the way of salient marking. Continuing references may be marked by pronominal or zero anaphora, but referential distance can be huge, and competing referents may be present as well. In narratives, it may be the discourse theme which is marked with more continuous devices and the non-thematic referents which are marked with discontinuous devices. This is similar to what Karmiloff-Smith (1980) found in the narrative production of young children.[2] This tolerance for long referential distances and ambiguity can be seen in extended narratives, such as the following NS example:

(32) **B:** Have you had any trouble with *Pat*?
   L: Not since—well you heard about the thing at The Loft?
   B: No. Tell me that one.
   L: We went to The Loft last August. Me and *Eddie* and *she* was there. So, we had fought all night on the telephone, *her* and I, over *she* was taking Cathy on the weekends. So, now when *she*'s on the telephone, *she*'s telling me that *she*'s our weekend baby-sitter. Well, *she*'s not taking this kid cause *she*'s not gonna be our babysitter. This was visitation with your baby, that's what it was. It wasn't—*she* wasn't babysitting for anybody. This was your daughter. So, anyway we had these words on the phone. And we went up The Loft and *she* came in around 2:00. So, I went up to *her* and I grabbed *her* by the wrists, and I said, 'Let's go outside now'. ø Cried, 'Lorraine,' *she* said, 'please, I don't want to fight with you. Please leave me alone'. So—this is--now everyone's coming. I'm not a scene causer. I can't be into that, so I let go of *her*. I said, 'Come on, Eddie, we'll walk away.' And I'll see *her* some other time--like *you*'re always telling me I'm a dyke, *Eddie's* afraid of me, *she* don't want me to raise her kids ... I been raising those kids--like this was four years now... So that's okay. I walked away from *her**. We were dancing, playing around. My cousin Lucy was down from Delaware and we had taken her out. So, now me and her get on the dance floor and we're up there, say good half hour. You know how the music keeps playing, playing, playing and you just keep going. Well, by now I'm feeling pretty good and I'm dancing. But as I come off the dance floor I see *Eddie* come away from the bar and walk into *these guys*, and as *he* did, they pulled *him* down. Now to me, they tell me there were five or six, I think there was seven or eight. I just got behind *them* and tried to pull *them* off of *him*, you know. *They* were throwing bottles, glass, and *they* hit me in the head

with a beer bottle, but the scar is gone. Twenty-six stitches I got in my head. When I approached *her**, *these guys* weren't there yet. But here *these guys* came from a club where *she* was at, so *she* started to talk to *them* and *she* told them that *Eddie* was gonna beat *her* up, that *he* was gonna give *her* a problem. (NS6–307)

There are participants other than *Pat* in this narrative, even a semantically compatible one (Lucy), and the referential distance between the first NP reference in the beginning of the narrative and the next reference is large, as is the distance between the two references to *Pat* marked with (*). However, the topic can continue with the pronoun *she* without any loss of meaning precisely because *Pat* is the topic. Compare, for instance, the recurrence of non-thematic referents, such as *these guys* or *Eddie*, with the use of the *she*. The full noun is repeated frequently in the former cases, while only the pronoun appears in the latter. In fact, the full noun representing the discourse topic in this narrative never recurs. There may be specific rules for reference which apply to narratives such as this which do not apply to conversation consisting of relatively short turns at talk. However, because the number of extended narratives in these data is small, it is not possible to state these rules definitively.

Introducing and continuing topics and referents

The measures of the predictability of topics and referents given in the section above provide general information as to the nature of these discourse devices. Based on the first two measures, the use of referential devices by all three speaker groups is essentially the same. A more detailed look at the specific contexts in which the subjects use one of these devices, zero anaphora, reveals other similarities, as well as some important but less obvious differences, between the NS and the NNS production. Table 7 shows the number of times zero anaphors are used in topic/referent-initiating, topic-reinstating, and topic-continuing contexts.

These figures indicate that zero anaphora can occur in a wider range of structural contexts in the production of the SingE speakers and SLLs than in that of the NSs. Specifically, these NNSs sometimes use this device to reinstate referents which appear more than eight clauses to the left in the preceding discourse. NSs, on the other hand, essentially limit their use of zero anaphora to what have been called topic-continuing contexts. Even in topic/referent-continuing contexts (those with referents less than eight clauses to the left), NS and NNS usage differs markedly. The NSs tend to restrict their use of zero anaphora (81%) to either *overtly* or *functionally*

TABLE 7. *Contexts of zero anaphora*

	SingE No.	SingE %	NS No.	NS %	SLL No.	SLL %
Introducing	2	2	0	0	0	0
Reinstating	16	13	1	2	10	22
Continuing	106	85	51	98	36	78
overtly co-ordinate	13	10	22	42	7	15
functionally co-ordinate	29	23	20	39	14	30
Non-coordinate	64	52	9	17	15	33
Total	124		52		46	

TABLE 8. *Zero anaphora in non-coordinate contexts*

	SingE No.	SingE %	NS No.	NS %	SLL No.	SLL %
i) Change in gram. role	15	23	0	0	3	20
ii) Separated by >1 clause	41	64	9	100	7	47
iii) Subordination	8	13	0	0	5	33
Total	64		9		15	

co-ordinate clauses, with the referent in the preceding parallel clause. The NNSs, and the SingE speakers in particular, use zero anaphora to a greater extent in *non-coordinate* contexts. The difference in frequency of the specific context of zero anaphora across speaker groups is highly significant ($X^2 = 44.24$, $p < 0.001$, d.f. = 8). Table 8 displays this breakdown of contexts for zero anaphora as used by the three speaker groups.

Again, the differences in usage across speaker groups are statistically significant ($X^2 = 9.66$, $p < 0.05$, d.f. = 4). Type (ii) is the most frequent context for zero anaphora for all three speaker groups, but it is the *only* context for the NSs; the NNSs use it in other contexts as well. Where the referent remains the grammatical subject, as in type (ii), it appears that continuity is more easily maintained, in spite of the distance between the zero anaphor and its referent, than if its grammatical function changes. NSs always mark a change in grammatical function with a less continuous device, usually a full NP, whereas NNSs will sometimes simply use a zero. In each case where this does occur, however, the previous referent appears within one or two clauses prior to the zero anaphor. In this way, continuity of reference is maintained by proximity. There are relatively few instances of zero anaphora after a subordinating conjunction, even by NNSs; but where it does occur, again, a less continuous referential device, such as a pronoun or full NP, always appears in the previous clause.

The category of topic-continuing contexts is a varied one. The most continuous context is one in which the previous clause is linked by a co-ordinating conjunction. The use of all referential devices in this study in this context is grammatical by both prescriptive (NSP) and descriptive (NSD) standards, although the use of pronoun copy would be rather odd. The second category is one in which the previous clause *could* be linked with a co-ordinating conjunction, but the conjunction is omitted. Again, most of these devices are grammatical in this context by NSP standards. The one exception is zero anaphora, which meets NSD, but not NSP, standards. In spite of its questionable grammaticality, this is a productive context for zero anaphora in the speech of all three speaker groups (SingE 29%; SLL 39%; NS 39%). Example (33) shows this for a NS.

(33) My girlfriends were saying, 'Anybody have a towel or napkin or anything?' But *he* just got in his car. ø Moved it away. (NS6–370)

Finally, there are contexts in which the clause containing the referential device is not, and could not be, attached to the preceding clause by a co-ordinating conjunction. It is in these contexts that the less continuous devices, such as pronoun copies and full nouns, are found. Zero anaphora is found in this context occasionally in the speech of NSs, but is generally considered to be nonstandard. This usage is much more common in the production of NNSs (SingE 60%; SLLs 42% of topic continuing zero anaphors).

Within this last category of topic-continuing contexts, there are several types. Examples (14) to (20) above illustrate these three types. Type (i) involves a change in grammatical function. For instance, the object of the previous clause may become the (unexpressed) subject of the following clause (18). In type (ii) contexts, referents maintain the same grammatical categories, but there may be several clauses, and possibly turns, intervening before the referent is taken up again (19). This is the only context in which non-coordinate zero anaphora is found in the production of NSs. The final context, type (iii), of which there are relatively few even in the NNS data, is one in which clauses are linked by subordination rather than co-ordination (20). Zero anaphora can be found in all three contexts in the production of NNSs; types (i) and (ii) are non-target-like (NTL), while type (ii) conform to descriptive norms (NSD).

Discussion

The results given above raise, and give at least partial answers to, three questions. The first has to do with the referring devices themselves. What function do these devices have in production? The second question concerns the three speaker groups. Having established some basic functions for these devices, we can then ask whether this usage differs depending on NS/NNS status, or between institutionalised and individual learner varieties. Finally, it is necessary to ask why the answers to the above questions should be so. Are there some underlying cognitive or psycholinguistically motivated reasons why certain devices should be associated with certain functions, and why the differences in these functions across the speaker groups in this study in many cases are small? Where differences among the speaker groups do occur, can they be explained in terms of these principles?

The functions of referring devices

It seems evident from the results of this study that subject pronoun copies are used in environments where, for some reason, the referent is difficult to construct or reconstruct in the consciousness of the inter-locutors. All indications are that subject pronoun copies are used when the referent is presented for the first time, is presented after a long absence from the discourse, or is a source of potential confusion with other semantically compatible referents in the immediate environment. In other words, pronoun copies are most likely to be found where there are potential processing difficulties. It also seems to be the case that pronoun copies are used to mark important themes that tend to continue in the subsequent discourse. Topics and referents which are introduced with this device are maintained far longer than with any other referring device. Together, these two attributes suggest that subject pronoun copies have a general highlight-ing or focusing function.

The functions of the other devices in this study are not as clearly delineated as that of pronoun copies. It does appear, however, that the functions of pronominal and zero anaphora generally do not overlap those of pronoun copies. Neither are used extensively in the introduction, or reintroduction of difficult to recover referents. For SLLs, the differences between these two devices in their referent recovering role is not significant, whereas for the NSs and the SingE speakers, pronouns show considerably more power to reach back into discourse and link up with previous referents than do zero anaphors. According to Klein (1986:121), this 'overuse of ellipsis as a syntactic device, considerably stretching the possibilities offered by the target language' is characteristic particularly of beginning learners. While these SLL subjects are not beginners, their proficiency is lower than that of the SingE speakers. It is possible that the combination of their limited linguistic resources and the demands of immediate production forces the SLLs to omit concrete references to NPs which even they doubt remain in the consciousness of their interlocutors.

The extended use of zero anaphora by both the NNS groups may also be attributed in part to the influence of the subjects' L1s. In the majority of the L1s, subject pronouns are optional, and in some cases are only used for special stress. Chinese is one of the main L1s in the SingE group. According to Li & Thompson (1979), the use of zero rather than a pronoun, especially in topic chains, that is, where the participant or topic remains the same across a large stretch of discourse, is the typical form of anaphora in Chinese. The use of pronominal anaphora is not highly predictable, but tends to be inversely related to what Li & Thompson (1979:334) have called *conjoinability*, or 'the extent to which a clause constitutes a unit with the preceding clause'. Anaphora, both zero and pronominal, is thus, according to Li & Thompson, a pragmatically rather than a grammatically controlled device. The work of Li & Thompson (1976, 1979) is based on Mandarin Chinese. The varieties of Chinese spoken as L1s by the SingE subjects are generally dialects of South China. However, the differences between Mandarin and these dialects tend to be primarily phonological rather than grammatical (Platt, 1983; Chao, 1969). Therefore, the analysis of the aspects of Mandarin presented above remain valid for these dialects. The use of zero anaphora is much more restricted in Malay than in Chinese, although less limited than in English. In spoken production, if the referent is either exophoric or can be found in the immediately preceding discourse, it is possible to omit the subject pronoun, although it is prescriptively correct to supply it. In written discourse, the pronoun must be used. Malay has no marking on the verb to indicate person, number, etc. Tamil is a subject-prominent language with extensive grammatical morphology. Pronoun omission occurs in speech, especially in subject position, since referents and extensive semantic information, including case relations, number and gender, are easily recoverable from verb inflections. As in the case of Malay, pronouns are used in more formal situations and in the written language.

The findings on potential ambiguity are more straightforward. Where there is some question as to which (usually of two) referents is to be revived, referential devices containing the most marking material are used. Where shorter forms, such as pronominal or zero anaphora, are used, there is potential for misreference. Conversely, where there is no potential for confusion, there is no need for salient marking. This trend is consistent across speaker groups. Moving from pronoun copy to full noun to pronoun, there is decreasing power to disambiguate among semantically compatible referents. From pronoun to zero anaphora, however, the decrease is small, since pronouns often have almost as little power to disambiguate as zero anaphors. In the NNSs' production, where zero anaphora is tolerated in a wider variety of contexts, there is a consequent increase in potentially ambiguous referents.

The figures on topic persistence are less clear. Full nouns and pronoun copies are more likely to be used to mark important themes or topics in discourse than are pronouns or zeros, although there is not a consistent differentiation between these two across speaker groups. Since neither pronouns nor zeros are used to any great extent to introduce topics, it is not surprising that the figures for topic persistence should be so low. Pronouns are used, however, to reintroduce themes and topics. In these cases, they are often found at the head of topic chains, which accounts for their significant, if limited, persistence in discourse. Zero anaphora, because of its very restricted use by NSs in introductory contexts, cannot even be considered as a marker of any significance in this category. Even for NNSs, the number of tokens is so small as to be nearly uninterpretable. Finally, there is some indication that these devices may operate differently within extended narratives. In these cases, once a theme for the narrative is established, it may be developed with more continuous referential devices. The use of a more discontinuous device signals a shift away from the discourse theme.

Referential functions across speaker groups

The second matter under consideration here is whether or not the functions of these devices change across the three speaker groups in this study. As shown above, the answer to this question is, by and large, that they do not. The extent to which these forms are used, however, does vary somewhat, although not always in predictable ways. For instance, the speech of SLLs, who produced the least speech in terms of sheer quantity, shows extensive use of subject pronoun copies, compared to that of NSs and SingE speakers, among whom frequency of use was comparable. Frequency counts for zero anaphora reveal that it is most prevalent in the production of the SingE speakers. This may be partly due to the extensive use of this device in the L1s of the SingE subjects. As for zero anaphora, that it was found to such an extent in the production of NSs was not expected. Over half of the zero anaphors are found in contexts which are not grammatical by NSP standards. It appears that for functions which operate to the left into the preceding discourse, the differences among speaker groups is not great. Based on the analysis given in the preceding section, it can be said that speakers in all three groups use these devices for a similar function, that is, to assist in the recovery or establishment of referents. The one measure which looks ahead into discourse, topic persistence, shows significant differences across speaker groups, and is also quite variable within speaker groups.

It appears that regardless of what variety of English is spoken—a native, institutionalised, or learner variety—the function of these linguistic devices remains relatively constant. In many cases, these devices, together with their NS-like functions, have spread to new contexts and are used more extensively by NNSs than by their NS counterparts. The question which remains to be answered is why this should be the case in the first place. Why should what Givón (1984) calls 'rock bottom discourse universals' exist at all? Are they acquired by the NNSs through NS input? If so, why should this spread to new contexts have occurred? If they are characteristic of language learners, what can account for their presence in the production of NSs as well?

Referring devices as a reflection of clarity and economy

Viewing these devices within a broader framework, their use can be seen as more than the arbitrary assignment of symbols to certain functions. Why should the discourse functions described above be marked in this particular way, and how can this usage be related to other production features which have been observed in these and other data? They seem to reflect the opposing discourse properties of clarity and economy (Slobin, 1973, 1977). Where referents are new or difficult to recover, or where there is potential confusion among referents, clarity suffers. In order to compensate for this loss of clarity, it is necessary to increase the redundancy and, as a consequence, the salience of the relevant referents. Pronoun copies are an example of a greater quantity of marking material leading to an increase in clarity and a decrease in ambiguity. In short, more marked, salient devices will be found in contexts where the referent may be difficult to locate and process. They can thus be seen as maximising clarity. This explains the high scores for pronoun copies on referential distance and potential ambiguity. High scores on these measures can be equated with heavy surface marking. The same cannot be said of the measures of discourse to the right of the referent. Heavy marking generally implies high scores for topic persistence; however, the converse is not always true. High scores do not necessarily imply heavy marking of referents.

At the opposite end of the continuum from pronoun copies is zero anaphora. This is a device of low salience, one which would be expected in environments with little ambiguity of reference and with high potential for redundancy. This is exactly what is found, for the most part, in the present data. Where referents are easily recoverable, heavy marking would be perceived as redundant and perhaps unnecessary. Zero anaphora is a case of minimum surface marking, that is, the non-marking of a continuing referent. This maximises economy by reducing salience and redundancy to their lowest point. Zero anaphora is communicatively efficient where there is little ambiguity. Where the referent of the zero or pronominal anaphor is somehow surprising, either because there are several compatible referents or because the referent cannot be found in the immediately preceding discourse, the price of this efficiency may be a breakdown in communication, as in (34).

(34) **R**: But don't forget my—the one month of reservist-training *the men*$_1$, you know what ah? It's defense camp, you know? You know what is defense camp? Okay, let me tell you. Okay we went in first week is our pre-preparation what you call it?—uh—advance party. Advance party means *all the NCOs and officers*$_2$ who are, you know, who are the leaders of their battalion, uh? $\emptyset_2$ supposed to go in for the one month—what you call—refresher course, so that you know what to do when *they*$_1$ come in.

  P: When *they*$_2$ come in?

  R: To train them lah. (SE5–103)

The variable use of these devices shows what the speaker believes to be the most efficient, but at the same time the clearest, form of communication. The speaker is making guesses as to what the listener still carries in short-term memory, and what might be potentially confusing, as well as keeping things easy for him or herself. The speaker can also give indications of what he or she deems to be important in the discourse or what the listener should pay particular attention to. Information which is assumed to be shared need not be expressed, while surprising or unpredictable information must be highlighted. For the NSs, it is possible that these strategies are the most apparent in unplanned speech. Ochs (1979) claims that the use of immediate context and the deletion of referents are characteristic of unplanned production. The task in this study is interactive and immediate; there is little time for the subjects to consider their responses. The pairs of subjects in this study are on close terms; there is a great deal of shared knowledge between them. If this is the case, NNSs may also be subject to these production constraints which seem even to affect the performance of NSs (Tomlin, 1984; Ellis, 1987). Because their linguistic resources are limited, they express only what is most important, sometimes leaving reference to be decoded by the listener through contextual information. At other times, where references are uncertain, their production may become redundant. This combination of forces may begin to explain the variable use of these referential devices in the production of all three speaker groups.

Notes to Chapter 9

1. Examples in the text which are followed by a numbered key to the transcripts are authentic: SE = Singapore English, NS = native speaker, SLL = second language learner; those with no number following them are either fabricated or taken from the indicated sources.

2. In the first language narrative production of children, Karmiloff-Smith (1980) offers counter arguments to the proposal that zero and pronominal anaphora are used for economy, and nouns are repeated to reduce ambiguity. Instead, she claims that full nouns are used to set major discourse themes and that pronouns and zero anaphora are signals to the listener that he/she 'should *not* recompute for retrieval of an antecedent referent but rather to treat the pronoun as the default case for the thematic subject of a span of discourse and to take it that deviations therefrom will be marked clearly linguistically by use of full NPs' (1980:235).

References

BUTTERWORTH, G. and HATCH, E., 1978, A Spanish speaking adolescent's acquisition of English syntax. In E. HATCH (ed.), *Second Language Acquisition: A Book of Readings*. Rowley, MA: Newbury House, pp. 231–45.

CHAFE, W., 1976, Givenness, contrastiveness, definiteness, subjects, topics and point of view. In C. LI (ed.), *Subject and Topic*. New York: Academic Press, pp. 25–56.

CHAO, Y. R., 1969, *Cantonese Primer*. New York: Greenwood.

DITTMAR, N., 1984, Semantic features of pidginized learner varieties of German. In R. ANDERSEN (ed.), *Second Languages: A Cross-Linguistic Perspective*. Rowley, MA: Newbury House, pp. 243–70.

DUSKOVA, L., 1969, On sources of errors in foreign language learning, *International Review of Applied Linguistics*, 7, 11–36.

ELLIS, R., 1987, Interlanguage variability in narrative discourse: Style shifting in the use of past tense, *Studies in Second Language Acquisition*, 9, 1–20.

FAKHRI, A., 1984, The use of communicative strategies in narrative discourse: a case study of a learner of Moroccan Arabic, *Language Learning*, 34 (3), 15–37.

FELIX, S., 1980, Interference, interlanguage and related issues. In S. FELIX (ed.), *Second Language Development: Trends and Issues*. Tübingen: Gunter Narr Verlag, pp. 93–10.

GIVÓN, T., 1976, Topic, pronoun and grammatical agreement. In C. LI (ed.), *Subject and Topic*. New York: Academic Press, pp. 149–88.

——, (ed.), 1979, *Syntax and Semantics, Vol. 12; Discourse and Semantics*. New York: Academic Press.

——, 1983, Topic continuity in spoken English. In T. GIVÓN (ed.) *Typological Studies in Language, vol. 3, Topic Continuity in Discourse: A Quantitative Cross-language Study*. Amsterdam: John Benjamins, pp. 343–63.

——, 1984, Universals of discourse structure and second language acquisition. In W. RUTHERFORD (ed.), *Language Universals and Second Language Acquisition*. Amsterdam: John Benjamins, pp. 109–33.

GUNDEL, J., 1978, Stress, pronominalization and the given-new distinction, *Working Papers in Linguistics*, 10 (2), 1–13.

GUNDEL, J., STENSON, N. and TARONE, E., 1984, Acquiring pronouns in a second language, *Studies in Second Language Acquisition*, 6, 215–25.

GUNDEL, J. and TARONE, E., 1983, Language transfer and the acquisition of pronominal anaphora. In S. GASS & L. SELINKER (eds), *Language Transfer and Language Learning*. Rowley, MA: Newbury House, pp. 281–96.

HALLIDAY, M. and HASSAN, R., 1976, *Cohesion in English*. London: Longman.

HILLES, S. 1986, Interlanguage and the pro-drop parameter, *Second Language Research*, 2 (1), 33–52.

HUEBNER, T., 1983, *A Longitudinal Study of the Acquisition of English*. Ann Arbor: Karoma.

——, 1985, System and variability in interlanguage syntax, *Language Learning*, 35 (2), 141–63.

HYAMS, N., 1983, *The Acquisition of Parameterized Grammars*. Ph.D. dissertation, City University of New York.

KACHRU, B., 1981, The pragmatics of non-native varieties of English. In L. SMITH (ed.), *English for Cross-cultural Communication*. New York: St Martins Press, pp. 15–39.

KARMILOFF-SMITH, A., 1980, Psychological processes underlying pronominalization and non-pronominalization in children's connected discourse. In J. KREIMAN & A. OJEDA (eds), *Papers from the Parasession on Pronouns and Anaphora*. Chicago: Chicago Linguistic Society, pp. 231–48.

KLEIN, W., 1986, *Second Language Acquisition*. Cambridge: Cambridge University Press.

KUMPF, L., 1984, Temporal systems and universality in interlanguage: a case study. In F. ECKMAN, L. BELL & D. NELSON (eds), *Universals of Second Language Acquisition*. Rowley, MA: Newbury House, pp. 132–43.

KUNO, S., 1975, Three perspectives in the functional approach to syntax, *Papers from the Parasession on Functionalism*. Chicago: Chicago Linguistic Society, pp. 276–306.

LI, C. (ed.), 1976, *Subject and Topic*. New York: Academic Press.

LI, C. and THOMPSON, S., 1976, Subject and topic: a new typology for language. In C. LI (ed.), *Subject and Topic*. New York: Academic Press, pp. 457–89.

——, 1979, Third person pronouns and zero anaphora in Chinese discourse. In T. GIVÓN (ed.), *Syntax and Semantics, Vol. 12: Discourse and Semantics*. New York: Academic Press, pp. 311–35.

LIM, K. B., 1980, Language learning and language use among some Singapore students, *RELC Journal*, 11, 10–28.

MEISEL, J., 1983, Strategies of second language acquisition: more than one kind of simplification. In R. ANDERSEN (ed.), *Pidginization and Creolization as Language Acquisition*. Rowley, MA: Newbury House, pp. 120–57.

MONTGOMERY, M., 1983, The functions of left dislocation in spontaneous discourse. In J. MORREAL (ed.), *The Ninth Annual LACUS Forum*. Columbia, SC: Hornbeam Press, pp. 425–32.

OCHS, E. 1979, Planned and unplanned discourse. In T. GIVÓN (ed.), *Syntax and Semantics, Vol. 12: Discourse and Semantics*. New York: Academic Press, pp 51–80.

PERDUE, C. (ed.), 1984, *Second Language Acquisition by Adult Immigrants: a Field Manual*. Rowley, MA: Newbury House.

PLATT, J., 1983, The Chinese background to Singapore English, *New Papers on Chinese Language Use*, 18, 105–17.

PLATT, J and WEBER, H., 1980, *English in Singapore and Malaysia: Status, Features, Functions*. Kuala Lumpur: Oxford University Press.

PRINCE, E., 1981, Toward a taxonomy of given-new information. In P. COLE (ed.), *Radical Pragmatics*. New York: Academic Press, pp. 199–255.

QUIRK, R., GREENBAUM, S., LEECH, G. and SVARTVIK, J., 1985 *A Comprehensive Grammar of the English Language*. London: Longman.

RINEHART, T., 1976, *The Syntactic Domain of Anaphora*. Ph.D. dissertation, Massachusetts Institute of Technology.

RITCHIE, W., 1986, Second language acquisition research and the study of non-native varieties of English: some issues in common, *World Englishes*, 5, 15–30.

SCHUMANN, J., 1984, Non-syntactic speech in Spanish–English basilang. In R. ANDERSEN (ed.), *Second Languages: a Cross-linguistic Perspective*. Rowley, MA: Newbury House, pp. 355–74.

SLOBIN, D., 1973, Cognitive prerequisites for the development of grammar. In C. FERGUSON & D. SLOBIN (eds), *Studies in Child Language Development*. New York: Holt, Rinehart & Winston, pp. 175–208.

——, 1977, Language change in childhood and history. In J. MACNAMARA (ed.), *Language Thought and Language Learning*. New York: Academic Press, pp. 185–214.

TOMLIN, R., 1984, The treatment of foreground and background information in the on-line descriptive discourse of second language learners, *Studies in Second Language Acquisition*, 6(2), 115–42.

WHITE, L., 1985, The 'pro-drop' parameter in adult second language acquisition, *Language Learning*, 35, 47–61.

WILLIAMS, J., 1987, Non-native varieties of English: A special case of language acquisition. *English World-Wide*, 8, pp. 161–200.

——, (in press), Variation and convergence in non-native institutionalized Englishes. In M. EISENSTEIN (ed.) *Variation in Second Language Acquisition*. New York: Plenum Press.

ZOBL, H., 1984, Uniformity and source-language variation across developmental continua. In W. RUTHERFORD (ed.), *Language Universals and Second Language Acquisition*. Amsterdam: John Benjamins, pp. 185–218.

10   Framing uncomfortable moments in crosscultural gatekeeping interviews

SUSAN FIKSDAL
Evergreen State College, Olympia.

Introduction

In this chapter drawn from a larger study[1], I build on work begun by Erickson & Shultz (1982) on uncomfortable moments in gatekeeping interviews between native speakers of English. Uncomfortable moments are a kind of interactional stumbling when one or both participants look and sound clumsy. In their study, Erickson & Shultz analysed filmed interviews between advisers and students at a community college. Since the advisers had the double role of guiding and monitoring the students' progress, Erickson & Shultz termed their role a 'gatekeeping' one. They note that more uncomfortable moments occur when speakers from different ethnic backgrounds talk together because they attend to different listening and speaking behaviours. However, these moments appear less disruptive to the interview when the speakers share some co-membership—that is, share an interest or some aspect of their backgrounds.

In the study under discussion here, I contrast native speaker–native speaker (NS–NS) discourse with native speaker–non-native speaker (NS–NNS) discourse in order to determine whether the variation in uncomfortable moments is due to ethnicity alone or to other factors. My approach is a descriptive one: I use the concept of frames and contextualisation cues (Bateson, 1972; Gumperz & Tannen, 1979; Erickson & Shultz, 1982) to discover how speakers cue the beginning and end of the uncomfortable moment. Therefore, I examine both verbal and nonverbal cues that have been noted in previous studies such as false starts, pauses, breathy noises, postural changes, gestures and smiles (Gumperz, 1982) for both NSs and NNSs.

Just as important as these cues, research on spoken discourse has revealed the role of tempo[2] to be a fundamental regulator of NS–NS discourse (Erickson & Shultz, 1982; Scollon, 1982; Buder, 1985), and NS–NNS discourse (Fiksdal, 1986). In their ground-breaking study, Erickson & Shultz show that one important measure of smooth flowing discourse is a regular tempo maintained by both speakers. Disruptions in the tempo seem to correspond to disruptions in the discourse; for example, arhythmia (disruption in the regular tempo) often occurs at uncomfortable moments. These moments of arhythmia do not last long, and speakers resume their previous, regular tempo afterwards. Tempo, then, may provide one measure of how speakers frame these moments: resumption of the previous tempo would signal an end to the uncomfortable moment.

In the gatekeeping interviews under investigation in the present chapter, two experienced NS advisers from the US interviewed two groups of foreign students: six native speakers of English from Canada, England, Ireland and Zimbabwe[3]; and nine non-native speakers of English from Taiwan. Gatekeeping interviews, as I mentioned above, involve an interviewer who is seeking to both guide and monitor the interviewee through an institution. This type of interview is prevalent in our society in corporations, health care institutions, and schools. In this case, the foreign student adviser is guiding foreign students through the rules and regulations of the Immigration and Naturalization Service. The adviser must also monitor the students' progress. If their progress is satisfactory, the adviser can grant students certain types of visa status.

Naturally occurring interviews were videotaped in the foreign student advisers' offices after the adviser had asked the student's permission. As the investigator, I remained in the office with the equipment, but the advisers and students reported being unaware of my presence except at the beginning and end of some interviews. I believe that for the most part I was able to counteract the 'observer's paradox'.[4] First, the students in the present study had important questions and goals for their interviews which they had decided upon in advance. Second, the advisers had become accustomed to my presence in their offices as I observed over 20 interviews and videotaped an additional 43. In support of the views expressed by the students and advisers in this study, Duncan & Fiske (1977) point out that it is possible to overestimate the intrusiveness of recording devices in natural settings.

Purpose

One of the purposes of this chapter is to describe how speakers frame uncomfortable moments in real time: tempo governs the verbal and nonverbal moves speakers make as seconds tick by. Another purpose is to determine the intensity of these uncomfortable moments by noting when repair appears necessary. These two approaches to the discourse correspond to a time-based model of conversation. In Fiksdal (in press), I show that NSs seem to rely on two systems of time to regulate or order conversation: the turn-taking system and the rapport system. These two systems are in turn based on two aspects of time captured by the Greek words for time: *chronos*, or real clock time, and *kairos* or the 'right time'. The turn-taking system relies on time as it passes moment by moment, or *chronos*. Speakers show their reliance on this aspect of time in their shared use of a regular tempo. The rapport system relies on speakers' understanding of when to introduce new topics or repair an uncomfortable moment—*kairos*. This sense of time is probably culturally based.

I assumed two factors would play a role in how speakers framed uncomfortable moments: first language background, and the activity or 'who was doing what'. I will discuss each of these factors in some detail before turning to the results of this study. I should underscore at this point, however, the complexity of the behaviour, and the difficulty of attributing factors as explanation.

I hypothesised that NS students would use different means to frame uncomfortable moments than NNSs. I based this hypothesis on Erickson & Shultz's (1982) findings: more uncomfortable moments occurred if the counsellor and student were ethnically dissimilar. Their work investigated NSs, but their findings suggest that variation in listening and speaking behaviour is at least partly due to ethnic background. Briefly, they found white listeners gaze at the speaker, giving accented nods at moments created by the speakers. On the other hand, black listeners do not gaze at the speaker, and give unaccented nods. These differences in listening style seem to be due to different ethnic backgrounds.

The second variable relates to the adviser's or student's activity under discussion. In this case, the most relevant activities revolved around the exchange of information and advice, and the speaker's role. (Advisers and students engaged in other activities such as asking for and giving reassurance, but uncomfortable moments did not seem to arise then.) Advisers gave information and advice; students asked for and gave information, and they accepted or rejected advice.

Most of the time advisers gave clear, relevant information and advice, but at times they made mistakes. If the student questioned information, an uncomfortable moment usually occurred. If the student did not take the advisers' advice about an important issue or showed in some way that s/he did not understand it, the uncomfortable moment which resulted seemed more intense than if the adviser were giving information. In addition, the topic played a role. If the advice had to do with a minor point such as finding an appropriate document, the uncomfortable moment seemed to have fewer cues acting to frame the moment. Alternatively, if the advice had to do with a major issue such as permanent residency, speakers seemed to use more cues to frame the moment. Thus, the intensity of the uncomfortable moment can be gauged by the number and extent of contextualisation cues.

Defining the uncomfortable moment

Erickson & Shultz began the work on uncomfortable moments which I investigate here. To discover what constituted an uncomfortable moment, they used independent raters to identify moments in the filmed discourse which appeared uncomfortable. They also asked the participants in their study to identify these moments in playback sessions. The participants selected the same moments as the raters. What intrigued Erickson & Shultz was that while their raters agreed in their assessment of uncomfortableness, they sometimes disagreed on when the uncomfortable moment began and ended. Apparently relying only on verbal interaction, such as misunderstandings and clumsy replies, was not sufficient to define the moment precisely. They decided to ask the raters to pay close attention to kinesic symmetry. To do this they asked the raters to note only when one person in the interview seemed to be making more and sharper movements than the other person. They found postural movement often accompanied uncomfortable moments, as did arhythmia.

I used a particular approach to define uncomfortable moments. First, I asked students and advisers to participate in a playback session. In order not to influence the students' and advisers' opinions, I asked them to comment whenever they wished. I stopped the tape at these moments and recorded their comments. Because these voluntary comments did not always address the moments I was interested in, I also stopped the tape at postural shifts and moments which seemed arhythmic and asked the subjects if they had any comments. I found that NSs volunteered information readily. NNS subjects, on the other hand, usually took the opportunity to gather more information about Immigration and Naturalization Service regulations and only occasionally talked about the moment I had signalled. My approach thus relied on my own criteria for uncomfortable moments as well as the comments by students and advisers. In addition, I found another cue used by NSs which contributes to this work on the uncomfortable moment: verbal frames or metastatements.

Uncomfortable moments may occur during the sorts of activities which are discussed in Erickson & Shultz (1982) and Fiksdal (in press): hyperexplanations and telling bad news. The hyperexplanation is an explanation which begins explaining the illustration or example given in an explanation. Fiksdal (1986) found that advisers accelerate the tempo at the point of hyperexplanation. Not all hyperexplanations constitute uncomfortable moments, but if the point being made is a major one, then the moment is often uncomfortable. (Example 1, below, shows a hyperexplanation which is also an uncomfortable moment.) Telling bad news can be an uncomfortable moment, but again, it depends on the task. In these interviews, if the student's telling of this bad news was indirect, it seemed to make the adviser uncomfortable. (Example 5, below, illustrates how a NNS corrected the adviser.) If the adviser told bad news, the effect seemed to be mitigated by the importance of the information to the student.

Findings and discussion

Speakers seemed to frame uncomfortable moments with great variation, yet NSs appear to use a different system to repair these moments than do NNSs. NSs seem to frame the moment with nonverbal cues, then usually move to repair it verbally by *seeking agreement*. This agreement usually includes a metastatement of some sort 'what I'm trying to do is ...' by the adviser, and/or a clarifying statement by the student framed by 'so ...'. Importantly, the adviser and student maintain good eye contact in these moments and signal the positive or negative aspect of their statements to their listener with repeated head nods or shakes. The listener usually mirrored these head movements in his/her next turn. This mirroring could be an indication of the kinesic symmetry mentioned in the Erickson & Shultz study.

In the present study, some sort of arhythmia seemed to be present in each of the 17 uncomfortable moments I found. In the surrounding talk the tempo remains steady. During an uncomfortable moment, however, the student or adviser may tug at the tempo, suspending it for a brief period or changing it temporarily in a hyperexplanation. A tempo tug ranges from a few tenths of a second to just over a second. A tempo change can last longer, ten to fifteen seconds, but the speakers return to the established tempo in these interviews.

Postural shifts occurred with most native speakers at moments that were uncomfortable to them. Native speakers seemed to make that postural shift at the moment of the discomfort. NNSs, however, did not always make a postural shift during an uncomfortable moment. If a NNS did make a shift, it also seemed to occur at the point of discomfort rather than the point of repair.

One complicating factor to this generalised view of how NSs and NNSs frame uncomfortable moments is that NSs seem to move towards verbally seeking agreement only if the issue is important to them. I will give two contrasting examples of NS–NS discourse to illustrate this point.

In the first example the student shows a measure of discomfort through postural shifts. The adviser hyperexplains, which distorts the tempo for about eight seconds. Neither moves to verbally repair the moment, however.

I use the following conventions for transcripts: S is student, A is adviser, R is researcher; double parentheses indicate nonverbal actions and lengths of pauses. They fall next to or below the speaker's verbal utterance. Brackets show overlapped verbal or nonverbal activity.

Example 1:   NS–NS

1. **S:**   = right so what do I do ... to process this 18 month?
2. **A:**   you need to bring me
3. **S:**   = oh right ((smiles))
4. **A:**   uh ... evidence that you *fin*ished in April
5. **S:**   which would be ((quietly))
► 6. **A:**   a copy of the di—a xerox copy of the diploma or a
7. **S:**   {((shifts))
8. **A:**   letter from the department
9. **S:**   yeah
   ((nods))
10. **A:**   uh uh did you—did you graduate from Rackham?
11. **S:**   yes
   ((nods))
► 12. **A:**   you may have already received the ((1.24)) end of
13.   the term ⌠academic grade report?
► 14. **S:**   ⌡yes ((shifts position))
15. **A:**   and if you received your degree in April that
   ((tempo quickens))

16.   probably is noted on that academic grade report
17. S: OK
           ((nods))
18. A: and a simple xerox copy of that will be sufficient
                                                ((tempo slows))

Comments during playback

At line 1:
S: I was suddenly aware that I'd already asked him that—he already told
    me and now I'm asking him again and that really is me being
    scatterbrained.
A: ((laugh))
R: so what did you think about that?
A: uh 'we just went through that fella, well here we go again' ((laugh))

At line 12:
S: I hadn't received that and that was really kind of irrelevant information
    .. and the way to get through it was not to ask questions.

In this example the student is embarrassed by his question in line 1, but
he needs the information. During the explanation in line 6 the student
makes a postural shift and does not give a listening response (usually 'uh
huh' accompanied by a nod) after the word 'diploma'. In line 10 the adviser
begins a side sequence which bothers the student; in fact, he gives an
affirmative answer which isn't actually true and shifts his posture in line 14
(see comments on line 12). The adviser quickens the tempo in line 15, at the
point of hyperexplanation. The student does not repair this uncomfortable
moment with a clarifying statement possibly because the point is a minor
one and he wants to 'get through'.

In the second example of NS–NS discourse, both adviser and student
make use of verbal metastatement to repair the moment.

Example 2: NS–NS

1. A: OK OK so it would be .. 9,236 tuition …
► 2.   what do you figure your living uh ... you're living
           ((tempo quickens))
3. S: what ((frowns))
4. A: in in the states 8 or 9 months out of the twelve?
5. S: = uh huh

▶   6. A: ((tempo slows)) or I'm just trying to figure out
    7.   what approximately to put down for figure
    8.   ⎧ I'm (   )
    9. S: ⎨ what what
▶ 10.   = what is it that you're looking to put down?

Comments during playback

R: just then you looked at her—do you remember anything?
S: well no, those are the numbers but I wasn't really sure what—she was
    what the figure *was* that she was looking to find I wasn't sure what she
    was driving at I didn't understand until the end.
A: yeah what I was trying to do was separate tuition (   ) but I didn't
    want it permanently separated. I—I yeah what was going on in my
    head—I was trying to sort out something and she was looking at the
    same thing

This uncomfortable moment was characterised by tempo changes at
lines 2 and 6. The student was standing, bending over the form on the
adviser's desk. No postural movement occurred, possibly because of the
positions the student and adviser had assumed. Note, however, that
arhythmia is present and that both participants use metastatements to
clarify the situation: the adviser in line 6, 'I'm just trying to figure out', and
the student in line 10, 'what is it that you're looking to put down?' The
comments during the playback session reflect the uncertainty both student
and adviser experienced.

Thus far in this discussion, I have shown the presence of arhythmia in
uncomfortable moments and suggested that the absence of a verbal repair
may be due to the relative unimportance of a point under discussion. I have
also noted an instance (example 2) where no postural movement occurred
and suggested that the positions of adviser and student may affect postural
movement.

Now consider a series of examples where uncomfortable moments
occur for non-native speakers. Instead of the explicit verbal metastatement
or clarification we saw in example 2, these students use a strategy of delay or
omission.

In the following example the student notices a contradiction in the
adviser's explanation but doesn't call it to the adviser's attention. For this
reason, only the student feels uncomfortable.

Example 3: NS–NNS

```
    1. A:  but you know that—in Michigan it's very difficult
                                            ((tempo tug))
►   2.     it's easy to go from F-1 to H-1 to permanent
    3.     residency
    4. S:  ((nods))
    5. A:  it's easy to go from F-1 to permanent residency
    6. S:  ((nods))
    7. A:  it's just very hard if you have to go from F-1
           ⎰  practical training to H-1
    8. S:  ⎱  ((nods during this turn))
    9. S:  ((2.07 sec)) so how about just go this way F-1 to
   10.     H-1
   11. A:  uh hum
           ((nods))
   12. S:  and then to
►  13. A:  = but ⎰H-1 isn't that simple if
   14. S:        ⎱yeah
   15. A:  ⎰if he's—all right
►  16. S:  ⎱H-1 is not that simple ((sotto voce, laughs))
```

Comments during playback

S: here she contradicts herself. I am surprised because H-1 is not supposed to be so hard

In this uncomfortable moment, the adviser contradicts her first statement in line 2 'it's easy to go from F-1 to H-1 to permanent residency' by her statement in line 13 'but H-1 isn't that simple'. The student notes the contradiction in line 16, but in *'sotto voce'* and overlapping the adviser's explanation (which begins with 'all right'). The student does not ask for a clarification of the adviser's explanation as the native speaker did in example 2. We could take the position, as we did in example 1, that the task did not warrant clarification—the student did not view the point as important. But in this case the student notes a contradiction in the information just given as well as a contradiction in what she has heard from other Taiwanese students. (See comments.) She thus appears to have omitted the verbal clarification native speakers seem to use in these circumstances.

In the next example the NNS student does choose to clarify the contradiction he hears, but he *delays* this clarification. Because the clarification is delayed, the example is in two parts—the first illustrates the contradiction with no clarification, an uncomfortable moment for the student; the second illustrates the delayed clarification, an uncomfortable moment for both the adviser and the student.

Example 4: NS–NNS

   1. **A:** ((3.9 sec))all right you can—you can ap*ply* to
                ((tempo slows in this turn))
   2.   ex*tend* this *any* time now
   3. **S:** = any time now
             ((nods))
   4. **A:** right. you can do it as early as thirty or I'm sorry
             ((tempo resumes))
   5.   *six*ty days before it expires
► 6. **S:** sixty days before ((raises eyebrows))
             ((nods))
   7. **A:** sixty. yeah. two months ⌈so you can do it any time
   8. **S:**   ⌊oh
   9. **A:** now and it'll probably *take* about a month.
 10. **S:** oh
             ((nods))

In line 6 the student is surprised to find out that he should apply 60 days before the expiration date because in line 2 the adviser says he can apply for his extension 'now'. 'Now', however, is 90 days before the expiration date. The student knows that he must wait a month, yet he says nothing at this point. The adviser goes on to explain the procedure for the application (not noted here). At the end of the explanation the student clarifies the point noted above:

Example 5: NS–NNS

   1. **S:** so I just ⌈uh start uh uh to—to put this since uh at
   2. **A:**   ⌊((nods))
   3. **S:** uh end of uh *March* right?
   4. **A:** uh hum you could even—let's see yeah. right.
          ((nods))   ((nods twice))
   5. **S:** it's ⌈uh early now
   6. **A:**   ⌊yeah   = yeah really uh ((5.11 sec))

```
     7.    well let's see March April nooo you can do it
     8.    any time after .. that's right March 31st right yeah
                    ((nods))                    ((nods))
►    9.    any time tha—after the first week in April. ⎧ sure
           ((leans back))                            ⎨ ((nods))
    10. S:                                           ⎩ OK
                                                      ((nods))
►   11. A: you can wait as long as two weeks before it expires.
           ((tugs at tempo))
    12.    they say anytime from sixty days before to fifteen
    13.    days before
    14. S: OK
           ((nods))
```

In this example the student clarifies the information he needs about when to begin the process in lines 1, 3, and 5. The point of the interview is when and how to apply for practical training, so this discussion forms an essential part of that explanation. He notes 'I want to make sure' in the playback session. But he didn't need the repetition in line 12 and it bothered him. This example shows a strategy of *delay* rather than the strategy of *immediate clarification* that the native speakers used in example 2. During the playback session the adviser noted only that he corrected her—she did not mention feeling uncomfortable. On the other hand, her false starts, postural shift in line 9, and arhythmia in line 11 show a measure of discomfort.

Here, then, we have a case of no verbal metastatement even though the NS adviser appears uncomfortable. The activity is serious because the student has *corrected* the adviser. We have, then, two examples where no verbal metastatement or clarification occurs for the NS: in example 1 the student wants to 'get through' the explanation; in the above example, the adviser stands corrected. In the first case the point is minor and the speaker affected is a student; in the second case the point is major and the speaker affected is the adviser.

The consequences of another delayed clarification seem more serious in another interview because the adviser is not simply giving information about when to file some forms; instead he is *advising* the student about how to solve a problem. When the student does not accept that advice or state what he intends to do, the adviser offers to do some paperwork for him. In the first part of this example, the student makes a decision about what to do but doesn't tell the adviser. (See reactions by both participants.)

Example 6:   NS–NNS

1. **A:** if you know that you can *get* your passport renewed
2. within uh uh let's say 3 or 4 weeks it ⌈might be to
3. **S:**   ⌊((nods))
4. **A:** your advantage to go ahead and do that *first* rather
5. ⌈than run the risk that they will delay granting the
6. **S:** ⌊((nods))
7. **A:** permit
8. **S:** ((nods))
9. **A:** by sending it back later
10. **S:** ((nods))
11. **A:** cause if we send it in ⌈now we won't know whether
► 12. **S:**   ⌊((leans back))
13. **A:** they're going to uh ((1.64 sec)) to reject it and
14. send it back
15. **S:** ((nods))
16. **A:** they *could* do either either one
► 17. **S:** uh huh
 ((nods))

Comments during playback

R: there [line 12] you leaned back. were you concerned there? do you remember at this point?

S: uh I'd say yeah I understand the—the interviewer keep on talking and I sit there and relax and listen you know I think I'm—I know what I'm going to do next uh so—but that's my *own* feeling. I feel that I—at this point I know what I have to do that—to (   ) I thought that I go and mail my passport to get it renewed in so but M will keep on talking about different things. I will listen—

R: did you notice that he leaned back

A: no the feeling that I'm getting now is that at that point it would not have affected me or meant anything to me. my reaction is that uh—seeing it there now he knows that—he knows he no longer has to read anything in that book so why—why be in that position

In this example, the student uses line 17 for a listener response ('uh huh') instead of a speaking turn. In other words, he does not accept or reject the adviser's plan. The adviser does not suspect that the student has made a decision (see comments). Because the process of discovering what the student has decided is lengthy, I paraphrase the events until the uncomfortable moment.

The adviser next suggests the second option (not shown here): 'well we can go ahead and send it in if you like'. This suggestion receives a listening response ('uh huh') rather than an answer. The adviser paraphrases the suggestion later: 'w-want to try that?' When the student does not respond, he says 'or do you want to hold it in for a few days until you find out?' After a side sequence initiated by the student, the adviser again suggests, 'why don't we go ahead and send it in'. During the viewing session the adviser volunteers a statement showing his reasoning during this process of making suggestions:

Comments during playback

A: now at this point see—although earlier in the interview I was kind of saying well you can send it in or you can hold it now I'm saying 'why don't we send it in' I've identified the different alternatives, in talking with him I've—I guess for some reason I've begun to feel that he would prefer it—that he would feel more comfortable if we did send it in I don't think I'm making that suggestion based on any conviction of my own that it's better from the standpoint of succeeding ... I think I'm just responding to ... the feelings that I'm getting as to what *he* would feel more comfortable with ...

The adviser decides that the student is having trouble coming to a decision; the student, having made his own decision, is debating when and how to say so.

The following example occurs after the student again introduces a side sequence and the adviser again suggests: 'well why don't we send it in'. When he again hears only a listening response, the adviser offers to do extra paperwork for the student. The student chooses this moment to explain what he would like to do:

Example 7: NS–NNS

1. **S:**   ((2.8 sec)) well I think—let me call the—the well
2.   it's the consulate in Chicago
3. **A:**   is that where you deal with them ⸨now for your
4. **S:**   ⸨yeah
5. **A:**   OK

6. **S:**   if they say that I can renew the passport I just
7.   mail it today
8. **A:**   all right
9. **S:**   and I—then I mail them the .. ten bucks for the Ex-
10. **S:**   ⎧Federal Express
11. **A:**   ⎩OK   = all right
12. **S:**   and I can get it back on Wednesday
13. **A:**   OK
            ((nods))
14. **S:**   and submit it on Wednesday
▶ 15. **A:**   ((1.91 sec)) ((louder)) let me look over this over
            ((leans forward))

Comments during playback

S: I think he is a little disappointed I think

R: because you didn't take his suggestion?

S: yeah my—my ways was not good. I don't know how the Americans respond when M say something that's opposite to your idea they will say 'no no no I will do what I—what I want' ... and he just pulled back a little bit, see after he finished he say—he said a lot of things and then he gave me the passport 'let me go ahead'

R: oh you mean he didn't say 'fine' or 'good'

S: yeah now I think that's uh a change over—you know he stopped doing one thing and started another

R: OK anything there that you wanna talk about

A: I guess the only thing that ... that I remember about it is his—his language seemed to be a little weak. but I guess looking back at it I was—I was relieved that he had—looking at him at first I had felt that maybe he's not going to uh .. to follow everything you know and uh—I'm *sure* I felt that his looks were deceiving that he's *quiet* but he did understand what it was about and that happens frequently.

In this example the student offers a simpler approach to the problem than the adviser did, but because he chooses to delay clarifying it for the adviser, he creates an uncomfortable moment for himself and the adviser when he does. The comments of the two participants during the playback session are revelatory: the student senses that he chose the wrong way to explain what he wanted to do. The adviser speaks only of being surprised, but he changes the topic using a louder tone, quicker tempo, and makes a large postural shift at line 15. In example 5, where the student corrects the adviser in a delayed clarification, the adviser does not repair the uncomfortable moment with a metastatement as is the norm. In addition, note that while both the student and the adviser appear to experience an uncomfortable moment, only the adviser shows a postural shift.

The consequences of an uncomfortable moment appear to be more serious to the adviser if the student recognises faulty advice or information and points it out to the adviser. In the above example, when the student presents his solution to the problem, it is obviously much simpler than the adviser's. Rather than acknowledge that fact with a metastatement, however, the adviser pushes ahead to a new activity ('let me look over this over'). In example 5 the student points out to the other adviser that her information is not quite correct. In that case, the adviser gives additional information which is not needed rather than acknowledge the error. In both cases, however, evidence of an uncomfortable moment is clear: postural shifts, arhythmia, and indication of a problem by the student. The adviser, however, does not 'recognise' the moment as uncomfortable by giving it a verbal frame.

Kairos, the Greek term for the 'right time', becomes important in this discussion of uncomfortable moments because it appears that there is a 'right' time and 'poor' time for making the clarifications necessary for repair of such moments for native speakers of English. Native speakers usually begin a repair in their first turn after an action disturbs or mystifies them. This first turn may be the 'right time' to begin repair for NSs. If a student waits to clarify until later, the effect on the interview seems to become more serious. The Taiwanese students in this study use a different repair system, one which seems to disrupt the NSs sense of appropriate timing.

Conclusion

This discussion underscores the necessity of eliciting participants' reactions during playback sessions, and analysing the interviews for both verbal and nonverbal contextualisation cues. Not all cues appear in all uncomfortable moments, and not all uncomfortable moments are identified as such by the participants.

The fact that NSs did not always make a postural shift during uncomfortable moments is inconsistent with findings by previous researchers (Scheflen, 1973; Erickson & Shultz, 1982). It is important to note that NSs made some sort of gesture during uncomfortable moments, although that gesture may not have changed the proxemics of the subjects. It may be that there are degrees of discomfort, and only higher degrees produce postural change. Another explanation comes from comments by one of the Canadian students during the playback of his interview (not discussed here). This student reported feeling uncomfortably close to the adviser during the interview because of the placement of chairs in the office. The student experienced a highly uncomfortable moment in the interview but, instead of a postural shift, he brought his hand to his tie.

Metastatements framed most NS uncomfortable moments: NS students did not use metastatements if the point was minor, while NS advisers did not use metastatements if the point was major. Tempo also plays an important role in uncomfortable moments. It appears that advisers tug at the tempo during an explanation or uncomfortable moment, or change the tempo for a turn to mark hyperexplanation. The fact that it is the advisers who do this and not the students may have to do with the adviser's rights and obligations during the interview. It is clearly the adviser who directs the activities—by explaining or advising.

Because of this directing role, the consequences of an uncomfortable moment may be more serious to an adviser or to a student at certain points in the interview. An adviser, for example, gives advice routinely in these interviews, but advice is often hyperexplained, thus taking up time for both participants. If an uncomfortable moment occurs after an advice hyperexplanation, it seems to have more impact on the interview as a whole than if it occurs in other places, whether the interview is NS–NS or NS–NNS. It may be that the investment of time and the act of offering advice together create a more sensitive environment for both student and adviser. Giving advice, it should be noted, is the adviser's primary responsibility, and it is offered rather than solicited. The student doesn't want to reject the suggestions offered by the adviser, but it is sometimes necessary to do that if immediate action is required. And the adviser expects that his or her advice will be recognised as the result of many years of experience in the position of adviser.

The NNSs were all students in this study, but unlike the NS students, they either delayed or omitted any verbal repair of an uncomfortable moment. In the delayed repair, they used an implicit rather than explicit statement.

This delayed, implicit clarification may be due to the considerations of face that Chinese have. They cannot risk forcing the adviser to lose face by indicating that s/he has not provided the best way of approaching a problem or has given apparently contradictory information. Hu (1944) explains that to expose another person's mistake or to even allude to it publicly constitutes losing that person's face ('mien-tzu'). In American society, criticising another individual's behaviour does not carry the strong association that it seems to carry with the Chinese.

Young (1982) suggests another explanation based on the grammatical structure of Chinese. Young extends the notion of topic/comment structure evident in the grammar of Chinese to the structure of discourse. In her study of Chinese businessmen reporting to their American counterparts, Young finds a discourse strategy of delaying the request, the major point and new information, in order to build up reasons. The request was often introduced indirectly (to American ears) by 'so'.

This approach to uncomfortable moments reveals the complexity of the frame itself and of the moments. Various cues mark these moments, and the moments themselves seem to vary in seriousness. Videotaping interviews and then using playback sessions as an indicator of these moments is essential to gauge this seriousness, as is work on how verbal and nonverbal cues cluster to frame them.

Notes to Chapter 10

1. The study was conducted at the University of Michigan, Ann Arbor in 1984.
2. These researchers use the term 'rhythm' but they are referring to the underlying beat.
3. The Zimbabwian speaker is white and speaks a dialect of British English.
4. Labov (1972) suggested that linguists wish to gather data from naturally occurring speech, but recording devices and the researcher's presence probably preclude the possibility of observing natural speech.

References

BATESON, G., 1972, *Steps Toward an Ecology of Mind*. New York: Ballantine Books.
BUDER, E. H. Jr, 1985, *Coherence of Speech Rhythms in Conversations: Auto-correlation Analysis of Fundamental Voice Frequency*. M.A. Thesis, University of Alberta.
DUNCAN, S. and FISKE, D. W., 1977, *Face to Face Interaction: Research, Methods, and Theory*. Hillsdale, N.J.: L. Erlbaum Associates.
ERICKSON, F. and SHULTZ, J., 1982, *The Counselor as Gatekeeper: Social Interaction in Interviews*. New York: Academic Press.

FIKSDAL, S., 1986, The right time and pace: a microanalysis of cross-cultural gatekeeping interviews, *Dissertation Abstracts International*, 47, 2563 A. Univ. Microfilms No. DA8621279.

——, (in press), *The Right Time and Pace: A Microanalysis of Gatekeeping Interviews*. Newark, N.J.: Ablex.

GUMPERZ, J., 1982, *Discourse Strategies*. Cambridge: Cambridge University Press.

GUMPERZ, J. and TANNEN, D., 1979, Individual and social differences in language use. In C. FILLMORE, D. KEMPER & W.-S. W. WANG (eds), *Individual Differences in Language Ability and Language Behavior*. New York: Academic Press.

HU, HSIEN CHIN, 1944, The Chinese concepts of 'face', *American Anthropology*, 46, 45–64.

LABOV, W., 1972, *Sociolinguistic Patterns*. Philadelphia: University of Pennsylvania Press.

SCHEFLEN, A., 1973, *Communicational Structure: Analysis of a Psychotherapy Transaction*. Bloomington, IN: Indiana University Press.

SCOLLON, R., 1982, The rhythmic organization of ordinary talk. In D. TANNEN (ed.), *Analyzing Discourse: Text and Talk*. Georgetown University Round Table on Language and Linguistics 1981. Washington, D.C.: Georgetown University Press.

YOUNG, L. W.-L., 1982, Inscrutability revisited. In J. GUMPERZ (ed.), *Language and Social Identity*. Cambridge: Cambridge University Press.

Section Five:
Power and Solidarity

11 Expertise and authority in native–non-native conversations: The need for a variable account

MILES D. WOKEN
Sangamon State University
JOHN SWALES
University of Michigan

Introduction

Conversations between native speakers and non-native speakers of a language are presumably almost as old as human speech itself, and have been richly caricatured for centuries in literary texts. However, it is only in the last few years that NS–NNS conversations have come under close scholarly scrutiny. It is our broad perception that in many such studies, SLA researchers have tended to take for their data samples of NS–NNS conversations in which (1) the NNS subjects were students of English in various kinds of pre-college ESL programmes, often with low proficiency (e.g. Abunahleh *et al.*, 1982; Day *et al.*, 1984; Fraser *et al.*, 1980; Gaskill, 1980; Gass & Varonis, 1984; Schwartz, 1980; Tarone, 1985; Varonis & Gass, 1985a), or (2) at least some of the NS subjects were ESL instructors or graduate students in applied linguistics programmes or their variants (e.g. Gaies, 1979; Varonis & Gass, 1982), or (3) both of the above participant characteristics applied (Hodne, 1985; Long, 1981; Pica, 1988, Sato, 1982).

While such 'economy' is understandable, there are, we suggest, a number of features about those settings that give rise to a certain partiality in the reported accounts of interactions. Thus, the natives in studies of types 2 and 3 have not only been experts *in* the language (as fluent and accurate speakers), but also, because of their training and experience, practised experts *on* the language. Further, these native speakers, as instructors and graduate students, have often brought to the experimental encounter a higher institutional status than that of the non-native participants.

It is, therefore, not surprising to find in this literature that the native speakers tend to take the lead in negotiating meaning, in nominating and terminating topics, in setting repairs in motion, and in offering assistance with syntax, lexis and pronunciation (Abunahleh *et al.*, 1982; Arthur *et al.*, 1980; Gass & Varonis, 1985; Pica, 1988).

Additionally, content expertise or knowledge of the topic under discussion (the topic-field) has been typically assumed to be either more or less equally distributed, or to be of minor importance (some exceptions being Gaies, 1982; Gass & Varonis, 1985; Selinker & Douglas, 1985; and Zuengler, in press). Thus, the tacit assumption in most studies has been that none of the participants in the conversations has any more expertise in the topics covered than the others do.

However, in settings where communication is functionally rather than socially directed, where the non-natives are placed in a position of authority by virtue of their possessing a greater field expertise, and where the natives are not experienced language teachers, one might expect to find a somewhat different configuration of native and non-native roles. Gaies (1982) and Gass & Varonis (1985), in fact, suggest that shared knowledge and the non-native's language proficiency level interact in creating expectations about the non-native's ability to participate in carrying some of the conversational load. Zuengler (in press) reports an earlier study in which non-natives appeared to take control of conversations when they and their native partners were simply *led to believe* the non-natives had greater knowledge of the 'discourse domain' (Selinker & Douglas, 1985).

Given the potential significance of the findings reported in the last paragraph, we set out to investigate NS–NNS conversations that had the following characteristics: (a) the non-native speakers were experienced (if flawed) users of English, (b) they had greater content-expertise, (c) they were ascribed higher authority by virtue of their instructor role, and (d) the conversations were goal-directed. Our hypothesis was that such conversations would turn out to have rather different patterns of interaction between natives and non-natives from those generally reported in the literature. We further believed that our experimental characteristics were not in fact bizarre or artificial, but occurred quite frequently in contemporary work settings; for example, in international business ventures, in teaching by non-native speakers in universities and elsewhere, and in aid-related activities throughout much of the developing world.

Method

Six female participants (three native English speakers, two native speakers of Mandarin Chinese, and one native speaker of Thai) were paired off into three dyads, each consisting of one native and one non-native speaker of English. The three non-natives were in their last semester before graduation with Master's degrees in computer science. At the time of the recordings, all had been in the United States between one and a half and two years, and during all that time they had been pursuing their degrees at Sangamon State University. They were fluent in English, but as the examples in this chapter show, their speech was sometimes grammatically inaccurate. Their pronunciation was distinctly non-native. All the non-natives had extensive experience on IBM Personal Computers with a word processing package called Volkswriter Deluxe, although none had ever instructed anyone else in the use of it. Each of them was asked to instruct a native speaker in learning how to use the Volkswriter Deluxe word processing program.

Two of the native speakers of English were undergraduates, and one was a graduate student. One of the undergraduates was a junior just beginning her major in computer science, and the other was a senior majoring in legal studies. The graduate student was majoring in communication. None of the three had ever used Volkswriter Deluxe before although all had expressed interest at one time or another in learning word processing in order to make writing their papers easier. One (the computer science student) had used a PC to write simple programs for her classes, but the other two had never used a PC at all. The dyads were composed solely on the basis of when the participants could conveniently meet; the members of each dyad had not previously met each other.

Each of the three sessions was videotaped, and transcripts made, labelled according to the first initials of the two participants. The transcripts of the two Mandarin speakers are labelled JC and ST, and that of the Thai is labelled PM. Two of the sessions took about 40 minutes, and one lasted about 30 minutes. Taken together, then, the transcripts represent nearly two hours of talk.

All the participants were informed at the time their help was requested that the sessions would be recorded. The recordings were made in an office where the participants would be undisturbed. An IBM Personal Computer was set up in the office, and a copy of the Volkswriter Deluxe program disk was made available along with a storage disk. The participants were also supplied with a brief list of the more commonly used Volkswriter functions.

The members of each dyad were introduced, shown the machinery set-up, and each native was told that the non-native, 'who knows Volkswriter very well', would give her an introduction to its use. They were then left alone.

In analysing the data it was important for us to keep in mind Long's (1983:183) observation that many devices such as clarification requests and confirmation checks are used in all kinds of conversations, including native–native, native–non-native, and non-native–non-native, and that the difference between them is one of quantity and not simply quality. Therefore, despite the difficulty of identifying the functional role of all utterances, we have none the less supplied the number of occurrences of various categorised phenomena throughout the chapter.

Analysis of the data

In reviewing the three sessions, it became obvious that most of what was going on was explanation, almost all of it by the non-native speaking experts. Explanations consisted of descriptions of how to begin, what functions the various keys performed, and so on (i.e. they were matters of procedure). Much of the rest was inquiry, most of it by the native non-experts.

While it was clear to us that the non-natives did most of the talking, we felt that an objective measure was necessary to support the impression. Therefore, we counted t-units and computed average length of t-unit for each session during the last ten minutes of each session. We chose to analyse only the last ten minutes because the first part of each session was when we would expect most of the preliminary explanations to take place, most of them necessarily being undertaken by the expert (the non-native). By using only the last ten minutes of each session as our data base, we could assume

TABLE 1. *Number of t-units by native and non-native speakers*

	by NNS	*by NS*	*Total*
Transcript JC	156	132	288
Transcript PM	234	41	275
Transcript ST	138	136	274
Total	528	309	837

TABLE 2.   *Average t-unit length (in number of words)*

	by NNS	by NS	Average
Transcript JC	5.76	3.61	4.77
Transcript PM	5.29	1.98	4.80
Transcript ST	4.46	3.40	3.93
Total average	5.21	3.30	4.51

that the heaviest part of the explanation and talk by the non-natives would be over. Thus, the last ten minutes should give a conservative measure of the relative amount of talk by natives and non-natives. The results of our counts, in Tables 1 and 2, confirmed our impression: the non-natives did most of the talking on all three transcripts.

The following fragments from the transcripts give the flavour of the recurring patterns of explanation and inquiry.

(1) **NNS:** And this is because DOS command, A greater than sign DOS, D-O-S,
  NS: M hm.
→ **NNS:** if, you know, next time when you use the PC, you know, when they mention about DOS, so you know that ... DOS f—uh ... DOS function or DOS uh command or whatever, for now ...
→ **NS:** So now I put VX?
  NNS: M hm ↗ .

PM/394

(2) **NNS:** After—if you ... [inhales] OK, I s—I think I should tell you ... [another thing] first.
  NS: [[Laughs]]
  NNS: There's a ... margin for this ...
  NS: oh, [OK.
  NNS: [typing] space. If you want to look at it, you can press this. [Points at screen]
→ **NS:** Oh, OK. So [just] F9?
  NNS: [Uh.] F9.

ST/129

We have seen in Tables 1 and 2 that the non-natives dominated in the overall amount of talk, and generally exceeded the natives in length of t-unit. We now see from Table 3 that the natives did most of the inquiring.

TABLE 3. *Inquiries by native and non-native speakers*

	of NS by NNS	of NNS by NS	Total
Transcript JC	13	119	132
Transcript PM	14	51	65
Transcript ST	13	167	180
Total	40	337	377

Review of the inquiries revealed that most were procedural. That is, inquiries by native non-experts revealed that they did not know the next step in a procedure, or did not know why something needed to be done. Inquiries by the non-native experts were devoted largely either to finding out the preferences of the natives (see example (3) below), or were instructional/rhetorical in nature (see example (4)). None of the inquiries by the natives were instructional/rhetorical.

(3) **NNS:** Insert is this one. [Points to instruction sheet]
    NS: M hm. [3 second pause while reading] Mm. [2 second pause] OK.
→ **NNS:** You want to go back and try that? [Points at screen]
JC/834

(4) **NNS:** OK. And now, you said you want to move this line ... go to up here, right?
    NS: Yeah.
→ **NNS:** Now what are you supposed to do?
PM/500

Typically, inquiries took the form of questions, including tags, as in examples (1) to (4). However, some took other forms: the use of 'Let's say ...' and its variants followed by a statement form were the most common of the non-question forms of inquiry. Examples are (5) and (6):

(5) **NNS:** This is a good disk.
→ **NS:** That would be in there whenever I would use it.
    NNS: Right.
JC/28

(6) **NNS:** Because right now I just give you some general idea, so you

don't have to waste your time, go back and reading it and all
that ⌈stuff.⌉
→ **NS:**   ⌊Not- ⌋ let's say you haven't set the
... [pointing at screen] left margin.

PM/257

Besides the dominance of the non-natives in amount of talk and in
clarification of procedure, we found that non-natives supplied the natives
with vocabulary, teaching them key terms from the subject area. Meanings
were sometimes solicited by the natives, as in examples (7) and (8), and
sometimes offered by the non-native without solicitation from the native
speaker, as in (9) and (10).

(7) **NNS:** Let's see. 'Highlight' ... [to NS] Just go on typing
    NS: ⌈OK. ⌉
    NNS: ⌊while⌋ I take a look at it.
→ **NS:**   Is there ... OK, what's ... this 'center text'?

JC/319

(8) **NS:**   OK. So then, when you say copy, you said copy this line
→   ⌈then, what⌉ do you mean by copy, to ⌈repeat⌉ it— ⌈again? ⌉
    NNS: ⌊Uh huh. ⌋   ⌊Right.⌋   ⌊Uh huh,⌋
    right.

ST/333

(9) **NNS:** And for drive B, we put your own diskette, to keep it, you
know, what—uh data file you want into your program, and to
boot—a PC, the—computer is already on,
→   right? And to boot it—boot is mean that to restart the
program again, so you just hit control, alternate, and
delete—at the same time.

PM/39

(10) **NNS:** OK. [Looks at screen] Now, this is the Volkswriter.
This called main menu.

ST/47

The overall number of NNS vocabulary explanations (Table 4) is quite
low, but not insignificant in the context of the NNS source.

We should note here what we did not find: nowhere in any of the three
conversations, contrary to what one finds when examining most reports of
task- and non-task-oriented NS–NNS conversations, did the natives offer
any kind of linguistic help, including help with vocabulary, nor did the
non-natives solicit any linguistic help from the natives. In the one case in
which the NNS might have seemed to be soliciting help, we judged that she

TABLE 4. *Vocabulary explanations by non-natives*

	Solicited by NS	Unsolicited	Total
Transcript JC	3	1	4
Transcript PM	1	8	9
Transcript ST	4	3	7
Total	8	12	20

was not, and that in fact she was asking a self-directed or rhetorical question. A major reason for our judgement was that she placed her chin on her hand and looked away from the native and the computer while asking the question, then answered it herself.

(11) **NNS:** So: it's—uh ... the colon, for PC, for the DOS—mm ... version—not the version—what I—what—what I gonna

→   say? [Rests chin on hand, looking away from NS] DOS mode.
PM/412.

When natives did question non-natives, the questions always concerned content (meaning or procedure), not the non-natives' use of language, and were followed by an explanation or clarification by the non-native in the next turn (example (12)) and not later.

(12) **NS:**   What's help?

→ **NNS:**   Oh, this is um ... you see when you're stuck in the middle, like um ... every—in—all the key d—doesn't work =

NS: = M hm. =

NNS: = or you hit some, some, um—some key by mistake, then you can always hit help ↗
JC/822

A possible explanation is that the English proficiency of the non-natives in this study was somewhat higher than that of the non-natives found in most other studies of NS–NNS conversations. The non-natives' status as topic experts may have interacted with language proficiency level (Gaies, 1982; Gass & Varonis, 1985) to suppress the tendency of natives to lead non-natives linguistically.

When non-natives inquired of natives, the questions were nearly always followed by some comment or action (by the native; see example (13)), also in the next turn, even when the non-natives' question was instructional/rhetorical (the only exception being example (11)). Examples like (13) show that an answer or turn need not be verbal.

→ (13) **NNS:** Now what are you supposed to do?
        NS: [Presses several keys; to self:] No, OK ↗ . [7 second pause in talk while she types some more]
        NNS: OK, you got it.

PM/503

Natives never corrected non-natives at all in these task-oriented conversations, not even their (mis)use of language. Non-natives, however, corrected natives fifteen times. This contrasts with much of the data reported in other, non-task-oriented NS–NNS conversations in which natives generally take the lead in negotiating meaning by clarifying and correcting, often acting as the expert resource person. Another finding that contrasts with the main body of the literature is that by far the majority of other-corrections by either party in most conversations show some modulation through the use of hesitations, pauses, rising intonation, and other uncertainty markers as described in Schegloff *et al.* (1977). In these task-oriented data, however, most other-corrections were unmodulated (Table 5).

TABLE 5. *Other-corrections, all transcripts*

	of NS by NNS	*of NNS by NS*	*Total*
Modulated	5	0	5
Unmodulated	10	0	10
Total	15	0	15

Example (14) shows modulation used in the correction, and (15) shows a multiple instance of corrections without modulation.

(14) **NNS:** You can try ... [pointing at screen] like ... this one.
      NS: OK. [Presses a key]
→ **NNS:** Um ... no no.

ST/968

(15) **NNS:** OK. And exit.
      NS: [Presses a key]
→ **NNS:** No, exit. Get out from—I ha—I haven't tell you this one yet. Now get out from this one. Get out from this (square?)

NS: OK. [Presses a key]
→ NNS: Nope.

PM/792

The location of these sorts of other-corrections is very restricted, however; all of them followed an incorrect action by the native non-expert, with the action taking a turn slot and the correction by the expert coming in the next turn and not later. It is obviously impossible for correction to take place any earlier than the next turn, but why does it never take place after that? And why are there more unmodulated than modulated other-corrections? Based on the work of Schegloff *et al.* (1977), Moerman (1977), Gaskill (1980), and the evidence from many of the other studies of conversation, one would expect unmodulated corrections by the other to be disfavoured.

The answer would again appear to lie in the context investigated. An incorrect action when dealing with a computer has the potential to result in something more than momentary conversational confusion. In a setting like this one, in which the informational aspect is dominant over the relational, procedural accuracy is very important. The expert in this case is likely to be under some pressure to repair immediately through the quickest means possible. Thus, the instructional context apparently allows bluntness without modulation, given the fact that the overriding purpose of the sessions was to teach the non-expert and not to establish a relationship (as may be the case in most non-task-oriented conversations).

However, unmodulated corrections were not the only form of bluntness found in the instructional conversations. (Example (15), for instance, contains two imperatives.) We have here considered some imperatives as directions rather than other-corrections because directions differ from corrections in function and location though they may be similar in form. Both directions and corrections may be imperative, as in the 'And exit' and 'No, exit' in example (15). However, corrections are always located directly after an incorrect action by the other while directions are embedded in an explanation—the self's own turn as in examples (16) and (17) below, or in a turn after a *correct* action by the other.

→ (16) NNS: First type C ↗ by what name ↗ pick out a name. I—I'll
              let you type it.

JC/138

(17) NNS: And now try to move the—cursor up ... to the first line.
            And after that uh, (p'rap) [= perhaps?] the end of the

→ statement, and I want you to hit the F8, to see what's the different ...

PM/462

Besides location, they also differ in function: an other-correction 'points backward' toward the last turn in that it is designed to repair an incorrect action. A side sequence, a departure from progress, is where the repair is accomplished. A direction, on the other hand, 'points forward' in that the topic or procedure progresses without resorting to a side sequence.

Directions are also much more common than other-corrections. Yet they are similar to corrections in one other respect besides form: the experts use them far more than the non-experts do (see Table 6).

TABLE 6.   *Directions by transcript*

	of NS by NNS	*of NNS by NS*	*Total*
Transcript JC	54	7	61
Transcript PM	71	1	72
Transcript ST	123	0	123
Total	248	8	256

Throughout the three transcripts, directions are commonly given by the non-native experts to the native learners, and most of the directions are accompanied by hesitations, pauses and rising intonation, i.e. signs of modulation, as in examples (16) and (17).

Because of the instructional context, with non-natives as authorities, it may seem surprising that the *natives* issued any directions at all. On examination, though, it is apparent that there are explanations for some of those that the natives do make. In two of them (examples (18) and (19)), both by the same person, the American is apparently bidding to move on to another stage of the instruction, and each seems more a suggestion than a direction.

→ (18) **NS:**   OK, I think that's—[laughs]
       NNS: OK.
       NS: about everything for now.

JC/1024

(19) **NS:**   OK. [Presses some keys during a 3 second pause in talk]
→   Um let's say that's all I have. [Laughs]

$$JC/400$$

A third (example (20)) also displays modulation by the native speaker:

(20) **NNS:**   Some time you put the—one to ten or whatever you can
change that one. And the last line of the text is mean that if
it—every time it's printing, its keep counting it until it hit

$\left[\begin{array}{l}\text{the—line sixty.}\\ \text{OK. Let's change}\end{array}\right.$ that one.

→ **NS:**

$$PM/679$$

The remaining five are of one type: the word 'wait' followed by an
inquiry, and all five appear only on one transcript. The 'wait' instances are
problematic in that one might reasonably suppose that that use is merely
one American's idiosyncrasy. We can, however, note that all five are either
within the American's own turn, or occur at the place where the American is
eligible to take her turn (see examples (21)) and (22)).

(21) **NNS:**   That's where we set the left margin. And capitalise, you have
to caps lock. Or shift ... $\left[\begin{array}{l}\text{if you ...}\\ \text{Oh ...}\end{array}\right.$

→ **NS:**   [Presses some keys]
wait, what ... what'd I do?

$$JC/256$$

(22) **NNS:**   ... it always ask you which drive it's $\left[\begin{array}{l}\text{in.}\\ \text{A?}\end{array}\right.$
NS:

[Presses a key]

NNS: Yeah. =

NS: = Is that right? =

NNS   = Right. So it's gone now.

NS: OK.

NNS: M hm.

→ **NS:**   Now wait. How would I—this is in no order, [pointing at
screen] right?

$$JC/1007$$

Directions, like corrections, may be modulated or unmodulated. Most
directions by the non-natives display some modulation, just as the corrections do, but examples (23) (in the third turn) and (24) display a lack of
modulation in the directions given by the non-natives.

(23) **NNS:** The B ↗ ... B drive ↗ .
    NS: Oh. All right. [Presses a key]
→ **NNS:** Hit the return key.
                        ST/1108

(24) **NNS:** Its depend on the printer also. OK. [Presses form feed
→   on the printer and extracts the paper] And now I want you
         to get out—from this one.
                        PM/787

Table 7 is a breakdown of directions according to whether they were modulated or not. The figures show that modulated directions far outnumbered unmodulated, but also indicate that the few unmodulated directions were given (with two exceptions) by the non-natives.

TABLE 7. *Modulated and unmodulated directions, all transcripts*

	of NS by NNS	*of NNS by NS*	*Total*
Modulated	220	6	226
Unmodulated	28	2	30
Total	248	8	256

Discussion

As the supposedly more linguistically competent participants in the conversations, native speakers might be expected to take on a significant portion of the linguistic work; after all, they have more cultural and linguistic resources available to them. The very possibility of unequal language competences might lead one to expect to find empirical evidence to support that expectation. Yet we did not, probably because of inequality of topic knowledge, a resulting gain in status by the non-natives, and the fact that the role (as teacher/expert) of the non-natives in these conversations is to support completion of a task.

Findings like those in our data suggest that the non-native experts have more conversational latitude in this context than the natives. In addition to that, however, there are other signs that the experts were freer to operate in this context. For example, the non-natives dominate in sheer amount of talk, in the use of rhetorical inquiries, directions and corrections (many of them unmodulated) of their partners, while the natives made more use of inquiries, and sought information, including lexical information, from the experts. Finally, native speakers did not correct non-natives at all, not even their language. All of these tendencies indicate that the non-native speakers are in a position of control.

If expertise in the language seems to allow the native speakers in non-task-oriented (relational or 'free') conversations to act like (and in some sense be) authorities, an analogous halo may surround the non-native expert in the instructional setting, creating a situation in which task-expertise spills over to greater latitude in language use. Schmidt & McCreary (1977), Harder (1980) and Thomas (1984), in discussing treatment of non-natives by natives in conversation, all refer to the unequal treatment of non-native speakers in conversation. For them, 'unequal' seems to be equated with 'unfair' or 'less than'. Yet here is a case in which unequal treatment (i.e. the imbalance in the use of otherwise disfavoured conversational practices) may have positive effects by facilitating the ongoing talk and work.

The present study (like Zuengler's in this volume, see chapter 12) has shown how certain features such as task-status and topic expertise can have a powerful impact on the conduct of conversation. This study was based on interactions whose function was instructional and limited in scope; more research on other functions than instructional, like that of Labov & Fanshel (1977), Arthur et al. (1980), and Varonis & Gass (1985b), is needed. By exploring the structure of NS–NNS conversations in a greater number of more purposeful settings, we would gain understanding of how authority and control are variably distributed. If similar results to those we have presented here emerge, we will need to recognise that there are real-world circumstances in which NS–NNS conversations assume the expected characteristics of NS–NS conversations.

Appendix: Transcript conventions

At the end of each example in the text is a notation which indicates which transcript the example was taken from and its location on that transcript using the form: transcript label/starting line number. The transcripts are labelled by the first initial of the first name of each of the two participants. Symbols used are:

'   clause-final intonation—breath pause—'more to come'
.   sentence-final with falling intonation

!	said 'with enthusiasm'
?	sentence-final with either rising intonation or with WH-questions. This is not used when it is not clear if a question is actually being asked; instead, a rising intonation symbol is used.
↗	rising intonation at other than end of a grammatical question, or when doubt exists as to the possibility of its being an intended question.
↘	falling intonation under similar conditions to ↗
:	lengthening of preceding syllable or sound
x	indecipherable word
xx	indecipherable words
x–x	longer indecipherable stretch of talk
—	quick hesitation, self-interruption or incomplete word
...	approximate half-second pause without falling intonation
=	latching (no pause between turn taking)
word	word emphasised by loudness
útter	primary stress on the syllable with the diacritic
" "	reading or quoting
[ ]	description of contextual accompanying behaviour
[=]	gloss
[= ?]	questionable gloss
( )	questionable transcription
[ ]	overlapping speech

References

ABUNAHLEH, L., ALLEN, S., ARTHUR, B., BEALS, S., BUTLER, M., DREZNER, B., FRYDENBERG, G., GALAL, M., GASS, S., HILDEBRANDT, K., MARLOS, E. and OSTRANDER, T., 1982, The scope and function of language repair in foreigner discourse, *Interlanguage Studies Bulletin*, 112–20.

ARTHUR, B., WEINER, R., CULVER, M., LEE, Y. J. and THOMAS, D., 1980, The register of impersonal discourse to foreigners: Verbal adjustments to foreign accent. In D. LARSEN-FREEMAN (ed.), *Discourse Analysis in Second Language Research*. Rowley, MA: Newbury House.

DAY, R., CHENOWETH, N., CHUN, A. and LUPPESCU, S., 1984, Corrective feedback in native–nonnative discourse, *Language Learning*, 34(2), 19–45.

FRASER, B., RINTELL, E. and WALTERS, J., 1980, An approach to conducting research on the acquisition of pragmatic competence in a second language. In D. LARSEN-FREEMAN (ed.), *Discourse Analysis in Second Language Research*. Rowley, MA: Newbury House.

GAIES, S. J., 1979, Linguistic input in first and second language learning. In F. R. ECKMAN & A. J. HASTINGS (eds), *Studies in First and Second Language Acquisition*. Rowley, MA: Newbury House.

——, 1982, Modification of discourse between native and nonnative speaker peers. Paper presented at the 16th Annual TESOL Conference, Honolulu.

GASKILL, W. H., 1980, Correction in native speaker−nonnative speaker conversation. In D. LARSEN-FREEMAN (ed.), *Discourse Analysis in Second Language Research*. Rowley, MA: Newbury House.

GASS, S. and VARONIS, E. M., 1984, The effect of familiarity on the comprehensibility of nonnative speech, *Language Learning*, 34, 65−89.

——, 1985, Variation in native speaker speech modification to nonnative speakers, *Studies in Second Language Acquisition*, 7, 37−57.

HARDER, P., 1980, Discourse as self-expression—on the reduced personality of the second-language learner, *Applied Linguistics*, 1(3), 262−70.

HODNE, B., 1985, Yet another look at interlanguage phonology: The modification of English syllable structure by native speakers of Polish, *Language Learning*, 35(3), 405−22.

LABOV, W. and FANSHEL, D., 1977, *Therapeutic Discourse: Psychotherapy as Conversation*. New York: Academic Press.

LONG, M. H., 1981, Questions in foreigner talk discourse, *Language Learning*, 31(1), 135−57.

——, 1983, Linguistic and conversational adjustments to nonnative speakers, *Studies in Second Language Acquisition*, 5, 177−93.

MOERMAN, M., 1977, The preference for self-correction in a Tai conversational corpus, *Language*, 53(4), 872−82.

PICA, T., 1988, Interlanguage adjustments as an outcome of NS−NNS interaction. *Language Learning*, 38(1), 45−73.

SATO, C. 1982, Ethnic styles in classroom discourse. In M. HINES & W. RUTHERFORD (eds), *On TESOL '81*. Washington, DC: TESOL.

SCHEGLOFF, E. A., JEFFERSON, G. and SACKS, H., 1977, The preference for self-correction in the organization of repair in conversation, *Language*, 53(2), 361−82.

SCHMIDT, R. and MCCREARY, C., 1977, Standard and superstandard English: Recognition and use of prescriptive rules by native and non-native speakers, *TESOL Quarterly*, 11, 415−29.

SCHWARTZ, J., 1980, The negotiation of meaning: Repair in conversations between second language learners of English. In D. LARSEN-FREEMAN (ed.), *Discourse Analysis in Second Language Research*. Rowley, MA: Newbury House.

SELINKER, L. and DOUGLAS, D., 1985, Wrestling with 'context' in interlanguage theory, *Applied Linguistics*, 6, 190−204.

TARONE, E., 1985, Variability in interlanguage use: A study of style-shifting in morphology and syntax, *Language Learning*, 35(3), 373−403.

THOMAS, J., 1984, Cross-cultural discourse as 'unequal encounter': Towards a pragmatic analysis, *Applied Linguistics*, 5, 226−35.

VARONIS, E. M. and GASS, S., 1982, The comprehensibility of non-native speech, *Studies in Second Language Acquisition*, 6, 114−36.

——, 1985a, Miscommunication in native/nonnative conversation, *Language in Society*, 14(2), 327−43.

——, 1985b, Nonnative/nonnative conversations: A model for negotiation of meaning, *Applied Linguistics*, 6, 71–90.

ZUENGLER, J. (in press) Assessing an interaction-based paradigm: How accommodative should we be? In M. R. EISENSTEIN (ed.), *Variation and Second Language Acquisition: An Empirical View*. New York: Plenum.

12 Performance variation in NS–NNS interactions: Ethnolinguistic difference, or discourse domain?[1]

JANE ZUENGLER
University of Wisconsin, Madison

Introduction

In the second language acquisition literature, some have asserted that when non-native speakers (NNSs) interact with native speakers of the language (NSs), the NS generally tends to dominate the conversation. (Such assertions can be found, for example, in Beebe & Giles (1984) and Scarcella (1983).) According to Beebe & Giles (1984), NS dominance may be due to the NS's higher linguistic, or ethnolinguistic, status *vis-à-vis* that of the NNS. That is, applying this to NS–NNS interactions in the US context, native speakers of English are at an advantage, status-wise, because they are *native* speakers (i.e. are proficient) in a language which is dominant in the US.

If such claims of NS tendencies to dominate are true, there are important implications for second language learners. Being dominated in a conversation represents what Levinson (1987) refers to as limiting the NNS's 'right to talk'. Such a limitation not only has serious psychological ramifications for the NNS, but may be acquisitionally limiting as well. Pica (1987) refers to this when she suggests that an NNS who plays a subordinate role in a conversation participates less in the negotiation of meaning, and it is active, frequent negotiation of meaning which Pica (1987), Long (1983), and others claim is necessary to propel language acquisition.

The question of dominance (or control) in NS–NNS interactions, important though it may be for the second language learner, has not been researched to any extent. While a study by Scarcella in 1983 included a measure of dominance (namely, interruptions), she did not separate the NNSs from the NSs in reporting her results. In a 1986 study, Gass & Varonis analysed some measures of dominance, but their dyads were NNS–NNS. However, one study in the literature does speak directly to the issue of dominance in NS–NNS interactions. Though Gaies (1982) is not a study of dominance *per se*, he addresses it in discussing his results. He suggests that NS control of NS–NNS interactions is not necessarily automatic. There are several variables which have an impact on the NS's behaviour. According to Gaies, shared knowledge and (the NNS's) proficiency level both act to set up expectations about the NNS's ability to share in the conversational work. The NS will have an expectation that the NNS can actively contribute to the conversation if they share knowledge of the topic (or what Selinker & Douglas (1985) refer to as the 'discourse domain'). This expectation will hold (i.e. the NS will not exert conversational control) *unless* the NNS's proficiency level is limited. When the NS perceives limitations in the NNS's proficiency, Gaies suggests, the NS will take over the conversation.

In other words, if the NNS's proficiency is adequate for interacting within a given domain of discourse, it is shared knowledge of that domain which will enable both interlocutors to participate in the conversation. Dominance by the NS will only occur if weaknesses in the NNS's proficiency obstruct his/her ability to actively participate.

A recent study by Woken & Swales (this volume, chapter 11) of three NS–NNS dyads in task-oriented interactions illustrates the importance of domain knowledge on conversational participation. The task they analysed consisted of subjects in clearly-defined roles: one subject (a computer specialist) taught another (a nonspecialist) how to use a word processing program. The NNSs were the computer specialists, the NSs the nonspecialists. Woken & Swales report evidence of NNS dominance throughout the conversations. They conclude that in their dyads, it is (greater) topic knowledge which leads to NNS dominance. Unequal *linguistic* competence (which would favour the NS) is not as important in explaining participation.

There is one additional recent study which focuses on topic knowledge. Zuengler (in press) reports an analysis of 45 interactions between NS and NNS women. One finding was that when NSs and NNSs assume relatively equal knowledge of the discourse domain, the NSs show signs of exerting control of the conversation. Although NNS proficiency weaknesses were not analysed *per se*, Zuengler points out that the NNSs may have given signs of limitations, causing the NSs to take control (thus supporting what Gaies (1982) suggests). However, when the NNSs were led to think that they knew more within the discourse domain than their NS interlocutors did, it was the NNSs who showed signs of taking control of the conversation (for example, interrupting more successfully). In other words, as Woken & Swales argue, relatively greater knowledge of discourse domain may lead the NNS to greater conversational participation, despite unequal linguistic competence. An important caveat, though, to the Zuengler study is that it involved induced, not actual, differences in knowledge of the discourse domain. That is, the researcher led one interlocutor to think that she knew more about what they were discussing than her partner knew. (It was not tied at all to real knowledge differences.) Thus, the only quantitative study to date of actual topic knowledge and its effects on conversational participation is that of Woken & Swales.

The study to be reported on here was undertaken to address the need for more research on topic knowledge and conversational participation in NS–NNS interactions. It addresses this question: does a speaker's actual knowledge of the discourse domain, relative to the knowledge of his interlocutor, explain patterns of participation in conversations between NSs and NNSs—that is, are both equal partners in building the conversation, or does one dominate the other?

The study

To address the research question, NSs and NNSs who are majoring in the same field at a large Midwestern university are paired together. All are male, are full-time graduate or undergraduate students, and are strangers to each other. None of the NNSs are enrolled in ESL classes. They come from a variety of native language backgrounds. In order to study any effects of the interlocutor's relative knowledge of the discourse domain, each dyad is asked to have conversations in two different domains. One domain involves a topic outside their field which both can be expected to have equal knowledge of, while the second domain is within their major. In the latter case, one set of dyads consists of an NNS who is more advanced in his major than his NS interlocutor is, one set constitutes the opposite (i.e. with a more advanced NS), and in one set of dyads both are judged to be at the same level in their major. The dyads with unequal knowledge consist, for example, of an undergraduate and graduate student, or a masters student paired with a doctoral student. The topic which is outside the major is 'food' (e.g. What is your most favourite food and why?, What is a really common meal in your country?, and so on). This topic was chosen because it was felt that it did not require special training to discuss, and both interlocutors could be expected to have roughly equal life experiences regarding food. The second topic was within the major. The students involved in the study represent four majors: mechanical engineering, electrical engineering, dairy science and statistics. To generate topics to discuss within the major, we asked a group of graduate and undergraduate students in that particular major (who were not subjects in the study) to suggest topics which interlocutors at both beginning and more advanced levels in their major could discuss, but which the more advanced-level interlocutor would presumably have more knowledge of. The questions that were agreed on by the students for the subjects to discuss, as well as the questions regarding food, are listed in the Appendix.

The subjects are given the questions about food, and asked to have a 10-minute conversation related to those questions. Following that first conversation, we talk briefly with them to clarify what stage they are at in their field. (We have already determined this ourselves before they are paired together, but want to indicate to each member of the dyad what stage his partner is at.) Then the subjects are asked to have a 10-minute conversation related to the second set of questions. Both conversations are audiotaped.

Measures

Several measures have been chosen to analyse the interlocutors' relative participation in the conversations. One of the measures is interruptions. There are numerous research studies which view the display of interruptions as an indicator of dominance. (See, for example, Ferguson, 1977; Kennedy & Camden, 1983; Leet-Pellegrini, 1980; Owsley & Scotton, 1984; Street & Cappella, 1985; Wiemann, 1985; Zimmerman & West, 1975.) However, there are researchers who argue that some interruptions might be supportive rather than dominating moves, therefore making it important to determine the function of each interruption before claiming it is an indicator of dominance (see, for example, Kennedy & Camden, 1983). It was decided, in the present study, to take this argument into account (rather than to simply count all interruptions as dominance markers).

Adapting the functionally-oriented coding system developed by Kennedy & Camden (1983) to our data, we are analysing only those interruptions which they claim function as dominating moves. First of all, we are locating the interruptions using an operational definition taken from West & Zimmerman (1977; see also Scarcella, 1983). To be classified as an interruption, the second speaker needs to begin at least one syllable away from a proper turn transition place. It is worth noting that this is difficult at times to determine, especially with respect to the interpretation of pauses. (See also the criticism raised by Edelsky, 1981.) In locating interruptions, we took a conservative position. That is, whenever there was any possibility that the first speaker was in the process of finishing his turn as the second speaker began talking, we did not count that as an interruption by the second speaker. Additionally, back-channel cues were not considered interruptions (Kennedy & Camden, 1983; Scarcella, 1983). The interruption analysis consisted of first determining the function of each interruption. Following Kennedy & Camden (1983), the interruption was categorised as a confirming move, or as a rejecting/disconfirming move. According to Kennedy & Camden, confirming moves show that the interruptor wishes to understand and show approval of the speaker. Confirming moves include clarification requests (e.g. 'What do you mean?') and expressions of agreement (e.g. 'Yeah, I feel that way, too'). An interruption labelled a confirming move is not considered an indicator of dominance. Kennedy & Camden argue that it is only the interruptions which function to 'lessen' the speaker in some way which are valid manifestations of dominance. Such interruptions serve to reject or disconfirm (i.e. deny the reality of) the speaker. Under the category 'reject/disconfirm', they include disagreement (e.g. the interruptor might say 'No, I don't think that's true,' or 'Well, but that's not the only important item'); 'tangentialisation' (e.g. the interruptor trivialises what the speaker is saying, such as interrupting with 'Cheer up, things'll get better' when the speaker is relating a serious personal problem he's having); and subject change (e.g. the speaker is in the process of talking about a movie he's seen, and the interruptor says 'Hey, did anybody make the coffee this morning?'). Preliminary analysis of the data led us to add two examples to Kennedy & Camden's dominating interruptions (i.e. to their classification 'reject/disconfirm'). One example was subject continuation, which occurs when the interruptor simply interrupts to add to what the speaker is saying (e.g. the speaker is talking about uses for computers, and the interruptor says 'Where I used to work, we used the computer at each stage of our analysis'). We felt that the general function of that type of interruption was to deny to an extent the existence of the speaker, and it would therefore serve as a dominating move. Another example was simply finishing the speaker's statement (e.g. the speaker says 'I think it was found in the—', and is interrupted by the interlocutor saying 'cabinet'). That type of interruption appears to be a dominating move, we felt, since it denies the speaker the opportunity to choose his own words in finishing the statement.

All interruptions were thus analysed as having a confirming, or rejection/disconfirming function. Since only those in the latter category are considered by Kennedy & Camden (1983) as being valid indicators of dominance, we discarded all interruptions falling within the former category.

Additionally, Kennedy & Camden include a coding system for *post-interruption behaviour*. By post-interruption behaviour, they mean how the interrupted speaker responds to the interruption. The interrupted speaker might give up his/her turn, thus submitting to the interruptor, or he/she might, instead, resist the interruptor and maintain the turn. In the latter case, Kennedy & Camden argue, the speaker is refusing to subordinate him/herself, and is attempting to maintain at least control of the turn. Our data analysis included the coding for post-interruption behaviour, with the objective of determining how often the NSs and NNSs resisted being interrupted. Such an analysis provides us with a measure of the subjects' tendency to refuse to subordinate themselves.

Two native speakers of English, including the researcher, coded the data collected to date following the adaptations of Kennedy & Camden's (1983) system as described above. Inter-rater reliability was determined early in the analysis; based on an arbitrarily-chosen subset of nine of the conversations, inter-rate reliability was as follows: nature of the interruption, 0.83; post-interruption behaviour, 0.98. The relatively lower reliability concerning the nature of the interruption was due, it was felt, to the challenge in assigning functions to the interruptions (which was not required in analysing the post-interruption behaviour). The two figures were considered to represent sufficient agreement, however, for the coders to continue the analysis.

Another measure of dominance is each speaker's amount of talk, which can be ascertained by measuring the length of time the speaker holds the floor, or by determining how many words the speaker produces (e.g. Gass & Varonis, 1986; Scherer, 1979; Wiemann, 1985). In the present study, we are measuring amount of talk in terms of the number of words each speaker produces.

A third measure involved in the ongoing study is questions. The analysis of amount of talk led to a look at NNS versus NS questioning behaviour, for reasons which will become clear when the findings are discussed.

Obviously, the measures referred to here provide only a limited account of an interlocutor's relative participation in a conversation. However, they do enable us to begin looking at control of the conversation, and to do so quantitatively, over a large number of subjects, thus providing us with the ability to generalise the results.

Findings

The findings which will be reported come from a subset of 27 dyads who have participated to date. Fifteen of the dyads consist of non-natives who are at a more advanced level in their major than their native partner is. (These will be indicated in the tables and figures as NNS +, NS −.) The remainder of the subset includes six dyads in which the native speaker is at a more advanced level (labelled NNS −, NS +), and six dyads consisting of interlocutors who are at relatively the same stage in their major (labelled NNS =, NS =). Needless to say, because of the low numbers, any patterns apparent in these latter groups need to be considered tentative.

To illustrate the size of the corpus of interruptions which were analysed, the total number of interruptions (dominating and non-dominating), and the average number of interruptions per dyad, are listed in Table 1.

The results of the analysis of dominating interruptions are displayed in

TABLE 1. *All interruptions, NNSs versus NSs*

	Topic outside major (all dyads)		NNS + NS −		Topic within major NNS − NS +		NNS = NS =	
	Total	X̄ per dyad	Total	X̄ per dyad	Total	X̄ per dyad	Total	X̄ per dyad
NNS*	119	4.4 (sd = 3.6)	68	4.5 (sd = 4.2)	27	4.5 (sd = 2.7)	13	2.2 (sd = 2.8)
NS*	120	4.4 (sd = 3.5)	59	3.9 (sd = 3.1)	30	5.0 (sd = 4.5)	28	4.7 (sd = 4.8)

* These figures include all of the subjects, including several who produced no interruptions. In the topic outside the major, $N = 27$ NNSs, 27 NSs. In the topic within the major, $N = 15$ labelled NNS +, $N = 6$ labelled NNS −, $N = 6$ labelled NNS =, $N = 15$ labelled NS −, $N = 6$ labelled NS +, and $N = 6$ labelled NS =.

Table 2. As explained above, we followed Kennedy & Camden (1983) in assessing whether a given interruption was a dominating move or not. For each subject, we determined the total number of interruptions that subject performed, and then the proportion of total interruptions which Kennedy & Camden (1983) would label dominating moves. Since all 27 dyads could be considered similar with respect to their knowledge of the topic outside their major (i.e. food), a t-test was conducted on NNSs versus NSs overall, in that conversation. This was to determine whether there were any differences between the NNSs and NSs in the proportion of interruptions they performed as dominating moves. As Table 2 illustrates, there were no significant differences found between NNSs and NSs when discussing the topic outside the major. Concerning the topic within the major, one sub-group was considered large enough to perform a test of differences on. These are the dyads labelled NNS +, NS −. We found, however, no significant differences in their proportions of dominating interruptions. Since the remaining dyads in the two right-hand columns are too small to do statistical tests on, they cannot be considered conclusive.

Additionally, we analysed each subject's post-interruption behaviour. As discussed above, Kennedy & Camden (1983) argue that it is important to look at how people respond to being interrupted. Speakers who resist an interruption, by continuing their turn, are attempting to maintain control.

TABLE 2. *Mean proportions of dominating interruptions to total interruptions, NNSs versus NSs*

Topic outside major (all dyads)	*Topic within major*		
	NNS + NS −	*NNS − NS +*	*NNS = NS =*
NNS* 0.25† (sd = 0.27)	0.53‡ (sd = 0.41)	0.37 (sd = 0.20)	0.39 (sd = 0.48)
NS* 0.29† (sd=0.33)	0.46‡ (sd=0.40)	0.50 (sd=0.31)	0.17 (sd=0.21)

* In the topic outside the major, $N = 27$ NNSs, 25 NSs. In the topic within the major, $N = 15$ labelled NNS +, $N = 6$ labelled NNS −, $N = 4$ labelled NNS =, $N = 14$ labelled NS −, $N = 5$ labelled NS +, and $N = 6$ labelled NS =. Since some subjects did not interrupt at all, they were not included in the analysis. Therefore, the number of NNSs and NSs involved in each analysis varies.
† Result of t-test on NNS versus NS, topic outside major: n.s.
‡ Result of t-test on NNS + versus NS −, topic within major: n.s.

TABLE 3. *Mean proportions of interruptions resisted to total post-interruption responses, NNSs versus NSs*

Topic outside major (all dyads)		NNS + NS −	Topic within major NNS − NS +	NNS = NS =
NNS*	0.47†	0.54‡	0.47	0.70
	(sd = 0.36)	(sd = 0.36)	(sd = 0.36)	(sd = 0.33)
NS*	0.60†	0.67‡	0.70	0.69
	(sd = 0.39)	(sd = 0.30)	(sd = 0.27)	(sd = 0.48)

* In the topic outside the major, $N = 25$ NNSs, 27 NSs. In the topic within the major, $N = 13$ labelled NNS + , $N = 5$ labelled NNS − , $N = 5$ labelled NNS = , $N = 12$ labelled NS − , $N = 6$ labelled NS + , $N = 4$ labelled NS = . In some cases, the number of subjects reported here does not correspond to their counterparts listed in Table 1. That is because in some cases the coders could not decide how to code a particular subject's post-interruption behaviour, and therefore the subject was not included in the analysis.
† Result of t-test on NNS versus NS, topic outside major: n.s.
‡ Result of t-test on NNS + versus NS − , topic within major: n.s.

Therefore, post-interruption behaviour, and resistance in particular, was included in the analysis, and the results are reported in Table 3.

Table 3 illustrates frequency of resistance to being interrupted. That is, the proportions represent how much of the time subjects displayed resistance when responding to an interruption. A t-test of NNS versus NS resistance behaviour when discussing the topic outside the major revealed no significant differences. Nor were the NNS versus NS proportions in the NNS + , NS − dyads found to differ significantly. (Determination of NNS–NS difference in the two remaining columns on the right will await statistical testing on a larger subject number.)

The next measure to report is amount of talk. Results of the analysis are illustrated in Figure 1. The analysis of all 27 dyads revealed that when discussing the topic outside the major (i.e. food), the NNSs spoke significantly more than the NSs. And, when discussing the topic within the major, the NNSs who were more advanced (i.e. those NNSs labelled +), spoke significantly more than the NSs. It is worth noting that in the other (albeit few) sets of dyads represented as NNS − , NS + , and NNS = , NS = , the pattern which has emerged is different. In the NNS − , NS + dyads, it is the NS, not the NNS, who is producing a greater amount of talk. Larger

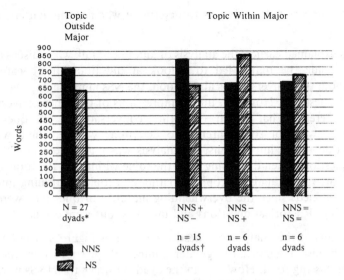

FIGURE 1. *Mean amount of talk (in words), NNSs versus NSs*
* *t* = − 2.39; *d.f.* = 52; two-tailed; *p* < 0.05
† *t* = − 1.92; *d.f.* = 28; one-tailed; *p* < 0.05

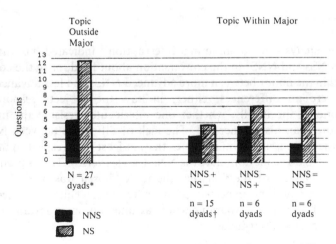

FIGURE 2. *Mean number of questions asked, NNSs versus NSs*
* *t* = 4.74; *d.f.* = 52; two-tailed; *p* < 0.001
† *n.s.*

subject numbers will enable us to determine whether this pattern will be borne out.

As explained earlier, the analysis of amount of talk when discussing the topic outside the major led to a look at questions. It appeared that throughout the conversations about food, the NSs in particular were asking a lot of questions. However, initial impressions of the other conversations were different. That is, in the other conversations, NS questioning behaviour was not so apparent. To determine whether there was any foundation to the impressions, an analysis was undertaken of NS versus NNS questions when discussing both the topic within and the topic outside the major. In the analysis, topic initiating and topic continuing questions were combined, since the overwhelming majority of questions were topic continuing. Rhetorical questions and tag questions were excluded.

Results of the analysis of questions appear as Figure 2. The NSs were found to pose a significantly greater number of questions than the NNSs when discussing food. However, in the dyads in which the NNSs were more advanced (NNS +, NS −), there is no difference between the interlocutors when discussing the topic within the major. In the remaining sets, the NSs appear to be producing more questions than the NNSs, although it cannot be determined at this point whether these differences will be borne out in a larger group.

Discussion

The analysis of dominating interruptions indicated no difference between NSs and NNSs in the conversation about food, or in the conversation within the major between more advanced NNSs and less advanced NSs. There were no differences, either, in how the subjects responded to interruptions, specifically, whether one interlocutor resisted the interruptions more than his partner did. The lack of difference between NSs and NNSs when discussing food indicates that, at least with respect to interruptions, the NS does not dominate the NNS (or vice versa). This is perhaps not surprising in view of the fact that the topic chosen was one which each interlocutor could be expected to have relatively equal knowledge of. Additionally, it was not what one would assume was an important topic for each interlocutor's self-image.

In the conversations within the major, there are also no apparent differences with respect to interrupting behaviour. The lack of difference in interrupting behaviour in these dyads contrasts with results reported in

Zuengler (in press). In that study, NNSs who were led to believe they knew more about the topic than their NS partner did, interrupted their partner more. (This did not happen when they thought they were equal.)

There are several reasons one could point to in explaining why interruption differences occurred in the preceding study but not in the present one. For one thing, a relative 'knower' might not need to use controlling moves such as interruptions if his/her active participation in the conversation is assured. And this, we would argue, is borne out by the present results which show that the NNSs labelled + spoke significantly more than the NSs labelled − . Although language proficiency *per se* was not analysed in the preceding study, many of the NNSs sounded less fluent than did those in the present study, producing a lot of hesitations, pauses, direct appeals to the native for help, and so forth. In the preceding study, the NNSs (including those who were the 'knowers') spoke significantly *less* than the NSs. Having trouble producing turns may have led those NNS 'knowers' to try to 'jump in', hence interrupt, as the NS continued to talk.

Generally speaking, the NNSs in the present study were very fluent when discussing the topics. Their greater amount of talk is at least one indication that they were quite actively participating in the conversation. When the subjects discussed the topic within the major, and the NNS was the 'knower', they may have accepted the knowledge differences, and therefore neither had to dominate the other by trying to 'butt in'. In fact, a questionnaire given to the subjects after the conversation indicated that most of the NSs did in fact view the more advanced NNS as the one who knew more.

A second reason for the difference in interruption behaviour between the preceding study and the present one, is possible gender differences, since the preceding study involved only females, and the present study, only males. Gass & Varonis (1986) found differences in conversational involvement between male–male pairs and female–female pairs. While they did not analyse interruptions, it is possible that gender influences interrupting behaviour for NNSs (as it does for NSs; cf. Zimmerman & West, 1975).

The analysis of amount of talk indicated that the NNSs spoke significantly more than the NSs when discussing the topic outside the major. Within the major, when the NNSs were at a relatively more advanced stage than their partners were, the NNSs also spoke significantly more. What could explain the NNSs talking more than the NSs when discussing food? The topic of food was chosen for the study because one could assume that the interlocutors would have relatively equal life experience regarding it. That the NNSs spoke significantly more than the NSs when discussing food may be a reflection of the positions the interlocutors negotiated *vis-à-vis* the topic. The topic questions that they were given to discuss asked each interlocutor to talk about favourite foods, holiday food, etc. However, many of the NSs (with the NNS's agreement) appeared to take the task and shift it primarily over to the NNSs. Frequently, in the beginning of the conversation, the NSs remarked that they assumed that the NNS already knew about common and holiday food in the US (and the NNS often concurred). The NS then made a suggestion such as the following: 'Why don't you start out and talk about food in your country, since I don't know anything about it.' In other words, acknowledging shared knowledge regarding food habits in the US, they refocused the domain toward that which they did not share knowledge of, namely, the NNS's experience. By so doing, they negotiated a 'knower' position for the NNS. That position was maintained throughout much of the conversation, as the NS continually asked questions, and the NNS elaborated, which resulted in his talking significantly more. Those dynamics could explain why the NSs produced significantly more questions than the NNSs in the conversation about food. Questions are potentially ambiguous, because sometimes they can signify dominance, while at other times they do not (Gass & Varonis, 1986). We would argue that in the conversations about food, the NS questions did not function as dominating moves. That is because the majority appeared to be what Goody (1978) calls 'information' questions. They are, simply, questions which are asked to elicit information. While they require a response, they represent a mode of questioning, according to Goody (1978), which is not a controlling move. With respect to talking about a topic within the major, there were no apparent NS–NNS differences in questioning. That is probably because the subjects in this case needed to jointly address the topic. In contrast to discussing food, crosscultural differences were not relevant when discussing the topics within the major. Though both were told to contribute to the conversation, we would argue that it was the interlocutor who was more advanced (i.e. the NNS 'knowers') who displayed signs of taking control. This is reflected in the NNS 'knowers' producing significantly more talk than the NS when discussing the topic within the major.

Conclusion

Several limitations in the present study should be kept in mind when considering the results. First of all, since the study is ongoing, results concerning the NNS 'knowers' need to be seen as tentative pending the completion of analyses of NNS relative 'nonknowers' and relative 'equals'.

Secondly, as we mentioned earlier, this study only concerns male NSs and NNSs, and therefore, cannot be generalised to females.

Nevertheless, there are several conclusions that can be drawn at this point, which the data make apparent. The analyses of interruptions and amount of talk illustrate that the NNSs in this study were *not* automatically dominated by the NSs. In fact, it is the NNS who could be said to dominate the conversation, with respect to talking more. Whether this would also be the case with NNSs at a lower level of proficiency than the NNSs had in this study needs to be investigated in future research. At any rate, at this point the evidence enables us to conclude that ethnolinguistic, or linguistic, differences alone do not explain amount of conversational participation in (male) NS–NNS interactions.

More specifically, we have evidence that an NNS's active conversational involvement can be explained as a function of relative knowledge of the topic, or discourse domain. It is important to consider topic knowledge as *relative*, since knowledge of a discourse domain is interactionally negotiated. It is not whether the NNS considers him/herself an absolute 'knower' or not of the discourse domain (cf. Selinker & Douglas, 1985), but what role is given to that knowledge within the interaction. Knowledge of discourse domain can provide an explanation for an NNS's extent of participation in an interaction, but only if we understand it to be a cognitive construct which has to be interactionally negotiated.

Appendix: Questions to guide conversations in the study

Conversation 1 (all subjects, topic outside the major)

Directions: Have a 10-minute conversation about *food*. You might talk about the following questions.

1. What is a really common meal in your country? Could you describe it?
2. Describe a special *holiday* meal.
3. What dishes do you like to prepare? Describe how you prepare one of them.

Conversation 2 (mechanical engineering)

Directions: Discuss or describe computer techniques and resources that are available to mechanical engineers.

1. When are computers used?
2. How are they useful?
3. How are they used?

Conversation 2 (statistics)

Directions: Have a 10-minute conversation in which you discuss *probability*.

Specifically discuss the difference between mutually exclusive versus independent events. Also discuss conditional probability and Bayes Theorem. Give examples where necessary.

Conversation 2 (dairy science)

Directions: Have a 10-minute conversation on the following topic: Bovine Growth Hormone.

Discuss the role of biotechnology on the future of the diary industry. For example, what nutritional problems will the bovine growth hormone create? Should it be used? If so, when should it be used? What are the possible long-term effects of the hormone on the market or on the animals themselves?

Conversation 2 (electrical engineering)

Discuss trouble-shooting circuits. What's the best way to approach the problem? What are the most likely causes of circuit problems?

Example: Suppose you build a microprocessor-controlled light dimmer, and it doesn't light (i.e. there's no output). How do you begin to solve the problem?

Note to Chapter 12

1. The research was supported in part by grants from the University of Wisconsin-Madison Graduate School Research Committee (Projects 170469 and 16103). The author would like to thank Barbara Bent, Jane Koenig, Anita Gallucci, David Conrardy and Nathan Grey for their assistance, as well as Learning Support Services at UW-Madison for providing recording and playback equipment.

References

BEEBE, L. M. and GILES, H., 1984, Speech-accommodation theories: A discussion in terms of second-language acquisition, *International Journal of the Sociology of Language*, 46, 5–32.

EDELSKY, C., 1981, Who's got the floor?, *Language in Society*, 10, 383–421.

FERGUSON, N., 1977, Simultaneous speech, interruptions and dominance, *British Journal of Social and Clinical Psychology*, 16, 295–302.

GAIES, S. J., 1982, Modification of discourse between native and nonnative speaker peers. Paper presented at the 16th Annual TESOL Conference, Honolulu, Hawaii.

GASS, S. M. and VARONIS, E. M., 1986, Sex differences in nonnative speaker–nonnative speaker interactions. In R. R. DAY (ed.), *Talking to Learn: Conversation in Second Language Acquisition*, Rowley, MA: Newbury House.

GOODY, E. N., 1978, Towards a theory of questions. In E. N. GOODY (ed.), *Questions and Politeness*. New York: Cambridge.

KENNEDY, C. W. & CAMDEN, C. T., 1983, A new look at interruptions, *Western Journal of Speech Communication*, 47(1), 45–58.

LEET-PELLEGRINI, H. M., 1980, Conversational dominance as a function of gender and expertise. In H. GILES, W. P. ROBINSON & P. SMITH (eds), *Language: Social Psychological Perspectives*, Oxford: Pergamon, pp. 97–104.

LEVINSON, K. 1987, The right to talk: A sociolinguistic investigation of conversational dominance and social prestige in non-native speaker interactions. Unpublished manuscript, Teachers College, Columbia University.

LONG, M. H., 1983, Native speaker/non-native speaker conversation and the negotiation of comprehensible input, *Applied Linguistics*, 4, 126–41.

OWSLEY, H. H. and SCOTTON, C. M., 1984, The conversational expression of power by television interviewers, *The Journal of Social Psychology*, 3, 261–71.

PICA, T., 1987, Second-language acquisition, social interaction, and the classroom, *Applied Linguistics*, 8(1), 3–21.

SCARCELLA, R. C., 1983, Discourse accent in second language performance. In S. GASS & L. SELINKER (eds), *Language Transfer in Language Learning*. Rowley, MA: Newbury House.

SCHERER, K. R., 1979, Personality markers in speech. In K. P. SCHERER & H. GILES (eds), *Social Markers in Speech*. Cambridge: Cambridge University Press.

SELINKER, L. and DOUGLAS, D., 1985, Wrestling with 'context' in interlanguage theory, *Applied Linguistics*, 6(2), 190–204.

STREET, R. L. Jr. and CAPELLA, J. N., 1985, Sequence and pattern in communicative behaviour: a model and commentary. In R. L. STREET, Jr. & J. N CAPELLA (eds), *Sequence and Pattern in Communicative Behaviour*. London: Edward Arnold.

WEST, C. and ZIMMERMAN, D. H., 1977, Woman's place in everyday talk: Reflections on parent–child interactions. *Social Problems*, 24, 521–9.

WIEMANN, J. M., 1985, Interpersonal control and regulation in conversation. In R. L. STREET, Jr. & J. N. CAPELLA (eds), *Sequence and Pattern in Communicative Behaviour*. London: Edward Arnold, pp. 85–102.

ZIMMERMAN, D. H. and WEST, C., 1975, Sex roles, interruptions and silences in conversation. In B. THORNE & N. HENLEY (eds), *Language and Sex: Difference and Dominance*. Rowley, MA: Newbury House, pp. 105–29.

ZUENGLER, J., 1987, NS–NNS interactions: Do NSs dominate them? Paper presented at the 21st Annual TESOL Conference, Miami, Florida.
——, (in press) Assessing an interaction-based paradigm: How accommodative should we be? In M. R. EISENSTEIN (ed.), *Variation and Second Language Acquisition: An Empirical View.* New York: Plenum Press.

13   The influence of the listener on L2 speech [1]

TOMOKO TAKAHASHI
Teachers College, Columbia University

Introduction

Research in sociolinguistics, bilingualism and second language acquisition (SLA) has indicated that interspeaker variation (e.g. the speech style and personal characteristics of the interlocutor) has significant effects on intraspeaker variation (e.g. the speakers' code-switching behaviour, style shifts, conversational adjustments). The work of Howard Giles and his associates, for example, provides evidence that speakers' style variation is often attributable to the effect of their interlocutors. That is, speakers often accommodate their speech style to their interlocutors (Giles & Powesland, 1975; Giles & Smith, 1979). In this framework, it is the speech style of the interlocutor that influences the speaker's style variation.

Speakers may also react to the personal characteristics of their interlocutors. Beebe (1977a, 1977b, 1981), for instance, examined the effect of the ethnic identity of the listener on the dialect code-switching behaviour of ethnic Chinese Thais. She found that Chinese–Thai bilinguals' pronunciation in Thai became more accurate when speaking Thai to an ethnic Thai than to another Chinese Thai. This phenomenon can also be explained in terms of accommodation theory, particularly psychological convergence (see Beebe & Zuengler, 1983). Beebe (1980) also found that Spanish–English bilingual children attempted greater syntactic complexity in English with an English monolingual listener than with a Hispanic bilingual listener. The ethnic identity of the listener, therefore, is a significant variable predicting phonological and syntactic variation.

Other studies have indicated that the standardness or formality of speech style is also subject to the relationship between the speaker and listener (see Bell, 1984, for a review of the related literature). Thus, there is evidence that the speaker accommodates to, or responds to, certain characteristics of the listener. Although most studies on this topic have focused primarily on native–native (NS–NS) or native–non-native (NS–NNS) interactions, there are some studies suggesting that certain characteristics of the *non-native* listener also influence second language (L2) learners' speech, some of the effects being unique to non-native–non-native (NNS–NNS) interactions.

For instance, in a study of Japanese bilingual women living in the United States, Ervin-Tripp (1964) reports on the effects of the listener on the style of the bilinguals' English. In the study, the Japanese women were interviewed either by a Caucasian American or by a Japanese interviewer in English. In 'a rather abnormal situation when [the Japanese women] were asked to speak English with another Japanese woman', it was found that 'there was much more disruption of English syntax, more intrusion of Japanese words, and briefer speech' (Ervin-Tripp, 1964:96). These findings are quite interesting and lead us to ask at least two questions: (1) are these changes in the subject's speech due to accommodation (i.e. the influence of non-native interlocutor's imperfect speech with a Japanese accent)? and/or (2) are they due to some psychological effects from the 'abnormality' of the situation (i.e. speaking English to another Japanese)?

In a more recent study on NNS–NNS interactions, Gass & Varonis (1986) demonstrated sex differences in L2 speech by presenting the ways in which male and female Japanese ESL learners conversed in English in same-sex and opposite-sex dyads. For instance, sex differences in the negotiation of meaning are summarised as follows: 'Males initiate more negotiation to females than they do to males, while females initiate more negotiation to males than they do to females' (Gass & Varonis, 1986:330). It has also been shown that women tend to exhibit a sharp range of style shifting between the cases of the same-sex and opposite-sex dyads. In other words, the L2 speaker exhibited a different amount of meaning negotiation depending upon the sex of the interlocutor.

In Varonis & Gass (1985) it has been pointed out that NNS–NNS pairs exhibited much greater incidence of meaning negotiation than their NNS–NS or NS–NS counterparts. Among the NNS–NNS pairs, however, it has been found that the pair of interlocutors who shared a native language and had the same ESL proficiency exhibited the lowest incidence of negotiation. These findings are significant in that they reveal the unique nature of NNS–NNS interactions. They are also important in that they show the L2 speaker's speech variation according to the NL background and the ESL proficiency of the interlocutor. These studies by Gass &

Varonis thus provide us with examples of the influence of the non-native listener upon L2 speech and invite us to look further into the topic of NNS–NNS interaction.

The study problem

The present study is an attempt to explain the influence of a non-native listener upon another non-native speaker using English as a second language (ESL). More specifically, it was asked whether and to what extent certain characteristics of the listener such as NL background and ESL proficiency contribute to the speaker's speech change, e.g. in style, fluency and amount of talk as well as in the use of meaning negotiation.

In this study it was assumed that the ESL speaker would react to non-native listeners differently, depending upon whether or not they are from the same NL background, and whether they have higher or lower English proficiency. It was further assumed that observed variation, if any, can be explained on the basis of this degree of psychological 'ease' or discomfort (e.g. feeling comfortable or uncomfortable, superior or inferior, close or distant, etc.) experienced by the subject while talking to a particular listener. These assumptions were drawn from episodes often told and feelings commonly expressed by Japanese ESL learners (although the same may apply to ESL learners of other nationalities). That is, it is often heard that they feel extremely uncomfortable speaking English to another Japanese (for instance, in the presence of Americans who don't know Japanese). Consequently, they either make more mistakes in English than usual or end up being very quiet in the conversation.

In order to test the above observation a written questionnaire survey was conducted. In the survey 44 Japanese ESL speakers living or working in New York City were asked to fill out a questionnaire in Japanese. The age, length of residence in the United States and proficiency in ESL varied among the subjects. The primary focus of the questionnaire was placed on the following question: 'In a daily conversation, you may sometimes have to speak English to another Japanese, for instance, in the presence of Americans. In such a situation, do you feel (or have you ever felt) uncomfortable speaking English?' To this question 31 out of 44 subjects (70%) responded 'yes'. One of the most striking results, however, was that this response was given predominantly by women, as indicated in Table 1.[2]

Another interesting finding was that among those who said 'yes' the majority of the women (12 out of 19) answered that they would feel uncomfortable speaking English *especially* when the other Japanese person

TABLE 1. *Distribution of responses by sex: 'Feel uncomfortable' vs. 'don't feel uncomfortable' in the Japanese–Japanese conversation in English*

	Female	Male	Total
'Feel uncomfortable'	19	12	31
'Don't feel uncomfortable'	3	10	13
Total	22	22	44

$X^2 = 5.35^*$;   d.f. = 1; $p < 0.05$
[*With the Yates correction factor, $X^2 = 3.93$; $p < 0.05$]

had higher English proficiency, while a much smaller number of men (2 out of 12) said the same.[3] The rest of the subjects answered that they would feel uncomfortable regardless of ESL proficiency of the Japanese interlocutor (with a few exceptions of those who specifically said that they disliked speaking English with a Japanese with lower English proficiency).

Why, then, do they feel uncomfortable? Ten subjects volunteered to give explanations for their negative feelings toward the Japanese–Japanese (J–J) conversation in English. Their comments were translated into English and summarised as follows:

1. It's very unnatural to speak English with the Japanese.
2. I feel as if my English were being evaluated by my Japanese interlocutor.
3. I become nervous because I try not to make grammatical mistakes in such a situation.
4. I suffer from an inferiority complex if my Japanese interlocutor speaks better English than I do.
5. I feel sorry for my Japanese interlocutor if he or she speaks poor English.
6. Because I am shy (or self-conscious).[4]

Interestingly, again, all these comments were given by women (and only by women!). This seems to indicate that many women felt so strongly negative toward J–J conversations in English that they needed to comment on their feelings. And their comments (especially numbers 2 to 6) provide us with an interesting psychological picture of how Japanese women would feel in such a situation.[5]

In sum, the overall results of the survey have indicated that a large number of Japanese ESL speakers *do* feel uncomfortable (or have experienced discomfort) in J–J conversations in English, and this is particularly true for women. It was also found that the interlocutor's proficiency in ESL is another possible factor reinforcing such feelings. The present study, therefore, was designed to investigate the influence of the non-native listener's NL background and ESL proficiency upon the L2 speech of Japanese females.

Methodology

Subjects for the study were six Japanese ESL learners (all females) living in the greater New York City area. They had spent about one to three years in the United States. Three of the six subjects had studied ESL at English language institutions in Manhattan, and they were at high-intermediate to advanced levels. The other three were at higher levels of ESL proficiency, enrolled in an MA programme at Teachers College, Columbia University (all were in the first year of the programme).

The six subjects were individually interviewed in English by each of the four non-native speakers of English with the following attributes:

(1) *Same* NL background (i.e. Japanese) with *higher* English
proficiency than the subject   [J–Hi]
(2) *Same* NL background (i.e. Japanese) with *lower* English
proficiency   [J–Lo]
(3) *Different* NL background (Spanish) with *higher* English
proficiency   [S–Hi]
(4) *Different* NL background (Spanish) with *lower* English
proficiency   [S–Lo]

The four interviewers were all females aged 25 to 27.[6] They were all college graduates. The higher proficiency interviewers (J–Hi and S–Hi) both had near-native proficiency in English having received highschool and college education in the United States. The lower proficiency interviewers (J–Lo and S–Lo) were both at the intermediate level of ESL proficiency, having lived and studied English in the United States less than one year. For control purposes, the six subjects were also individually interviewed by an American female (NS) who belonged to the same age group as the other four non-native interviewers, and was also a college graduate. None of the five interviewers had previously met the subjects.

Each interviewer was told (1) to introduce herself to each subject so that the subject would know what kind of linguistic background the interviewer was from, (2) to get to know the subject by asking questions (ones prepared by the interviewer as well as spontaneous questions) and (3) to carry out a conversation in English as naturally as possible for about 15 minutes. All interviews were done over the telephone and were tape recorded by the interviewer (and permission to use the tape recorded data was granted by each subject).[7] The order of the five interviews was randomised across subjects. Furthermore, after all five interviews each subject was interviewed again, but this time in Japanese, in order for her to freely express the feelings she had had during each interview.

The first five minutes of each conversation in English were transcribed.[8] The transcripts of 30 conversations (6 subjects × 5 interviews) were used as the data for the study.

Results and discussion

The results are discussed with respect to the following aspects: (1) the length of speech and fluency, (2) the amount of talk, (3) the number of questions, and (4) the use of meaning negotiation. The results from the follow-up interview will be presented at the end of the section to account for the overall results.

Length of speech and fluency

One of the most striking findings in the study was that the length of the subject's speech varied according to different interviewers. When conversing with the Japanese interviewers (J–Hi and J–Lo), for instance, our subjects sounded hesitant, and thus their speech at times sounded disconnected and each utterance was very brief. In other words, fluency of their speech was hindered to varying degrees in an encounter with a Japanese interlocutor. These results are quite similar to the finding reported by Ervin-Tripp (1964): Japanese women's speech tended to be much briefer when they were forced to speak English with another Japanese woman.

In the observation of interaction between Americans and Japanese, Hattori (1987) has found that Japanese used verbal feedback (such as 'yeah' and 'uh-huh') approximately 20% more often than Americans. This observation also seems to match the findings in the present study. This claim is especially true with the J–J conversation. That is, the use of back-channel cues tended to increase when a Japanese spoke English to another Japanese. As a result, each utterance of the speaker—i.e. a string of words between the cues—appeared to be very brief. It is thus possible that the amount of verbal feedback is usually high in the conversation between the Japanese.

At the same time, however, it seems that more cues were actually triggered by many pauses used by the subject. In other words, cues were used by the listener in order to fill the gap between the speaker's utterances when they were slow and hesitant. As can be seen in the following exchange, one sentence can be divided into several segments by pauses or rising intonation which were consequently followed by back-channel cues (See Appendix for transcription conventions):

Excerpt 1: Reiko (JS1) and Setsuko (J–Hi)

Setsuko: uh Are you taking uh classes? (↗) Or course? (↗)
Reiko: Yeah, I used to
Setsuko: Uh-huh (↗)
Reiko: I: learned English .. in .. Manhattan ..
Setsuko: uh-hum (↗)
Reiko: .. private school ..
Setsuko: Oh ..
Reiko: for nine months ..
Setsuko: uh-huh (↗)
Reiko: and graduated (↗) ..
Setsuko: uh-huh (↗)
Reiko: the school (↗) ..
Setsuko: uh-huh (↗)
Reiko: Now .. I'm .. taking .. umm private lesson .. every .. Tuesday
           ..
Setsuko: Ohh ..
Reiko: only once a month ..
Setsuko: uh-huh (↗)
Reiko: no once a week
Setsuko: uh-huh .. Are you able to speak in English home? (↗) like uh
           Do you have a friend? (↗)
Reiko: Yes, my teacher is native American
Setsuko: uh-hum (↗)
Reiko: She .. worked for umm New York Times (↗) ..
Setsuko: Oh wow!
Reiko: for long time ..
Setsuko: uh-huh (↗)
Reiko: and she's very good teacher. I'm very lucky ..
Setsuko: Oh wow!
Reiko: I THInk
Setsuko: That's gREAT!
Reiko: Yeah .. because of HER ..

Setsuko:	uh-huh (↗)
Reiko:	I .. I could impROVE ..
Setsuko:	uh-huh (↗)
Reiko:	I THInk
Setsuko:	Wow!

This example is an extreme case in that the average length of utterance between cues in Reiko's speech is only four words long, but it best describes the overall tendency, especially in the subjects with lower proficiency.

Furthermore, as in the above example, each utterance can be divided into smaller segments either by filled pauses (e.g. 'umm') or by unfilled pauses (indicated by ' .. ' in the transcript). With respect to the high frequency of pauses in the J–J conversation there are at least three explanations. First, hesitation pauses were used for discourse/cognitive planning (Beattie, 1983; Goldman-Eisler, 1968). In this sense, the subject was probably trying to make her speech as accurate as possible (see explanation 3 given in the written questionnaire survey). Secondly, pause

TABLE 2.   *Each subject's average length of utterance between cues (LUBC)*

Subject	Interviewer situation					
(*JS*)	*J–Hi*	*J–Lo*	*S–Hi*	*S–Lo*	*NS*	*Mean (sd)*
1	4.85	4.75	6.02	5.05	6.69	5.47 (0.85)
2	6.32	6.84	7.32	6.89	9.45	7.36 (1.22)
3	6.19	6.89	10.46	4.53	10.00	7.61 (2.54)
4	6.94	6.30	8.87	6.55	7.23	7.18 (1.01)
5	7.55	6.00	6.90	8.69	10.31	7.89 (1.67)
6	8.02	7.67	17.04	6.98	9.25	9.79 (4.13)
Mean (sd)	6.65 (1.13)	6.41 (0.99)	9.44 (4.04)	6.45 (1.49)	8.82 (1.51)	7.55 (2.40)

frequency or length is related to the anxiety level of the setting, i.e. the abnormality of the situation (see LoCastro, 1986). In other words, pauses could be either the cause and/or the result of uncomfortable moments arising in the interaction. Thirdly, pauses tend to be longer (LoCastro, 1986) and probably used more frequently in Japanese interactions. In this respect, it can be hypothesised that the subject was transferring Japanese patterns of interaction into English. All three explanations seem to be reasonable to account for the subject's disrupted speech in the J–J conversation in English.

Each subject's average length of utterance between cues in each dyad is given in Table 2. The subjects' ID numbers (1 to 6) reflect their approximate proficiency (with 6 being the highest).[9] The table indicates the following tendency: the higher the subject's proficiency, the longer the average length of utterance between cues. This relationship is statistically significant with a Spearman rank order correlation coefficient of 0.829 ($p = 0.02$). This is quite natural in that the speech of the subjects with higher proficiency was more fluent and thus it triggered fewer cues, which resulted in longer utterances. At the same time, we notice that the length of utterance varies according to different interviewers: the effect of the interviewer is significant when tested with a repeated measures analysis of variance (ANOVA) ($F[4,20] = 3.79$, $p < 0.025$, see Table 3). The average lengths of utterances between cues are plotted in Figure 1.

As seen here, each subject's utterance was short not only with the two Japanese interviewers but also with Veronica (S–Lo), while it tended to be the longest either with Maria (S–Hi) or with Linda (NS). This point can be illustrated by the comparison between excerpts 2 and 3.

TABLE 3. *Results of repeated measures ANOVA for average length of utterance between cues (LUBC)*

Source	d.f.		SS		MS	F
Between subjects	5		48.19			
Within subjects	24		118.29			
Interviewer		4		51.04	12.76	3.79*
Error		20		67.25	3.36	
Total	29		166.48			

* $p < 0.025$

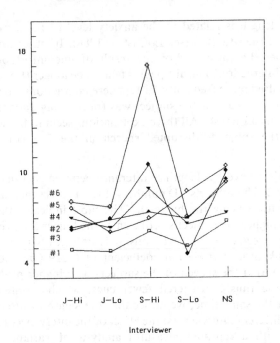

FIGURE 1. *Average length of utterance between cues (LUBC)*

Excerpt 2: Yoko (JS3) and Veronica (S–Lo)

Veronica:	eh .. Did you eh study English uh here? (↗)
Yoko:	Yes, I went to Columbia (↗) ..
Veronica:	Yeah (↗)
Yoko:	University (↗) for while ..
Veronica:	Yeah (↗)
Yoko:	to take American language course (↗)
Veronica:	uhhh Yeah .. I did uh also ..
Yoko:	You did too? (↗)
Veronica:	Yes
Yoko:	Oh really .. still doing it too? (↗)
Veronica:	eh No .. I .. I did .. the last semester
Yoko:	You finished last semester? (↗)
Veronica:	Yes
Yoko:	I see. Which which class did you take?
Veronica:	eh Until .. 5 .. Level 5
Yoko:	uh-huh (↗) Full-time? (↗)

Veronica: eh Yes
Yoko: Really
Veronica: How about you? Which level were .. you?
Yoko: uh I was .. in Level 8
Veronica: Eight! oh very GOOD [chuckle]

Excerpt 3: Yoko (JS3) and Maria (S–Hi)

Maria: You wouldn't like to work for a bank? (↗)
Yoko: No, uh I just avoid financial company and also .. umm I
preferably .. I'd I'd like to work for a American company but
it's VE:ry difficult ..
for Japanese people ┐
Maria: └ You think so? (↗)
Yoko: uh-huh ┐
Maria: └ because if you're bilingual like now ┐
Yoko: └ Yeah
Maria: the trading between the United States
and Japan is increasing ┐
Yoko: └ Yeah but ..
There are many Japanese companies and if I, you know, ask
most most of Japanese company (↗) to let me work there .. they
will say okay at that day but mm I'm .. really interested to in-
terested in [self-correction] working in American company this
time .. because I like to study more English ⌈ there [chuckle]
⌊ Yeah
Maria:
[Yoko continues to talk about her job hunting]

Again, these examples represent extreme cases, where the same subject's
length of utterance between cues appears to be the shortest and the longest.
In excerpt 2 we notice that Yoko uses rising intonation three times in an
affirmative sentence ('Yes, I went to Columbia University for while to take
American language course'). This could be interpreted as checking Veronica's comprehension. Likewise, the shortness of Yoko's utterance may
also be due to her effort to accommodate to her lower-proficiency interlocutor. Similar phenomena are also observed in conversations between
other subjects and the two lower-proficiency interviewers (J–Lo and S–Lo).
There is thus a tendency for Japanese subjects to make each utterance
briefer (and slower) when talking to a lower-proficiency interlocutor. If the
low proficiency of the interlocutor is one explanation for the subject's brief
utterance, the case with Setsuko (J–Hi) remains a question.

In excerpt 3 it can be speculated that Maria could have used more cues since there are several instances where prolonged pauses and rising intonation appear in Yoko's speech but Maria does not try to fill them with any cues. It is thus possible that Maria has a speech habit of using less verbal feedback. Even if she did use more cues, however, the length of utterance in Yoko's speech would still be quite long. Furthermore, Yoko appears to be much more 'willing' to talk when conversing with Maria than when speaking to Veronica. Her willingness to talk is reflected in the faster speech as well as in instances where her utterance is latched onto the end of Maria's utterance. It is also clear that the type of topic influences the speech style. Apparently, Yoko is more interested in talking about her job hunting than finding out about where Veronica had studied English. Naturally, due to the more complicated nature of the topic, the discussion between Yoko and Maria is also enriched with more sophisticated vocabulary.

What is interesting, however, is that Yoko was asked about her job hunting by Setsuko (J−Hi) but did not talk about it as much as when talking to Maria, as seen in excerpt 4.

Excerpt 4: Yoko (JS3) and Setsuko (J−Hi)

Yoko:	umm-hmmm .. and .. now .. I'm looking for a job now ..
Setsuko:	uh-huh (↗)
Yoko:	I just came back from the interview [chuckle]
Setsuko:	Oh wow!
Yoko:	Yeah ..
Setsuko:	Where did YOU go?
Yoko:	.. uh .. in Manhattan ..
Setsuko:	uh-huh
Yoko:	Yeah ..
Setsuko:	What kind of job are you LOOKing for?
Yoko:	uh ... kind of, you know, bilingual b-but uh ... I used to be a secretary, too ...
Setsuko:	uh-huh (↗)
Yoko:	I .. 'd like to be a kind of trainee .. of some office manager (↗) .. or ...
Setsuko:	uh-HUH (↗)
Yoko:	ummm I just learned about export and import ...
Setsuko:	Oh wow! That's gREAT!
Yoko:	[laugh] That's great but very difficult .. to find .. uh ... what .. I want .. [chuckle]

Setsuko: [laugh] Yeah .... [pause] So, what do you DO everyday? uh ..
            you're not working now .. are you? (↗)

Here, as seen in many pauses and short utterances, Yoko sounds hesitant to
talk about her job preference. It also looks as if she voluntarily tried to end
the discussion of the topic by saying 'yeah' twice after Setsuko's feedback
cues ('uh-huh'). Consequently, Setsuko encourages her to talk more by
asking further questions, but she eventually gives up questioning about the
job. It is reasonable to assume that Yoko was reluctant to go further into
the topic knowing that Setsuko worked for a Japanese computer company
(which had been mentioned in Setsuko's self-introduction). Since Yoko's
aim was to find a job in an American corporation, she might have thought it
would be impolite to tell someone working for a Japanese company that she
preferred an American firm to a Japanese one. Or perhaps Yoko was
avoiding talking of her private matters simply because Setsuko was also
Japanese, i.e. someone in her own network. In any case, one also observes a
tendency for other subjects to be more or less hesitant and/or short in
speech in an encounter with the non-native interviewers, with the exception
of Maria.

Amount of talk

If Maria was the interviewer most subjects felt comfortable with, this
comfort would also be reflected in the amount of talk in the conversation.
Table 4 presents the number of words spoken by each interviewer and
subject in each dyad.

We notice here that most pairs used almost equal numbers of words:
the stability in each pair was confirmed by means of a goodness of fit test
which indicated in most cases the nonsignificant deviation from a 50%:50%
split—especially between the interviewer and the advanced subject. There
is, however, observed variation in the amount of talk by the subject. As
with the length of utterance, the number of words is related to the level of
proficiency (Spearman correlation = 0.714, $p = 0.055$). Figure 2 illustrates
the number of words spoken by each subject in each dyad.

Here we notice that there are two patterns. In the first pattern the
number of words spoken by the subject is parallel with that of the
interviewer (as in JS3, 4, 5 and 6). Naturally, the interviewers with high or
native proficiency (J−Hi, S−Hi, NS) spoke extensively. Accordingly, many
subjects accommodated to them and spoke many words. In this pattern,
therefore, the amount of talk by the subject is in direct proportion to that

TABLE 4. *Number of words spoken by each interviewer and subject*

Subject (JS)	Interviewer situation				
	J–Hi	J–Lo	S–Hi	S–Lo	NS
1	450:265 (37%)*	279:330 (54%)	286:265 (48%)	196:331 (63%)*	409:352 (46%)
2	384:326 (44%)	288:376 (57%)*	467:329 (41%)*	253:365 (59%)*	358:392 (52%)
3	359:340 (49%)	270:325 (55%)	218:405 (65%)*	270:287 (52%)	320:360 (53%)
4	312:368 (54%)	262:304 (54%)	308:352 (53%)	283:310 (52%)	419:276 (40%)*
5	363:384 (51%)	312:295 (49%)	375:323 (46%)	253:450 (64%)	326:482 (60%)*
6	332:361 (52%)	322:305 (49%)	299:466 (67%)*	287:350 (55%)	375:383 (51%)
Mean	367:340 (48%)	289:289 (50%)	314:357 (53%)	257:349 (58%)	368:374 (50%)

Note: Number of words by *interviewer*: number of words by *subject* (% of words by *subject*)
* the difference in the pair with * is found significant by means of a goodness of fit test with the critical value set at the 0.01 level (i.e. $X^2 = 6.63$ on 1 d.f., $p < 0.01$)

by the interviewer. In the second pattern (indicated by bold lines in Figure 2) the subject's talk is in inverse proportion to the interviewer's (as in JS1 and 2).

In order to determine if these patterns were statistically significant, three ANOVAs were performed. A mixed-model 2 by 5 ANOVA was done in which the two levels of subject proficiency were used as the between-group factor and the identity of the interviewer was the repeated measure. In addition, repeated measures ANOVAs were performed on the two groups separately. The results of all three ANOVAs are presented in Table 5 and indicate that only for the low proficiency subgroup were there significant differences between word rates in different dyads ($F[4,4] = 28.35$, $p < 0.01$).

In this second pattern it appears as if the subject were dominated by the higher-proficiency interviewer, while she surpassed the lower-proficiency

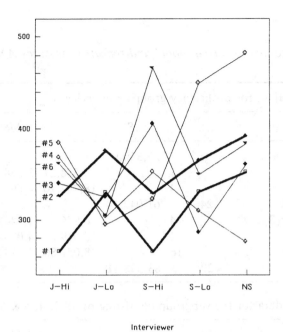

FIGURE 2. *Number of words spoken by each subject*

interlocutor. These subjects (JS1 and 2) are, of course, relatively lower in ESL proficiency compared with the rest of the subjects. The advanced subjects (JS3, 4, 5 and 6), on the other hand, were apparently able to adjust their level of speech according to the interlocutor. This difference between the two proficiency groups is further emphasised by the fact that in five (50%) of the ten interviews with the low-proficiency subjects (JS1 and 2) their word rates differed significantly from that of the interviewer. For the higher-proficiency subjects (JS3, 4, 5 and 6), however, in only four (20%) of 20 interviews were word rates significantly different. (See the significant difference in word rate indicated by an asterisk in Table 4.)

For instance, when talking to Yuri (J–Lo), Kimiko (JS5) and Akiko (JS6) spoke less than Yuri whose proficiency was much lower than theirs. They spoke not only less but also very slowly and clearly with many pauses. That is, these subjects with very high proficiency actually modified their speech just as in foreigner talk or caretaker speech. See excerpt 5 for example.

TABLE 5. *Results of mixed model and repeated measures ANOVAs for words spoken*

Summary of data for proficiency groups × interviewer:

Source	d.f.		SS	MS	F
Between subjects	5		22,350.97		
Group(A)		1		3,588.27	3,588.27	0.76
Error		4		18,762.70	4,690.68	
Within subjects	24		61,047.14		
Interviewer(B)		4		6,976.27	1,744.07	0.73
A × B		4		16,019.07	4,004.77	1.67
Error		16		38,051.80	2,378.24	
Total	29		83,398.11		

Summary of data for the subgroup consisting of JS 3, 4, 5 & 6:

Source	d.f.		SS	MS	F
Between subjects	3		12,760.20		
Within subjects	16		52,810.00		
Interviewer		4		15,100.20	3,775.05	1.20
Error		12		37,709.80	3,142.48	
Total	19		65,570.20		

Summary of data for the subgroup consisting of JS1 & 2

Source	d.f.		SS	MS	F
Between subjects	1		6,002.50		
Within subjects	8		10,038.40		
Interviewer		4		9,696.40	2,424.10	28.35*
Error		4		342.00	85.50	
Total	9		16,040.90		

*$p < 0.01$

Excerpt 5: Kimiko (JS5) and Yuri (J–Lo)

Kimiko: uh where .. are you studying? ($\nearrow$) [slow]
Yuri: uh in .. Engl English ($\nearrow$)
Kimiko: uh-huh ($\nearrow$)
Yuri: Yes
Kimiko: uh which .. SCHOOL .. are you studying now?
         [each word said slowly and clearly]
Yuri: uh-huh .. uh .. maybe you don't know .. uh just CES ($\nearrow$)
Kimiko: CES? ($\nearrow$)
Yuri: Name is the Center for English Study ($\nearrow$)
Kimiko: ohhh ..
Yuri: um-hmn do do you know? ($\nearrow$)
Kimiko: uh I don't know .. I'm sorry .. uh-huh ($\nearrow$)
Yuri: uh in Manhattan
Kimiko: Where is it? ($\nearrow$) Is it near Columbia University ($\nearrow$) or ..
         downtown?
Yuri: Yes uh just uhm umm located is ... uhm 7th Avenue ($\nearrow$)
Kimiko: um-hmn ($\nearrow$)
Yuri: and 28th ($\nearrow$) and .. uh! between 28th and 29th Street
Kimiko: Ohhh I see

In this exchange, after realising that Yuri misunderstood the first question regarding *where* she was studying, Kimiko rephrases it as *which school* she was attending. In order to get more details on where the school was located in Manhattan, Kimiko again employs the strategy of rephrasing as in 'Where is it? Is it near Columbia University or downtown?' This is quite reminiscent of foreigner talk, in which WH-questions are often restated as yes/no or alternative questions (Hatch, 1978). In addition to these modifications, each of Kimiko's statements was articulated clearly and with many pauses, and given at a slow rate with important words emphasised (see Ferguson, 1975; Hatch, 1978). Another high-proficiency subject, Akiko (JS6), basically did the same as Kimiko when conversing with Yuri. Thus, in sum, there was a tendency for the subject with high proficiency to speak less and to use foreigner talk features in order to adjust to the level of the low-proficiency interlocutor (cf. Porter, 1986).[10]

Number of questions

Apart from the amount of talk, we also notice in excerpt 5 that Kimiko (JS5) assumed a role of interviewer by asking Yuri (J–Lo) questions. That is, the roles were reversed in this instance. Since all the interviewers knew that their major task was to 'interview' each subject, they knew they were supposed to ask more questions than the subject. In some cases, however, as in the case of Kimiko talking to Yuri, the subjects asked more questions than the interviewer because their proficiency was higher than the interviewer's. In other words, the subjects led the conversation due to their higher ESL proficiency.

In their study of sex differences in L2 speech, Gass & Varonis (1986) examined who would lead the conversation in same-sex and opposite-sex dyads. One of the signs of dominance was found in the much larger number of questions asked by men. In the case of their picture description task, for instance, men tended to dominate the conversation in opposite-sex dyads regardless of the role they were assuming (e.g. even when they were playing the passive role of drawing the picture which women verbally described). This is quite interesting in that the effect of the interlocutor's sex tends to override that of the role determined by the task.

Similarly, in a good number of cases in the present study, the roles of interviewer and interviewee tended to be reversed depending upon who the interviewer was. In Table 6 the number of questions asked by the interviewer is compared with those asked by the subject in each dyad.

The clearest pattern found here is the conversation between Linda (NS) and each subject: in all five interviews Linda asked a much greater number of questions than the subject. This is quite natural in that her native proficiency in English simply enabled her to ask overwhelmingly more questions, which were somewhat reminiscent of 'machine-gun questions' (Tannen, 1984). In other words, she was able to stay in the role of interviewer and lead the conversation due to her superiority in English proficiency. In the case of the conversation between Setsuko (J–Hi) and the subject, a similar pattern was obtained, with a few exceptions (see Note 6). The pattern in the case of Yuri (J–Lo) represents the opposite case in that most subjects asked more questions than she did. That is, they led the conversation thanks to their higher proficiency in English.

The case with Maria (S–Hi) is rather unexpected in that despite her higher proficiency she asked fewer questions in three out of the six interviews. In her case, however, let us recall that the subjects seemed to feel most comfortable with this particular interviewer. The most perplexing is the case with Veronica (S–Lo). Despite her lower proficiency she asked more questions than most of the subjects and virtually led the conversation. One possible explanation is that most subjects found it difficult to talk to Veronica because of differences between them in ESL proficiency and NL background. Although they also experienced difficulty talking to Yuri

TABLE 6.   *Number of questions asked by each interviewer and subject*

Subject	Interviewer situation				
(JS)	J–Hi	J–Lo	S–Hi	S–Lo	NS
1	3:5	4:8	6:7	9:3	14:2
	(− 2)*	(− 4)	(− 1)*	(+ 6)*	(+ 12)
2	7:7	6:5	7:7	11:10	13:0
	(0)	(+ 1)*	(0)	(+ 1)*	(+ 13)
3	9:5	7:2	6:2	7:9	11:1
	(+ 4)	(+ 5)*	(+ 4)	(− 2)	(+ 10)
4	14:3	3:8	5:8	13:5	16:4
	(+ 11)	(− 5)	(− 3)*	(+ 8)*	(+ 12)
5	9:4	9:11	6:9	6:4	14:1
	(+ 5)	(− 2)	(− 3)*	(+ 2)*	(+ 13)
6	9:8	6:10	10:3	14:5	9:4
	(+ 1)	(− 4)	(+ 7)	(+ 9)*	(+ 5)
Mean	8.5:5.3	5.8:7.3	6.7:6.0	10.0:6.0	12.8:2.0
	(+ 3.2)	(− 1.5)	(+ 0.7)	(+ 4.0)*	(+ 10.8)

Note: No. of questions by *interviewer* [A]: No. of questions by *subject* [B]
( ) the difference between A and B (A − B)
* unexpected pattern

(J–Lo), there were a number of things they had in common and the subjects were able to return many questions to the interviewer, especially on the topics they knew well or found interesting (e.g. which cities they were from in Japan, what they used to do there, what they miss there, etc.). In other words, their familiarity with the interviewer's background enabled them to overcome the difficulty in talking caused by the interviewer's low proficiency (cf. Gass & Varonis, 1984). Furthermore, the subjects were supposedly of a superior status in terms of ESL proficiency. With Veronica, on the other hand, most subjects seemed to be occupied with trying to understand her and adjusting their speech to her level.[11] They also seemed to be reluctant to talk about general topics and felt it difficult to ask her questions. Consequently, they simply let Veronica ask the questions which she had prepared prior to the interviews.

Negotiation of meaning

Let us now ask how difficult or easy it was for the subject to understand each interviewer's English. One of the most interesting findings reported by

Varonis & Gass (1985) is that the pair of interlocutors with different NL as well as different ESL proficiency levels exhibited the highest incidence of meaning negotiation. Negotiations of meaning are defined as 'exchanges in which there is some overt indication that understanding between participants has not been complete and there is a resultant attempt to clarify the nonunderstanding' (Gass & Varonis, 1985:39). According to Varonis & Gass (1985), indication of nonunderstanding is signalled by two types of indicators: (1) direct (e.g. 'What?' 'Excuse me?' 'huh?' 'I don't understand'); and (2) indirect (e.g. repetition of the interlocutor's previous utterance).

The present study has indicated results which are similar to, but not the same as, those found in Varonis & Gass (1985). Table 7 presents the average use of meaning negotiation by the subject and the interviewer. The results indicated that the interviewer had a statistically significant effect on the subject's use of meaning negotiation ($F[4,20] = 3.17$, $p < 0.05$). As shown in Table 8, there was also a significant difference between the use of indirect and direct negotiations ($F[1,5] = 69.94$, $p < 0.01$).

In Varonis & Gass (1985) it was found that NNS–NNS pairs exhibited much higher incidence of negotiation than NNS–NS or NS–NS pairs. If this is so, the conversation between Linda (NS) and the subject is expected to show the lowest incidence of meaning negotiation. It was, however, found to be slightly higher than the average use of meaning negotiation between Setsuko (J–Hi) and the subject. In the case of Linda, the average amount of negotiation initiated by her (5.0 indirect and 0.83 direct) is higher than that initiated by the subject (3.17 indirect and 0 direct). This could be accounted for in terms of Linda's lack of familiarity with the Japanese

TABLE 7.   *Mean negotiation by interviewer and subject*

Indicator Type	Interviewer situation				
	J–Hi	*J–Lo*	*S–Hi*	*S–Lo*	*NS*
Indirect					
by interviewer	2.17	6.00	4.00	7.17	5.00
by subject	2.85	5.17	4.83	7.67	3.17
Direct					
by interviewer	0.00	0.67	0.83	1.33	0.83
by subject	0.00	1.50	1.00	0.83	0.00

TABLE 8.   *Results of repeated measures ANOVA for type of negotiation by interviewer*

Source	d.f.	SS	MS	F
Between subjects	5	131.33		
Within subjects	54	554.60		
Type(A)	1		248.07	248.07	69.94*
Error	5		17.73	3.55	
Interviewer(B)	4		68.93	17.23	3.17†
Error	20		108.67	5.43	
A × B	4		30.60	7.65	1.90
Error	20		80.60	4.03	
Total	59	685.93		

* $p < 0.01$
† $p < 0.05$

speaker's English (see Gass & Varonis, 1984). It is true that Linda is not accustomed to hearing English spoken by the Japanese. In fact, she had difficulty understanding some words pronounced with a Japanese accent. In several instances, Linda also repeated or rephrased the subject's previous utterances. It sometimes looked as if she were correcting them (see Brock *et al.*, 1986, for discussion of NS's corrective feedback in NS–NNS interactions). The exchanges between Reiko (JS1) and Linda (NS) are especially rich with such examples as seen below.

Excerpts 6A–6F: Reiko (JS1) and Linda (NS)

(6A)   **Linda:**   How do you like it here?
       Reiko: So MUch..
→   **Linda:**   You like it a lot? (↗)
       Reiko: uh-huh (↗)
       Linda: Good!

(6B)   **Reiko:**   I went there .. ummm last .. hm wait .. May .. in May ..
       Linda: Yeah? (↗)
       Reiko: One years ago
→   **Linda:**   A year ago? (↗)

(6C)   **Linda:**   Yeah .. well, you have the tempura .. I can eat that and I can get fat

	Reiko:	I don't like tempura so much [chuckle]
→	Linda:	No? (↗)
	Reiko:	I like sashimi (↗) or sushi (↗)
	Linda:	Yeah: ...
	Reiko:	uh-hmn [/? ...../
	Linda:	[But actually that's very expensive
	Reiko:	I know .. but SOMEtimes I have ..
→	Linda:	Oh .. you mean you don't usually eat it (↗)
	Reiko:	No ..

(6D)	Reiko:	and I've been to .. Orlando .. Disney World
	Linda:	Oh, that's beautiful. I was there, too. How did you like that?
	Reiko:	Yes, I went there .. two times
→	Linda:	Oh .. I guess you loved it
	Reiko:	So much ..
	Linda:	Yeah ..

(6E)	Linda:	Is most of your family in Japan? (↗)
	Reiko:	uh-hmn (↗)
	Linda:	Oh..
	Reiko:	.. All of my family and my husband's .. [sounds like 'my husband']
→	Linda:	Your husband's there? (↗) Oh .. [sympathetic]
	Reiko:	No no, my HUSband is here [chuckle] but my husband's .. FAMily ... is in Japan ..
	Linda:	Oh ..

(6F)	Linda:	How long did you go out with your husband before you got married .. or before you got engaged?
	Reiko:	Uh .. it was very .. [chuckle] urgent [pronounced without 'r']
→	Linda:	It was very what? (↗)
	Reiko:	Urgent [chuckle]
→	Linda:	Ancient? (↗)
	Reiko:	Urgent .. urgent .. means .. I saw him (↗) .. January 3rd ...
	Linda:	uh-huh (↗)
	Reiko:	and we engaged ... January 8th
→	Linda:	Oh, one week afterwards? (↗)
	Reiko:	uh-huh (↗) ⌐
	Linda:	└ Oh my gosh!
	Reiko:	It was arranged marriage

Linda: Oh .. okay .. good .. Well, I was getting scared to hear ..
like, love at first sight
Reiko: [laugh]

It seems that many of Reiko's responses were rather 'unusual' or 'unexpected' for someone who is not used to talking to Japanese speakers. They sometimes required special interpretations based on native-speaker intuitions (as in 6A, 6C and 6D). The words pronounced with a Japanese accent were often so 'foreign' to the native ear that they sometimes resulted in misunderstanding or nonunderstanding (as in 6E and 6F).

The subjects, on the other hand, experienced some difficulty understanding Linda (probably due to her fast speech), but that was not as serious as the problem Linda was faced with. Thus there was a slight asymmetry between the use of meaning negotiation between the subject and Linda, which can be seen in Figure 3.

In other cases there was almost the same amount of meaning negotiation initiated by both the subject and the interviewer. As presented in Figure 3, the dyads between Setsuko (J–Hi) and the subjects exhibited the lowest incidence of meaning negotiation, whereas those between Veronica (S–Lo) and the subjects exhibited the highest. Furthermore, in terms of the content

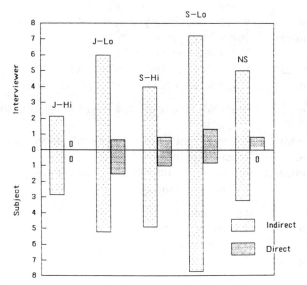

FIGURE 3. *Mean negotiation by interviewer and subject: indirect vs. direct indicators*

of negotiation, we can see that the nonunderstanding involved in the case of Setsuko (J–Hi) was least serious (most of the negotiations observed there are not even due to nonunderstanding). The negotiations there were mostly in the form of echo with rising or falling intonation as in: 'How long have you been in New York?' 'For one year' *'One year?'* 'Yeah'.

In the case of the conversation between the subject and the other non-native interviewers, the problems seemed to be much more serious. As seen in Figure 3, the difficulty of understanding was the greatest between Veronica (S–Lo) and the subject. This finding is in agreement with the results reported by Varonis & Gass (1985): namely, there was the highest incidence of negotiation between the pair of interlocutors with different native languages and different proficiency levels. Many of the problems manifested in such conversation are related to the interlocutor's pronunciation or to the speaker's lack of knowledge of certain words. Take the following exchanges for instance:

Excerpts 7A–7C: Yoko (JS3) and Veronica (S–Lo)

(7A) **Veronica:**   So, uh what else do you LIke? umm the specTAcles here .. like eh Broadway show ['show' sounds like 'chow']
→ **Yoko:**   uh bird-watching you said? (↗)
  Veronica: Broadway shows
→ **Yoko:**   What did you say? (↗)
  Veronica: musicals .. uh and .. ballet .. or ...
  Yoko: Oh, yes, uh I really like .. classical music

(7B) **Yoko:**   umm Which city are you from? (↗) ['city' sounds like 'Chile']
→ **Veronica:**   [pause] from Chile (↗) [sounds uncertain]
  Yoko: from Chile but which city?
  Veronica: uh eh from Santiago .. it's the capital
→ **Yoko:**   uh really .. Santiago

(7C) **Yoko:**   He commutes
→ **Veronica:**   Excuse me? (↗)
  Yoko: He commutes (↗)
  Veronica: Yeah
  Yoko: Take, you know, he takes .. a .. train
  Veronica: uh-huh (↗)
  Yoko: to Manhattan every day
  Veronica: Every day .. maybe he's very tired

Excerpts 8A & 8B: Yoko (JS3) and Maria (S–Hi)

(8A) Maria: Yeah I like to crochet ⎡That's my hobby
  →   Yoko: ⎣uh What's that?
      Maria: Crochet (↗)
  →   Yoko: Crochet? (↗)
      Maria: You know what that is? (↗)
  →   Yoko: No, I don't know.
      Maria: Okay, that's uhm, you know, like, the thread you take ya yarn?
      Yoko: uh-huh (↗)
      [Maria continues to explain what crochet is]

(8B) Yoko: Are you interested in quilt ['kilt']? (↗) uh what's that uh quilting ['kilting']? (↗)
  →   Maria: Excuse me? (↗)
      Yoko: Quilting ['kilting']
  →   Maria: Quilting ['kwilting']? (↗)
      Yoko: Quilting ['kwilting']
      Maria: I uh I haven't learned that ... yet

The above examples suggest that the problem of understanding was mutual, i.e. shared by the interlocutors who had different native languages.

In the conversation between Yuri (J–Lo) and the subject, there seem to be very few problems which are related to pronunciation, but in many cases negotiation exchanges are used by the speaker in order to check her own comprehension.

Excerpt 9: Akiko (JS6) and Yuri (J–Lo)

      Akiko: How long have you been in this country?
      Yuri: uh Yes, almost uhm nine (↗) nine months (↗)
  →   Akiko: Nine months? (↗)
      Yuri: Yeah
      Akiko: I see ..
              uhhhh so you came last uh last fall? (↗)
  →   Yuri: Last fall? (↗)
      Akiko: hmn
      Yuri: uh Yeah, uhmn November 22nd
      Akiko: ohhhh
      Yuri: Yeah ... uh-huh
      Akiko: I see

Yuri:	And this this April (↗) uh I went back to Japan
→ Akiko:	Oh really? (↗)
Yuri:	and I came back here ..
Akiko:	uh-huh (↗)
Yuri:	May 1st (↗)
Akiko:	uh-huh (↗)
Yuri:	Yes ..
Akiko:	How was it?
→ Yuri:	oh .. Japan? (↗)
Akiko:	uh-hmn (↗)
Yuri:	uhhh yes, so so [chuckle]
Akiko:	[chuckle]

In some special instances the same NL background was a facilitating factor in the understanding between the two Japanese speakers. For instance, Reiko (JS1) was asked by Yuri (J–Lo) if she liked cats. She answered: 'Yes! I love cat, especially *Sham*'. Apparently, the word 'Sham' here was derived from the Japanese word 'Shamu' which means either 'Siam' (noun) or 'Siamese' (adjective) in English. Reiko was not sure if this name was correct to refer to the breed she had in mind, repeating 'Sham' with rising intonation. Yuri immediately responded: 'Yes, I know... Sham!' If this name had been mentioned to a Spanish speaker, it would have had a negative effect similar to the case of 'kilting' (for 'quilting') as seen in excerpt 8B above. It was thus generally true that the speakers' comprehension was helped by their familiarity with each other's pronunciation in English and/or their shared knowledge of loan words in Japanese.

Results from the follow-up interview

Intelligibility of each interviewer's English

Let us turn next to the results of the follow-up interviews. During the interview each subject was asked to assign a rank, from 1 to 5, to each interviewer according to how easy her English was to understand. The results are given in Table 9.

The overall pattern J–Hi > NS > S–Hi > J–Lo > S–Lo was obtained with a high agreement (Kendall's Coefficient of Concordance $W = 0.811$). This pattern matches the order in terms of the amount of negotiation initiated by the subject with each interviewer (see Table 7 and Figure 3). This is quite interesting in that the learner's perception of the interlocutor's English is accurately reflected in the amount of meaning negotiation which they must have been mostly unconscious of.

TABLE 9. *Rank order of interviewers: intelligibility*

Overall pattern: J–Hi > NS > S–Hi > J–Lo > S–Lo				

Average rating:				
	J–Hi	J–Lo	S–Hi	S–Lo	NS
Mean	1.17	4.33	2.83	4.50	2.17
s.d.	0.41	0.52	0.41	0.84	0.98

Agreement of rank order:
Kendall's Coefficient of Concordance $W = 0.811$
The average Spearman correlation between all possible
pairs of ranking $= 0.77$

Comments made by the subjects on each interviewer's English are very informative. Regarding Setsuko (J–Hi), most subjects felt her English was almost identical to a native speaker's. It was also extremely intelligible for the subjects because she used easy vocabulary and simple sentence structures and spoke slowly. One of the subjects (JS6) noticed a slight Japanese accent in Setsuko's English, but she felt it made her English even easier to understand. Another subject (JS5) also pointed out that there was something 'Japanese' about her English and yet it was 'beautiful English', which was fascinating to her.

Linda (NS) was rated as the second easiest due to her 'fast' and 'overwhelming' speech although her English was 'very clear' and she was also 'very attentive'. Maria (S–Hi) was identified as 'almost native' but her slight Spanish accent placed her third in the ranking. The other two non-native interviewers (J–Lo and S–Lo) were ranked lowest (i.e. most difficult to understand) because of their lack of fluency in English.

Psychological ease

The most basic assumption in this study was that Japanese ESL speakers would feel uncomfortable speaking English to another Japanese. This discomfort was thought to be manifested in the Japanese speaker's English. In the follow-up interview each subject was also asked to rank order each interviewer in terms of psychological ease they had experienced during each conversation. The results are given in Table 10.

As seen in the overall pattern, the two lower-proficiency interviewers (S–Lo and J–Lo) are placed on the lowest ranks. Most subjects agreed that it was difficult to talk to somone with lower ESL proficiency. In other words, it became a psychological burden to talk to (and adjust to) someone

TABLE 10. *Rank order of interviewers: psychological ease*

Overall pattern: S–Hi > NS > J–Hi > S–Lo > J–Lo

Average rating:

	J–Hi	J–Lo	S–Hi	S–Lo	NS
Mean	2.50	4.83	1.83	3.50	2.33
s.d.	1.38	0.41	0.75	1.05	1.21

Agreement of rank order:
Kendall's Coefficient of Concordance $W = 0.567$
The average Spearman correlation between all possible
pairs of ranking $= 0.48$

who lacked fluency in English. Although many subjects felt that those lower-proficiency speakers (especially J–Lo) had 'tried very hard to speak English' and they received favourable impressions, they felt uncomfortable talking about topics which were rather 'superficial' in nature. Some subjects commented that they felt 'threatened' because their English seemed to become less fluent, converging towards the lower-proficiency interlocutor. This impression was particularly true with Yuri (J–Lo). One subject said that she felt 'annoyed' with Yuri's English because it reminded her of her own struggles in earlier stages of English learning. She was also afraid of seeing her English regress to that point. Another subject pointed out that Yuri's English was 'so noticeably Japanese' that it constantly reminded her of speaking English to a Japanese. It also made her think of Japanese equivalents of what had been said, and this forced her to make many mistakes due to transfer from Japanese.

Regarding the two Japanese interlocutors (J–Hi and J–Lo), most subjects found it 'unnatural' to talk to the Japanese in English. They felt 'nervous' with them, especially at the beginning of the conversation. Some subjects also found themselves trying to evaluate the level of the interviewer's English. Such feelings, however, were quickly overcome with Setsuko (J–Hi) because her proficiency was so high and close to the native speaker's that they even forgot they were talking to a Japanese. Some said they actually enjoyed talking to Setsuko because they were interested in knowing how she had reached such a high level of English.

There were, however, two opposing views towards Setsuko, either very favourable or unfavourable (as reflected in the relatively high s.d. 1.38 in Table 10). The subject who expressed the latter view and feelings most typical of Japanese was Yoko (JS3). She was uncomfortable speaking to the two Japanese throughout the conversation: she actually rated them lowest.

She said she was concerned that Setsuko was evaluating her English. Since both of them were strangers to her, she also tried to be 'formal' with them. She also said: 'Because they are Japanese, I found myself trying not to give too much information especially on private matters'. In other words, she had fear of revealing information to those in her own network. This fear, she added, was probably related to the sense of rivalry among those from the same native background. With other interviewers, on the other hand, she was able to become more 'frank' in the conversation. In this respect, it can be said that Yoko was transferring Japanese sociolinguistic rules of privacy into English when conversing with the Japanese interviewers (see Beebe, 1983), while in other situations she was applying what she thought were American sociocultural norms (probably based on the stereotype, e.g. 'frankness' of Americans). It thus seems that speaking English to a Japanese tends to induce transfer from the NL—either linguistic or sociolinguistic—which has two results: (1) negative feelings in the speaker and (2) negative effects on her speech (also see Selinker *et al.*, 1975).

Linda (NS) was ranked in the middle along with Setsuko (J–Hi), being rated either very high or quite low (as reflected again in the relatively high s.d. in Table 10). Some subjects felt very comfortable with Linda because it was 'natural' to speak English with a native speaker. Others felt very 'nervous' with and 'overwhelmed' by her English. The latter group became so conscious of the NS's linguistic superiority that they could not enjoy the one-to-one interaction with her.

Maria (S–Hi) was ranked first by the subjects. This explains the highest average length of utterance and the proportionately large number of words spoken by the subjects when conversing with her. All the subjects actually expressed very favourable impressions regarding Maria. They said she was 'very friendly', 'polite', 'kind', 'warm' and 'had a good sense of humour'. They commented more on her personality than on her being bilingual in Spanish and English. It seems, however, that Maria's English also played an important role in this respect. First of all, although there was a slight Spanish accent to her English, it was near-native and very intelligible. Secondly, she was able to adjust her English to her interlocutor's level. Third, she was quite similar to Setsuko in that she used easy vocabulary and simple sentence structures and spoke slowly. Since Maria was from a different NL background, the subjects were also free from feeling 'unnatural' about speaking English to her.

Lastly, it must be added that the subjects said they would choose the NS or someone like Maria as their linguistic model to practice English with (cf. Beebe, 1985; Goldstein, 1987). On this point, one subject precisely commented: 'The native speaker of English is most preferred because we can try various expressions with him/her to see if they really work or not' (see Beebe, 1980).

Summary and conclusion

The present study has shown that the listener (i.e. interlocutor) is an important factor influencing the non-native speaker's speech. It has been observed that L2 speakers are sensitive towards certain characteristics of their interlocutors. Their sensitivity was manifested at the linguistic as well as psychological level. At the linguistic level, the following tendencies were observed:

(1) The non-native speaker's utterance became hesitant and brief in an encounter with (a) the listener with low ESL proficiency and (b) the listener with the same NL background.

(2) With respect to the amount of talk, (a) advanced L2 speakers converged towards the proficiency level of their interlocutor by speaking more with their higher-proficiency interlocutors and by speaking less with their lower-proficiency interlocutors, and (b) intermediate L2 speakers surpassed their lower-proficiency interlocutors by speaking more, while they spoke less than their higher-proficiency interlocutors.

(3) L2 speakers asked more questions than their lower-proficiency interlocutor and dominated the conversation but they asked fewer questions than their higher-proficiency interlocutor. This tendency, however, was subject to other factors such as the speaker's familiarity with the interlocutor's speech and background as well as the availability of common topics.

(4) The use of meaning negotiation by the L2 speaker increased when conversing with (a) the interlocutor with the different NL background and (b) the interlocutor with the different proficiency level in English. The combination of (a) the different NL background and (b) different proficiency resulted in the highest incidence of meaning negotiation (confirming the finding by Varonis & Gass, 1985).

At the psychological level, the subjects experienced the following feelings during the interviews:

(1) The subjects felt uncomfortable speaking English to (a) the listener with low ESL proficiency and (b) the listener with the same NL background. This discomfort seemed to be reflected in the first tendency described above: the non-native speaker's speech became hesitant and brief with these particular listeners.

(2) Some subjects also felt uncomfortable with the NS listener who they found was unable to adjust her level of speech to them.

(3) The personality of the interlocutor was also found to be an important factor contributing to the subject's psychological ease (as in the case of Maria).

In sum, it has been found that there are many interacting factors that have complicated the effects of the listener on the L2 speaker's speech. The NL background and the English proficiency of the interlocutor are among the most important factors. The familiarity with the interlocutor's speech and background and with the topic discussed are also significant. Personality of the speaker and the interlocutor, and possibly the interlocutor's age, also seem to be relevant.

The present study has examined the NNS–NNS interaction, focusing primarily on quantitative aspects such as the length of speech and the amount of talk and meaning negotiation. Needless to say, there is much more to examine in this direction; for example, number of overlaps, interruptions, topics nominated or shifted, and so on. The qualitative change in L2 speakers' speech as well as in interactions also remains for future investigation. It is promising to inquire into such aspects as (a) paralinguistic features, (b) pronunciation, (c) syntactic complexity attempted by the L2 learner, (d) self-correction or monitoring, (e) hedges, (f) word choice and (g) sociolinguistic appropriateness and pragmatic features. The questions we must pursue in future research also include the following:

(1) Does speaking to another L2 speaker benefit the learner's L2 development? If yes, what type of non-native interlocutor is most beneficial to the learner's L2 development?

(2) How does input from the non-native interlocutor differ from input from the NS?

(3) Is the NS always the best model for a non-native speaker to practise English with?

(4) Does speaking to another NNS with the same NL background increase the rate of NL transfer?

(5) What would be the best way to organise an ESL class? According to the NL background and/or proficiency level?

Together with many other related questions asked elsewhere (e.g. Long *et al.*, 1976; Porter, 1986), there are a number of issues awaiting elucidation.

ESL learners are often placed in an environment where they must practise English with various types of non-native speakers of English (e.g. in the ESL classroom) regardless of their model preferences. For this reason also, it is important for us to inquire further into issues related to NNS–NNS interactions.

Appendix: Transcription conventions

..	noticeable pause or break in rhythm
CAPS	mark emphatic stress
↗	marks rising intonation
:	indicates lengthened vowel or diphthong (e.g. I: pronounced [a:y], while I [ay])
[ ]	are used for comments on speech
/?../	indicates an undecipherable utterance
[	Brackets between lines indicate overlapping speech
	Two people talking at the same time

Brackets on two lines ⌐
└ indicate second utterance latched onto first, without perceptible pauses.

(adopted from Tannen, 1984, with modifications)

Notes to Chapter 13

1. I wish to thank Setsuko Mochida, Yurie Kinugawa, Maria L. Cruz, Veronica Gorigoitia, and Linda Gutowsky for interviewing the subjects for the study; Tamiko Akimoto, Kumiko Kishi and Michiko Yuki for their help in the data collection for the written questionnaire survey; and all subjects for participating in the study. I would also like to acknowledge that the present study as well as its title were inspired by Leslie Beebe's study entitled 'The influence of the listener on code-switching' published in *Language Learning* Vol. 27, No. 2 (1977) and my special thanks are due to Leslie Beebe for her encouragement and for her helpful comments on an earlier version of this paper.

2. It must be noted here that such negative feelings toward the Japanese–Japanese conversation in English were expressed by a number of female subjects regardless of age, occupation, length of residence in the US and proficiency in English. A large number of them had lived in the US for more than three years and had a high level of ESL proficiency.

3. One of the female subjects made a further comment on this, that she would feel even worse if her Japanese interlocutor with higher ESL proficiency was also a woman. Another female subject also commented that whether she feels uncomfortable or not in such a situation would depend on the degree of intimacy or familiarity of the interlocutor.

4. These comments could be contrasted with the following responses as to what

they would do when they feel uncomfortable speaking English to another Japanese. Eighteen out of 31 said that they would employ one of the following strategies: (a) try to remain silent as much as possible by taking a listener's role (39%); (b) speak Japanese to the other Japanese as much as circumstances allow (39%); (c) try to speak English as accurately as possible (11%); (d) others, e.g. use simple and short sentences (11%).

5. If such strong feelings are peculiar to Japanese women, they could possibly explain some aspects of sex differences found in Gass & Varonis (1986).

6. The subjects were between 27 and 36 years old, while the interviewers were between 25 and 27. It would have been ideal to control for the age of the subjects and interviewers. It was, however, hoped that the age effect could be avoided by using telephone conversations instead of face-to-face interactions which would have made the age difference more apparent. In some situations, however, the subject asked the interviewer how old she was, and this seemed to have some psychological effects on the speaker, e.g. in the number of questions asked. As seen in Table 6, Reiko (JS1) asked more questions than the interviewers J−Hi, J−Lo and S−Hi. During each of the conversations with these three, she asked their age and found out that they were younger than she was. In the follow-up interview, Reiko (age: 30) said that she had thought they were very young at the beginning of each conversation. Miki (JS2) also asked the J−Hi and J−Lo interviewers how old they were and found out that they were the same age as she was (age: 27). The number of questions asked in these dyads happened to be equal or almost equal. These instances may simply be coincidences. JS4, 5 and 6 said that the age of the interviewer had no effect on their speech. Thus, it seems that age *could* be a possible factor for some speakers, but not for everyone.

7. It is generally accepted that speakers accommodate mainly to their addressee, but it is also possible that third persons (auditors, overhearers and reference groups or 'significant others' not even present) may have an influence on the speaker to a lesser but regular degree (see Bell, 1984). In this study telephone conversations were used and it was made sure that the interviewer and interviewee spoke to each other when nobody else was listening to their conversation. This arrangement was made in order to avoid the influence of auditors or overhearers. For the same reason, the subjects had been told that we were interested only in the impressions they would get from each interviewer, and they had not been told that the conversation was being tape recorded. That is, if they had been aware that there was another listener (a listener to the taped conversation—i.e. the researcher), this would probably have made them conscious of their speech and thus had an unwanted effect on their speech. After all five interviews, permission to use the tape recorded data was obtained from each subject. All subjects also accepted that their agreeing to participate in the study could be taken as granting the permission to tape record the conversation before taping. In fact, the subjects were rather appreciative that it had been done without their awareness because they felt they would have been unable to talk naturally if they had been aware that the conversation was being tape recorded.

8. Each 5-minute transcription excluded the initial negotiation between the interlocutors, e.g. for the caller (the interviewer) to obtain permission to talk and to introduce herself. It took the interviewer about 20 seconds to 1 minute to

complete the initial routine. During the self-introduction the interviewer naturally spoke much more than her interlocutor. Transcription was thus begun immediately after the introduction was completed.

9. The proficiency of each subject was determined on the basis of number of years spent in the US and the opportunity to practise English as well as on the experimenter's and the NS interviewer's judgements based on the subject's performance in the interview.

10. As seen in Table 4, Kimiko (JS5) was an exception: she spoke extensively—450 words (65%)—when conversing with Veronica (S–Lo). This looks as if Kimiko had neglected adjusting her speech to her lower-proficiency interlocutor. In the follow-up interview, however, it became clear that at the beginning of the conversation Kimiko had thought Veronica was at a much higher proficiency level than she actually was. In fact, in the initial routine of the conversation, Veronica introduced herself quite fluently (probably due to the expertise she had gained through the previous interviews). Kimiko then gradually noticed that Veronica was not as proficient as she had thought. Kimiko described this point as follows: 'As I talked more, answering Veronica's questions, I became worried that she might not have understood what I had said. I also noticed that she made grammatical mistakes, which became more and more noticeable.' Consequently, she adjusted her speech to Veronica. Since the transcript included only the first 5 minutes of their talk, this adjustment simply did not appear in the data.

11. Yoko (JS2) and Miki (JS3) are exceptions here since they were able to return many questions to Veronica (S–Lo). As mentioned in excerpt 2, Yoko and Veronica attended the same school to study English. So did Miki. It seems that they had a lot more in common and thus many topics were available to them. It must then be implied that the shared familiarity of the topic discussed plays a facilitating role in the conversation (cf. Gass & Varonis, 1984).

References

BEATTIE, G., 1983, *Talk: An Analysis of Speech and Non-Verbal Behavior in Conversation*. Milton Keynes: Open University Press.

BEEBE, L., 1977a, The influence of the listener on code-switching, *Language Learning*, 27, 331–9.

——, 1977b, The dialect code-switching of bilingual children, *CUNY Forum*, 3, 141–58.

——, 1980, Measuring the use of communication strategies. In R. SCARCELLA & S. KRASHEN (eds), *Research in Second Language Acquisition*. Rowley, MA: Newbury House.

——, 1981, Social and situational factors affecting communicative strategy of dialect code-switching, *International Journal of the Sociology of Language*, 32, 139–49.

——, 1983, Examining transfer from a sociolinguistic perspective. Paper presented at Second Language Research Forum (SLRF), University of Southern California, November 1983.

——, 1985, Input: choosing the right stuff. In S. GASS & C. MADDEN (eds), *Input in Second Language Acquisition*. Rowley, MA: Newbury House.

BEEBE, L. and ZUENGLER, J., 1983, Accommodation theory: An explanation for style shifting in second language dialects. In N. WOLFSON & E. JUDD (eds), *Sociolinguistics and Language Acquisition*. Rowley, MA: Newbury House.

BELL, A., 1984, Language style as audience design, *Language in Society*, 13, 145–204.

BROCK, C., CROOKES, G., DAY, R. and LONG, M., 1986, Differential effects of corrective feedback in native speaker–nonnative speaker conversation. In R. R. DAY (ed.), *Talking to Learn: Conversation in Second Language Acquisition*. Rowley, MA: Newbury House.

ERVIN-TRIPP, S., 1964, An analysis of the interaction of language, topic, and listener, *American Anthropologist*, 66, 86–102.

FERGUSON, C. A., 1975, Towards a characterization of English foreigner talk, *Anthropological Linguistics*, 17, 1–14.

GASS, M. and VARONIS, E. M., 1984, The effect of familiarity on the comprehensibility of nonnative speech, *Language Learning*, 34, 65–89.

——, 1985, Variation in native speaker speech modification to non-native speakers, *Studies in Second Language Acquisition*, 7, 37–58.

——, 1986, Sex differences in NNS/NNS interactions. In R. R. DAY (ed.), *Talking to Learn: Conversation in Second Language Acquisition*. Rowley, MA: Newbury House.

GILES, H. and POWESLAND, P. F., 1975, *Speech Style and Social Evaluation*. London: Academic Press.

GILES, H. and SMITH, P., 1979, Accommodation theory: Optimal levels of convergence. In H. GILES & R. ST. CLAIR (eds), *Language and Social Psychology*. Oxford: Blackwell.

GOLDMAN-EISLER, F., 1968, *Psycholinguistics: Experiments in Spontaneous Speech*. London: Academic Press.

GOLDSTEIN, L., 1987, Standard English: The only target for nonnative speakers of English?, *TESOL Quarterly*, 21, 417–36.

HATCH, E., 1978, Discourse analysis and second language acquisition. In E. HATCH (ed.), *Second Language Acquisition: A Book of Readings*. Rowley, MA: Newbury House.

HATTORI, T., 1987, A study of nonverbal intercultural communication between Japanese and Americans—focusing on the use of the eyes, *JALT Journal*, 8, 109–18.

LoCASTRO, V., 1986, The pragmatics of pauses. Paper presented at the Second Kyoto Conference on Discourse Analysis, Doshisha University, Kyoto, Japan, September 1986.

LONG, M., ADAMS, L., McLEAN, M. and CASTANOS, F., 1976, Doing things with words—verbal interaction in lockstep and small group classroom situations. In J. FANSELOW & R. CRYMES (eds), *On TESOL '76*. Washington DC: TESOL.

PORTER, P., 1986, How learners talk to each other: Input and interaction in task-centered discussions. In R. DAY (ed.), *Talking to Learn: Conversation in Second Language Acquisition*. Rowley, MA: Newbury House.

SELINKER, S., SWAIN, M. and DUMAS, G., 1975, The interlanguage hypothesis extended to children?, *Language Learning*, 25, 139–52.

TANNEN, D., 1984, *Conversational Style: Analyzing Talk Among Friends*. Norwood, NJ: Ablex.

VARONIS, E. M. and GASS, S., 1985, Non-native/non-native conversations: A model for negotiation of meaning; *Applied Linguistics*, 6, 71–90.

Contents of Volume II

Index